GODS OF MYTH AND STONE

PHALLICISM IN

GODS
OF
MYTH
AND
STONE

JAPANESE FOLK RELIGION

by
MICHAEL CZAJA

with a foreword by
GEORGE DE VOS

New York · WEATHERHILL · Tokyo

First Edition, 1974

Published by John Weatherhill, Inc., 149 Madison Avenue, New York, New York 10016, with editorial offices at 7–6–13 Roppongi, Minato-ku, Tokyo 106. Protected by copyright under terms of the International Copyright Union; all rights reserved. Printed and first published in Japan.

LCC Card No. 73–88468   ISBN 0–8348–0095–0

To Antonin and Noèmi Raymond
who first introduced me to the arts of Japan
and to the everlasting truths
that nurture the creative spirit

CONTENTS

PART THREE: FOLK WORSHIP

GODS OF MYTH AND STONE

FOREWORD

THIS PERCEPTIVE STUDY, both visual and verbal, by Michael Czaja of the worship of fertility in Japan is instigated by a restless curiosity of mind as well as an original artistic sensibility. Czaja as artist and architect has dedicated his talents in the past primarily to projects of a visual and physical nature. Luckily, in this work he has turned his unusual untrammeled capacity for insight to a description of folk religion that includes both sculpture and dramatic ritual. He was prompted by a need to understand the mentality of the unknown Japanese artists who gave representation to beliefs reaching back to the prehistoric beginning of agriculture in the Japanese archipelago. These carvers of stone have contributed to an art tradition given little regard by the Japanese themselves. The carved roadside sculptures as well as the remaining folk rituals of rural Japan portray a view of human sexuality that is direct, simple, and affectionate. This "phallic tradition" is neglected and even suppressed from view not because it lacks artistic worth but because it has offended, and still offends, the prudery of those made uncomfortable by the simple earthy sexuality of rural agriculturalists.

Czaja's scholarly work has been stimulated circuitously by a second love. Affection for horses has motivated him to reading on man's domestication of the horse and the cultural traditions developed as a consequence. Again, the swift current of his curiosity has carried him into a pursuit far afield from the ordinary interest of the artist. He has read everything available to him on the North Asian shamanistic ceremonies of horse riders. Czaja finds preserved in the folk myths of the Japanese, as recorded in the ancient chronicles, remnants of Altaic shamanistic practices. The eighth-century *Kojiki* and *Nihongi,* the sacred scriptures of Shinto, echo distantly to the shaman's drum. One finds recorded, for example, the flaying of the horse backward as ultimate pollution. The fuller meaning of such desecration was no longer clearly understood even by those early scribes writing down an older oral tradition in the newly acquired Chinese ideographs. Many of the modern commentaries on Shinto beliefs fail even to attempt a satisfactory interpretation.

Czaja's work weaves together in a unique synthesis areas of self-initiated scholarship usually not combined in the same person. By so doing, he has transcended the pedestrian efforts of many more orthodox, academically trained specialists who have plodded before

13

him without vision through the incomplete, inconsistent, ambiguous, and fragmentary nature of Shinto folk beliefs. What pulls it together for Czaja are first, an implicit psychodynamic understanding of the centrality of human sexuality as a universal source or wellspring in human religious beliefs, and second, a sense that the cultural transmission of beliefs may be imperfect, partial, and incomplete. It depends therefore little on direct understanding, yet it somehow can remain vital. What preserve these fragments of more ancient beliefs and practices are the continuities to be found in the psychology of man in Japan seeking harmony both within and between nature and culture.

If there is any organizing principle to Shinto, it is not to be found by laying its corpus of beliefs on Levi-Strauss's procrustean binary bed and reducing the complexities of human mythology to the pairing of opposites. For the Japanese do not conceptually oppose "the raw and the cooked" or "culture and nature." They embrace them as inseparable unities of experience to be tasted and savored together. What is raw or natural is both absorbing to and is absorbed by man, and bent to his purposes rather than devitalized or transformed out of recognition into cultural artifact. Japanese cooking, like Japanese art, is based on this nonconflicting harmony of what is natural with what is done with nature. As Czaja elucidates in his discussion of Fushimi-Inari Shrine, sex and food are worshiped as a unit, both singular and plural, natural and cultural, as an affirmation of fertility.

Using the Japanese language, one does not need to distinguish the singular or the plural except in careful context. Godhood, *kami,* is/are not carefully defined. *Dosojin*—earth-ancestral-god(s)—is/are worshiped in a conceptually ambiguous way. A Western mind insists on "cleaner" definitions in an either/or way; and so must it be to communicate well in intellectual terms. Often in translating to English a Japanese experience one makes it too precise and hinders comprehension of the soothing possibility of a conceptual reality blurred and unfocused, given to nuances, not categorizable ideas. Such a hazy form of reality raises anxiety and discomfort in a Western-trained mind. Such fluid and evocative thought patterns cannot be approached too immediately without careful preparation to ease away the need to define and catalogue.

Japanese thought is considered "illogical," "artistic," and "intuitive," even "feminine," by some as opposed to the "clean," noncontaminatory categorization savored by a Western-trained "masculine" philosophic mind. A heritage of Judaic as well as Aristotelian logic is trained into Western thought so thoroughly and at such a young age that to find oneself without it threatens one's sense of reality—or better still, one's sense of control over reality—so violently as to be equated with uncontrollable insanity.

Mary Douglas, the eminent British anthropologist, describes well, in her analysis of the definitions of pollution formulated in the Judaic law, the Western horror and intolerance of ambiguity. Unfortunately, Douglas and others cannot escape their own Western minds when they create psychological universals. It seems very cogent therefore for them to generalize crossculturally and to equate pollution and "cognitive inconsistency." Japanese thought belies any such an attempted universalization. Japanese have a profound fear of pollution but certainly not in respect to cognitive inconsistencies! Even "official" Shinto, derived from inchoate folk beliefs, does not demand organization, consistency—or even a desire for comprehension—to affirm life. Shinto belief shows no need to exclude alternatives. What is useful is absorbed; what is not is not aggressively disparaged or repelled but simply ignored. Local rituals remain vital representations of human needs and social processes without any reference to a body of systematic dogma.

In Japanese folk belief, purity is not a matter of clean conceptualization. There is no Talmudic, convoluted exegesis to comment on Japanese myths of genesis. There is no obsessive worry about logical overconsistencies that might raise doubt and disbelief. Nor is there fear of anomaly. Japanese mythology is a sensual, nonintellectual, nonideational affirmation of life. Its vague conceptual content remains spasmodic and fragmented at best. One can, with difficulty, attribute some schematic order to the deities recorded in the *Kojiki* and the *Nihongi*. But whatever ordering is evident bespeaks the political usage made of these writings to legitimatize and affirm at the time of their advent an amalgamation of diverse, previously warring groups more than it affords logical consistency in a religious creed. Myths in Japan were created more to avoid disturbances in hierarchical harmony than to avoid conceptual "sinning" in the realm of religion.

Modern literate urban-oriented Japanese are not comfortable with the phallic tradition of agricultural Japan. As is true almost everywhere, anthropological or psychological investigation can be considered a source of embarrassment. A straining, socially pretentious bourgeoisie prefers hypocritical coverup to the acknowledgment of a peasant past as part of its heritage. In Europe the fountain statues that streamed water out of female breasts have all had their plumbing cut off. A singular exception, Mannikin-pis, still performs in a nook of central Brussels as a quaint throwback to a more honest avowal of natural functions that was much more in evidence prior to the social triumph of the urban bourgeoisie throughout Europe. Crude peasant realities are now well hidden from view.

In the forms of art brought into Japan by Buddhism, the human body and its functions never received representation. These Buddhist religious traditions in painting, sculpture, and dance became the chief art forms available to the socially dominant groups. Nevertheless, the more directly erotic representations in stone and wood produced by rural folk continued surreptitiously despite government suppression. Later, after the seventeenth century, a thoroughly secular townsman culture also introduced sexuality in representational art. Such art was not acceptable to the social and governmental establishment. The Kabuki theater, for example, was several times suppressed by puritanical samurai administrators. The ukiyo-e woodblock prints were openly appreciated outside the bordello areas in Japan only after receiving praise from modern revolutionary Western art circles with which the Japanese came in contact after the Meiji Restoration of 1868. As an artist, Czaja was perceptive in seeing the inseparability of Japan's folk and fine arts, which the Japanese now do not differentiate as we tend to do in the West. Spontaneous appreciation lured him into making a large number of rubbings of roadside sculptures as a record of this unique folk art.

Czaja's social insight picked up the fact that the Dosojin statues reflect historical vicissitudes in the social status of women in Japan. Until the Tokugawa period (1603–1868) these statues suggest a neutrality in status equivalence between men and women in the rural inheritance. In Tokugawa and Meiji (1868–1912) times this equality of status as depicted in earlier Dosojin sculptures deteriorates into a relationship in which women are subject to male dominance. Czaja's illustrations show love to be a tender and mutual expression in prior periods and the need for male dominance to be a late phenomenon.

Another theme handled with great clarity and insight by Czaja is his description of various present-day rituals. He traces their continuity through a long Japanese tradition utilizing ecstatic states as a part of folk religion. This use of some form of an altered state of consciousness is an almost universal characteristic of folk religions as they are reported in the anthropological literature. As elsewhere, a more controlling priestly bureaucracy finds it hard to give official sanction to ecstatic practices. They appear only at the periphery of recognized Buddhism. Part of the present vitality of new religions in modern Japan again depends upon the utilization of some form of altered state of consciousness, be it conceptualized as trance, possession, or meditation.

With the rapid depopulation of the countryside, Japanese culture may be exhausting its supply of effervescent rural vitality, which has been the broad base of Japan's creative energy. Japanese farmers, to some, may seem to have been only simple hard-working serfs. This superficial view does them injustice. For centuries they have been a vital force in Japanese social change, economic development, and artistic expression. Each generation has sent many of its sons and daughters into the city. They not only carried with them a capacity for hard work and endurance—they also came fired by an implacable optimism nurtured from birth by a warmth of family life. They brought also an aesthetic sense of composition developed by daily contact with an ordered countryside divided and patterned into irrigated paddies, made alternately verdant by a seasonal cycle beautiful to behold, never too far from a craggy coast that stubbornly thrust out its brave, weathered pines above water-beaten rocks. Japanese farm youth each generation also carried into the city a vital desire to learn: not simply to submit slavishly but to innovate, to become, to change.

These fresh waves are no longer there to vitalize the urban environment with their own view of life. The farm population is falling below ten million people. In many villages there is no one left who can carry out the seasonal rites and festivals; there is no youth to welcome the kami ancestors and the god of the New Year. In many instances rural ceremony has degenerated into a commercial enticement to bring in urban tourists and is no longer a vital expression of an agricultural community representing its hopes and anxieties, as well as its gratitude for a fertile earth. The spiritual expression of a former way of life close to nature, its ceremonies and folk art, cannot be kept alive artificially. Such efforts must become either plastic caricatures or hopefully, in time, there will arise new religious and artistic expressions of modern man, in tune both with himself and his new cultural environment.

GEORGE DE VOS

Berkeley, California

AUTHOR'S PREFACE

THIS STUDY OF THE SACRED roadside sculptures of Japan began in 1960–61, during the time I was in Japan as a Ford Foundation–Fulbright research fellow. My official project was entitled "The Integration of the Arts in Japanese Architecture." As an artist-architect I had become interested during an earlier visit to Japan in the way all of the arts had been integrated into the daily pattern of Japanese life, at least as it is found in parts of the country away from the centers of commercial and industrial environment. In the course of this search for the philosophic ideas and creative forces that had produced Japan's culture I interviewed many architects, artists, priests, teachers, business people, students, and farmers. I also undertook the study of a very special craft, *kyogi,* working with paper, with Yuji Abe, owner and director of the Yoseido Gallery in Tokyo, whose father and grandfather had been kakemono-makers to the emperor before World War II. I felt that through trying to master a craft I would gain some insight into the Japanese way of doing things and into their feelings and attitudes.

Yuji Abe arranged for me a trip to Matsumoto in Nagano Prefecture and a meeting with Sanshiro Ikeda, owner and president of a furniture company, who was the local authority on the folk arts of the area and on wayside sculptures in particular. The purpose of our trip was to make rubbings of some of these sculptures, with the intention of mounting them as a class exercise when we returned to Tokyo. This introduction to the art of making rubbings, in which we were guided by the expert Otosaburo Moriizume, a local kakemono-maker, was successful and inspiring. Several months later I returned to Matsumoto as a guest of Mr. Ikeda for the specific purpose of making as many rubbings of wayside sculptures as I could, particularly of the man-wife Dosojin, images of the phallic deities of agriculture and procreation. These images of folk-Shinto deities are still found in rural villages where rice and silk are produced. Often they stand side by side with Buddhist images, although usually a greater number of the latter is present in a community.

Ever since that first attempt to make rubbings which might be exhibited, I have continued to search for meanings relating this folk art form to the beliefs, customs, and institutions of the common people of Japan.

In the beginning my study of the background for these sculptures was concerned simply with gathering enough information to produce captions explaining each of the rubbings, which eventually I arranged to exhibit at the Lowie Museum of Anthropology at the University of California, Berkeley, from November 28, 1966, to January 3, 1967. After considerable frustration in searching for source material, complicated by my lack of ability in reading Japanese, I did produce the captions and a brief text explaining the symbols, location, nature, character, and purpose of these roadside sculptures. In that first research I found no source of information specifically pertaining to these folk deities as a class, and nothing at all that had been published about Dosojin in the Western world. Even in Japan very little had been published before 1960 on folk religion, Dosojin, phallicism, or shamanism.

In any event, the field notes and sketches which I had gathered in 1960–61 proved to be inadequate for the full interpretation of the symbolism of these sculptures. Even so, it was obvious that they could be separated into two groups, those which were Shinto, or indigenously Japanese, and those which were "foreign" because they reflected characteristics imported through Buddhism, Taoism, Confucianism, or other alien influences.

For the first category I developed a reference library of source materials by having translations made of books and articles written in Japanese by Hisakichi Takeda, Eiichi Ashida, Kunio Yanagita, Kei Wakasugi, Kenkichi Ito, Kenji Kawaguchi, Hachiro Daigo, Mukusaburo Mitsuishi, Hideo Nishioka, Chomei Shimizu, Kei Kato, and others.

Following the exhibition in the Lowie Museum I produced a paper entitled "The Folk Art of Japan's Roadside Gods," and on April 5, 1967, I presented it at a colloquium of the Center for Japanese and Korean Studies at the Berkeley campus of the University of California. The lecture was illustrated with ninety-nine slides showing different kinds of prehistoric figurines, plaques, and sacred roadside sculptures and monuments. The paper included chapters on folk religion, phallicism, various roadside gods, the couple Dosojin, and the festival of Dosojin, and a final chapter attempting to trace the continuity of folk religion in Japan until the present time. In making this effort I discovered the rich and diverse studies published by the Asiatic Society of Japan, which include works by Ernest Satow, M. W. de Visser, Karl Florenz, D. C. Buchanan, D. C. Holtom, R. J. Kirby, Arthur H. Lay, F. V. Dickins, and Robert Spencer. Then, too, there were the translations of the *Kojiki* (Record of Ancient Matters) by Basil H. Chamberlain and the *Nihongi* (Chronicles of Japan) by William G. Aston; Aston's work *Shinto: The Way of the Gods;* Dr. Genchi Kato's *A Study of*

Shinto: The Religion of the Japanese Nation; and Kato's early study of Japanese phallicism, as well as that by Edmund Buckley. Almost all those works were published before World War II and reflected, more or less, that period's lack of research in anthropology, archaeology, and aspects of folk religion, especially the subjects of phallicism and shamanism.

The religious ideas originating in ancient Japan are better understood today because of new knowledge and recent discoveries in formerly neglected subjects. Some new work has appeared upon the history of phallicism, though less has been done for shamanism. A considerable number of archaeological excavations since World War II have brought to light a wide variety of tombs, artifacts, accouterments, religious sites, and information about early religious practices, which help to establish the origin, character, and ritual of religious beliefs in prehistoric Japan.

It was only at this point that, after a great deal of study, the idea of writing this book and presenting the material that follows was suggested. This book does not make claim to being entirely original in research or thought, but it does attempt to bring together the results of the work of many scholars, both amateur and professional, whose scattered individual efforts I have tried to focus upon one subject of study, namely, the sculptures of Japanese folk worship and the religious ideas and practices of the common people who produced them. This religious activity among the common people established the characteristics of the Japanese folk religion, which in turn served as a foundation for Shinto and for some aspects of Japanese Buddhism. My creative contribution, if it can be called that, lies in presenting an analysis of Japanese religious thought outside of the presently accepted institutionalism, in interpreting the meanings of certain myths and stories as they relate to concepts originating in phallicism and shamanism, and in identifying the character and the purpose of certain ceremonies in the same context.

In summary, folk religion, of which these sculptured roadside deities are an intimate part, is significant not only because of its historic role in shaping the basic themes of beliefs, rituals, and customs, but also because it offers a means of understanding contemporary life in Japan. The bewildering material changes on the surface of contemporary life obscure the comparatively stable spiritual substructure of the society, which changes ever so slowly.[1] The ability to comprehend and to interpret societal activity at this substructural level is one key to an ordering of the chaotic surface phenomena. Jung gave us this insight, to help us achieve that understanding: "Comparative religion and mythology are rich mines of archetypes, and so is the psychology of dreams and psychoses. The astonishing parallelism between these images and the ideas they serve to express has frequently given rise to the wildest migration theories, although it would have been far more natural to think of the remarkable similarity of the human psyche at all times and in all places. Archetypal fantasy forms are, in fact, reproduced spontaneously anytime and anywhere, without there being any conceivable trace of direct transmission."[2]

The condition of the spiritual life of the Japanese people since World War II is revealed in their religious activities, as numerous cults and sects have been rejuvenated or born. These embrace many components, drawn in varying amounts from Buddhism, Taoism, Confucianism, Shinto, Christianity, animism, phallicism, shamanism, reverence for political and military heroes, remembrance of mythological deities, or *kami,* ancestor worship (in the family sense), preachings of self-appointed evangelists, and rituals of cults attached to a variety of annual celebrations, such as the "naked festivals," which, in one form or another, occur during every month of the year.

I wish to express my appreciation to the many people who played a part in this study: foremost among these are Mr. Yuji Abe, Mr. Sanshiro Ikeda, and Mr. Otosaburo Moriizume, who introduced me to the art of roadside sculptures and the making of rubbings; Dr. Osamu Funasaka and Mr. Akira Shirakawa, for their companionship and help as guides and translators during field work; Dr. Albert Elsasser of the University of California at Berkeley, and his aide, Mr. Alex Nicoloff, for originating and designing the Lowie Museum exhibition of my collection of rubbings; and again to Dr. Elsasser, for encouraging me in writing this book and for editing an early draft of it. I am grateful to the University of California Center for Japanese and Korean Studies for producing and distributing my paper "The Folk Art of Japan's Roadside Gods"; to Dr. George De Vos of the Department of Anthropology for his expert guidance, criticism, and suggestions for improving the original manuscript; and to Dr. Alan Dundes, Chairman of the Department of Folklore, and Dr. Felicia Bock, Lecturer on Japanese and Chinese Cultural History and Far Eastern Buddhism, for similar help.

I am especially indebted to Mr. Eiichi Ashida for supplying a large number of the photographs that are included here and for his helpful correspondence relating to Dosojin and religious folk customs, and to the Ikeda Publishing Company, Limited, Tokyo, for permission to reproduce Mr. Ashida's photographs in this book. I am also obliged to Mr. Sanshiro Ikeda for the loan of his entire collection of photographs of Dosojin, animal sculpture, and other deities. Mr. Gunji Ishikawa, Director of the Fuji Library of Fuji City, Shizuoka Prefecture, was very helpful in making his collection of photographs and notes available for study. I am grateful to those Japanese authors who presented me with copies of their books, and to the officials of various cultural groups who sent me copies of their studies of religious practices in local areas: Mr. Hachiro Daigo, Mr. Kenkichi Ito, Mr. Kenji Kawaguchi, and Mr. Mukusaburo Mitsuishi; officers of the Kofu Second High School Social Studies Club in Kofu City, Yamanashi Prefecture; the Committee for the Investigation of the Cultural Properties of Gotemba City, Shizuoka Prefecture; and the Board of Education of the Kanagawa prefectural government.

I am most grateful for funds provided by the University of California Committee on Research, which enabled me to begin this study.

I am thankful for the help of Miss Kinue Nagatomo of Yokohama, who has served me as researcher, typist, and translator since 1962, and to the other typists who have struggled with my difficult writing, Mrs. Betty Reid and Mrs. Michiko Peters.

The contribution of my wife I leave for final acknowledgment. Hers has been a continuing, quietly inspiring involvement at every stage of the work, especially in contributing to our long discussions about the varieties of meaning in dreams and symbols and in the imagery of rituals and myths that I have attempted to interpret in this book.

PART ONE

A RELIGIOUS FOLK ART

I

THE DOSOJIN SCULPTURES

Among the Japanese people themselves a renewed interest in sculptured wayside stones began after World War II as part of a folk art movement headed by the late Soetsu Yanagi, who was then an art critic, lecturer, and director of the Japan Folk Crafts Museum at Komaba in Tokyo. In his travels throughout Japan, while searching for craft products and encouraging a return to the manufacture of folk crafts, Yanagi inspired cultural leaders in the larger country towns to take an interest in the crafts of their respective localities. The artistry of many an anonymous craftsman was rediscovered in examples of woodcarving, pottery, netsuke, embroidery, weaving, dyeing, prints, ironwork, and other articles made for common use. Among these many discoveries were the sculptured wayside stones, particularly those in the Matsumoto area of Nagano Prefecture. Several people became interested in these wayside sculptures and started to make photographic records of them.

Coincidental with the discoveries of surviving folk crafts was a growing interest in roadside sculptures among teachers and students of schools, such as the Kofu Second High School in Yamanashi Prefecture. In 1957 and 1958 the Social Studies Club at that school carried out a two-year field survey of fifty-two towns and villages where Dosojin sculptures of one kind or another were found. The results of their study were published in 1959. A similar study by the Committee for the Investigation of the Cultural Properties of Gotemba City in Shizuoka Prefecture was published in 1960. The Board of Education of the Kanagawa prefectural government published a study concerned with the Dosojin festival. These investigations seem to have been inspired by the rediscovery of the book *Dosojin* written by Dr. Hisayoshi Takeda and published in 1941. Takeda was one of the pioneer investigators of Dosojin and the place of this deity in folk religion.

In rural settings, such as the countryside around Matsumoto, along dirt roads leading into small villages, there often stand groups of sculptured stones, three, four, or five upon a single site. These wayside images represent folk deities. Although they may take a variety of forms, their general function is to protect the village from evil spirits and also to grant such favors as people think lies in their power to do. A typical grouping of such stones may include a Koshin god, with fierce face and eight arms; the gentle monk Jizo (the bodhisattva Kshitigarbha); a miniature pagoda inscribed with a prayer to the Buddha Amida (Amitabha); and, almost always, a man-and-wife couple, a Dosojin.

The late Kunio Yanagita, an anthropologist, was among the first to search for the meaning and origin of those wayside deities. During the past thirty years other interested people, such as Eiichi Ashida, Kei Wakasugi, Hisayoshi Takeda, Mukusaburo Mitsuishi, Hachiro Daigo, Kenji Kawaguchi, and Kenkichi Ito, have explored thousands of square miles of countryside in search of wayside sculptures. They have located about forty thousand Dosojin sculptures alone, not including the more numerous Buddhist representations. Attempts have been made to classify the Dosojin, some of which are inscribed with dates of dedication and the names of donors. Neglect and vandalism, however, are causing the rapid destruction of these distinctive stone sculptures, and probably few will remain in place by the end of this century.

The worship of wayside deities was and still is carried on mostly by rural and agricultural people. Farm folk were far removed from centers of urban culture, and their feelings and attitudes were deeply rooted in the soil, their families and villages, and local heroes and histories. In this environment they created a style of life that was distinctively their own, complete with the deities that served them best. Japan is a land of festivals and ceremonies, in which almost daily some deity, somewhere, is acknowledged and given the remembrance that is his due.

Among these, Dosojin is an extraordinary deity—an invention of the minds of simple people in a time when belief in magic was commonplace. Dosojin is a benevolent deity, understanding, kind, generous, and—like the people who created him—long-suffering. People find it easy to approach him, to ask for things that will make their lives easier, happier, and more meaningful. He is made in their own image.

Types of Dosojin Images The variety of Dosojin images found in the field is very large; and it is interesting to note that the earliest types, which were natural objects, stand side by side with sophisticated carvings of more recent times. The earliest material form of this deity as a couple seems to have been a pair of trees, the pine and the myrtle being one combination. An old gnarled cypress with a hole in its lower trunk is another example. The tree is the male element, while the female element may be a hole in its trunk, a cavity formed by a coiled root, a round rock enwrapped by the roots, or a second kind of tree, usually an adventitious one. Such a Dosojin image can be seen near Myobu Shrine at Fushimi-Inari near Kyoto, where a certain pine tree has two main roots protruding and extending in a shape which is thought to be very suggestive of the pudendum. The name of this tree is Sho-ichi Kimyo Dai-Myojin, First-class Marvelous Great Enlightened Deity.[1]

The two great rocks standing just offshore in the sea near the village of Futami-ga-ura on the Ise Peninsula, not far from Toba village, are joined by a gigantic woven rope and are referred to as the "husband-and-wife deities." Very much smaller in scale are those compositions consisting of naturally shaped stones, found in stream beds and on rocky seashores, which are arranged side by side. In these pairings the male element is sometimes thirty to thirty-six inches high, and the female stone is rounded, flat, and much pitted with holes and crevices. Similar to these are images which have been partly or wholly shaped by the tools of a stone-cutter. The male stone can be a very realistic representation of a penis, or it may be so abstract as to resemble a mushroom. The female stone usually is a perfect sphere, which is placed beside the male "pillar." Sometimes the sphere is mounted atop a square-cut pillar three or four feet high, in a variation on the usual side-by-side arrangement. Small male pebbles found in stream beds are placed in miniature stone shrines, and sometimes the tiny chamber of the shrine is filled with a dozen or more of these smoothly polished stones. A large naturally shaped phallic boulder can be used as a base upon which the three characters *do, so,* and *jin* are carved. This is the calligraphic type of image. Specimens of this kind are greatly admired because often the calligraphy is done in the style of a famous master.

Dosojin also appears in some places as a single figure in the form of Saruta-hiko (Monkey Rice Field Prince) or Ugadama, goddess of food. And on the Izu Peninsula Dosojin often appears in a triad, as three separate divinities. These are variously identified, but the most popular version calls them Ugadama, Saruta-hiko, and Ame-no-Uzume-no-Mikoto (Heaven-alarming Female Augustness).

The Couple Dosojin   The type of image which is found in largest numbers is the so-called "man-wife deity," or the "couple Doso-jin." This kind of image is especially interesting because it so clearly expresses the duality of the deity's sex. It is truly unique. A few other gods in Japanese mythology are described as being both male and female, such as Fujin, deity of the wind,[2] but these are not shown graphically as such.

The merging of the male and female elements into one form is significant on several levels. Most often the Dosojin couple is identi-fied as being Saruta-hiko and Uzume, both phallic deities of some importance in Japanese mythology. Depicted as a couple, they ex-press the universal concept of genesis, or the universal wellspring of the creative impulse. In this sense, as Erich Neumann has stated, "masculine" and "feminine" are seen not as "personal sex-linked characteristics, but as symbolic expressions. . . . The symbolism of 'masculine' and 'feminine' is archetypal and therefore transper-sonal."[3] Some images of Dosojin show the couple in the act of coitus, and often this is judged on a personal level rather than on a symbolic one. "To call such images 'obscene,' is to be found guilty of a pro-found misunderstanding. Actually, life in those times was far more disciplined sexually, far purer, than in most of the later cultures; the sexual symbolism that appears in primitive cult and ritual has a sacral and transpersonal import, as everywhere in mythology. It symbolizes the creative element, not personal genitality. It is person-alistic misunderstanding that makes these sacral contents 'obscene.' "[4]

The male and female of the Dosojin couple are shown nearly always as equal in size and height and as being the same in shape of face and facial expression. Often it is difficult to determine which figure is male and which female. This technique seems to symbolize an equality between men and women generally, and between these two deities specifically, inasmuch as they represent the archetypal principles of creativity.

During the Yayoi period in prehistoric Japan (c. 200 B.C.–c. A.D. 250), cultivation of rice was the basis of the economic system, and the socioeconomic structure was a matriarchy. Women assumed important roles as priests and shamans. There were many female chiefs and several empresses. In consequence, it seems natural that the figures paired in Dosojin should be equal in size. The status of women deteriorated during the wars in the years when the country was being subordinated and consolidated by males. The connection undoubtedly is not direct, but the oldest Dosojin images never portray the female in a definitely subjugated position or as inferior to the male, whereas those of recent times, such as the Meiji era (1868–1912), definitely do so.

Characters Represented   The characteristics of the couples represented in the Dosojin sculptures resemble people drawn from all walks and stations of life, including the peasant and his wife, prince and princess, priest and nun, bride and groom, the young, middle-aged, and old husband and his mate, the concubine and her lover, mythological deities, and court figures. The poses assumed by the couples show them in wedding ceremony, in prayer, eating, drinking, holding hands sedately, chasing each other, dancing, embracing each other in different ways, kissing, and even in the act of coitus. The free, bold depiction of everyday life in all its progressions reveals the warm friendliness of the village people who created these deities in their own likenesses. The titles given by villagers to some of the sculptures suggest the range of their characteristics: Lovely Couple, Dancing Couple, Kissing Jizo, Love of Nuns, Whispering Dwarfs, Chubby Cheeks, Night and Day Love, Prince and Princess.

Not all such sculptures are inscribed with dates, names of deities, or sponsors, but often the following names are engraved upon them: Dosojin (Earth Ancestor Deity), Gaishin or Yoshin (Deity of the Town), Chimata-no-Kami (Road-fork Deity), Michi-no-Kami (Deity of Roads), Sae-no-Kami (Preventive Deity), Sai-no-Kami (Deity of Happiness), Funado-no-Kami (Pass-not Place Diety), Kunado-no-Kami (Come-not Place Deity), Yachimata-hiko (Eight Crossroads Prince) and Yachimata-hime (Eight Crossroads Princess), Yachimata-no-Mikoto (Eight Crossroads Deity), Sagami (Deity of the Sea or Deity of the Mountains), Saruta-hiko (Monkey Rice Field Prince) and Ame-no-Uzume (Heaven-alarming Female), Izanagi (Male Who Invites) and Izanami (Female Who Invites), and many others.

These variations in the names of Dosojin are based upon the particular use each community made of its deity—in other words, upon whether he functioned as a guardian of the village, or as a deity of sex or of agricultural fertility, or as some other kind of expression of his total powers inherent in the duality of phallicism.

Donors of Dosojin Images   On the back or the base of a Dosojin stone may be inscribed the name of its donor, the date of its installation, and, sometimes, a commemorative epigraph. In some instances the expense of buying and carving the stone may have been borne by a wealthy individual or by a group of men; in others a whole community may have contributed to pay the cost of erecting the deity-stone. In addition, a site for the image had to be provided, and the maintenance of the whole had to be assured for posterity. In this way certain families have inherited the privilege of caring for Dosojin from one generation to the next. During more recent times the names of donors and other details of the dedication of the site and of the statue in the name of the congregation have been recorded in official documents that are preserved in the village office. One village may have several congregations, each with its own Dosojin image.[5]

The forerunner of the Dosojin congregation is found in the open public meetings of earlier times. In the Edo period, from 1603 to 1868, congregations of commoners were organized according to place of residence or degree of kinship. Under that long rule of the Tokugawa shogunate, which was proud of being the strongest of all military governments, each commoner was assigned to one of three classes—the agricultural, the industrial, or the mercantile. All classes were required to pay very heavy taxes in cash or in produce (usually in rice), and if certain individuals were unable to do so a member of the family was conscripted for labor. This rigorous policy was put into practice systematically everywhere, regardless of whether it was applied to a farming community or to a fishing village. Village chiefs were responsible for the administration of the shogunate's laws. Farmers in general were divided into two groups, landowners and tenants.

Among commoners, sets of five neighboring families were organized by the law into a group known as a *gonin-gumi*, "five-person group," which assumed such responsibilities as paying taxes and preventing fires and theft. No farmer was permitted to sell the dry fields and irrigated paddies in his possession. In fact, during the Tokugawa dictatorship sumptuary laws regulated the personal life of all Japanese in great detail. In consequence, the extreme repression suffered by the common people built up in them a desire for freedom which burst out in many ways—and found readiest expression in sexual play at parties and festivals and in the worship of folk deities, such as Dosojin.

A congregation for the worship of Dosojin was gathered easily, for the worshipers had already been assigned by force of law (if sometimes against their will) to a gonin-gumi. In any locality, then, the congregation for the worship of a common deity could be found in such a group, already joined by the spirit of mutual aid. Once established, the congregation found or developed many other mutual benefits. As a group they offered assistance to needy people at times of rice planting and harvest, the construction and repair of a house, arrangements for a wedding or a funeral, and so on. The smallest congregation was formed by only a few neighboring families, but in most cases about fifty or sixty families in a community were organized into a congregation. The Dosojin congregation enjoyed a kind of extraterritoriality within the community, with certain benefits accruing to its members only.[6]

Characteristics of Form in Couple Dosojin Images   The stone sculptures of the couple Dosojin are found in a very great variety of designs and types. The differences in character are the result of many factors, such as the size, shape, texture, color, and structure of the stone; whether it is a natural or sculptured rock; and whether it has been provided with a base, a shaft, and a roof. Which of these elements are included, and how they are handled by the sculptor, are matters of local custom. The structural and formal elements of the design include such components as the size and shape of the stone, the base and roof, the size of the couple in relation to the stone, their posture in stasis or in action, facial expression and character, the head (without or with hair, headgear, or crown), the position of hands and feet, the presence or absence of clothing or costume, articles held or appearing as symbols, decorative elements, and the site.

Size of the Stone   The size of a particular Dosojin sculpture indicates the seriousness with which it was worshiped by the community, the financial condition of the congregation, and the availability of stone suited to the purpose in that locality. The largest number of couple Dosojin carvings are done on stones of moderate size, having a height of 16 to 28 inches not including the base (where there is one). In a total of 3,000 stones which Kenkichi Ito measured, 660 were 16 to 20 inches high, and 904 were 20 to 24 inches high. Only 150 were between 40 and 72 inches in height.

Base and Roof   Many couple sculptures are carved on naturally shaped stones which have been simply stuck in the ground to a sufficient depth to stand them upright. Many, of course, fall over as the ground is softened or worn away by rain. Other sculptured stones are set upon bases. These are level, flat stones either of unworked natural shape or fashioned into square-cut slabs, sometimes set up in two or three layers. In some instances the base is a stone wall or the extended foundation wall of a farmhouse or shrine.

Frequently the top of the stone is covered by an overhanging roof in order to protect the sculpture from rain and snow and from becoming stained and streaked by dripping water. Three other solutions to the weathering problem are found. The most common is to shape the top of the stone so that its sides slope upward to the center, making a peak like a gabled roof. In addition, this peak projects forward and overhangs the sculptured face of the stone. The effect is something like that of the prow of a ship, or the head of a hooded cobra, or, most strikingly as well as appropriately, like the glans penis. A second device is to slope the sides inward to form a peak or a shallow rounded canopy at the top. Then the vertical front face of the stone is cut back all around the figures so that, in effect, they stand in an alcove, out of the rain. The third solution is the direct one of placing a natural stone on top of the sculptured shaft, thereby achieving the effect of a hat. Often this capstone is given a conical shape and looks exactly like the roof of a house. There are many subtle variations on these three devices. Finally, some sculptures are housed within small wooden shrines which completely cover the stone but are too small for a person to enter. This is by far the most effective protection as long as the miniature building is maintained in good condition.

Degree of Intimacy   Dosojin stones can be separated into two groups according to the general posture and degree of intimacy or affection that is displayed between the two carved deities. This can vary from no sign of affection at all to the warmest of embraces. In the first group the figures stand erect, looking forward, without contact of any kind, and each seems to be unaware of the other. In the second group the deities appear to be aware of each other, facial expressions are evident, and there is body contact of some kind, expressing affection, love, or passion in varying degrees. Kenkichi Ito has observed that the degree of affection portrayed seems to vary in a direct relationship with the elevation of a locality above sea level. Thus the degree of intimacy displayed by the couple in five prefectures ranges downward from Nagano through Shizuoka, Gumma, and Kanagawa to Yamanashi. In other words (and only generally), the number of images observed in intimate poses is far smaller in the warm lowlands as compared with the number found in isolated and colder mountain villages.

The loving character of couple Dosojin is expressed by these symbolic or realistic positions of affection and lovemaking. In the unemotional types of sculpture, however, it is often hard to determine the gender of the figures. The female may be distinguished from the male by a small difference in the size of the figure or in the shape of the headdress or by a softer line of the face. Otherwise there is almost nothing to help in this determination. The equal size of the two figures would seem to indicate that the two partners are considered to be equals in love, and that the attitude toward love is idealized or spiritual. The number of sculptures of this symbolic kind is much smaller than is the number of the realistic or emotional type.

The following table compiled by Ito shows the distribution of the two types in the five prefectures where most couple stones are found:[7]

	Yama-nashi	Naga-no	Gum-ma	Shizu-oka	Kana-gawa	Total
Deities showing affection toward each other	183	648	347	564	327	2,069
Deities standing side by side	152	206	97	497	197	1,149

The posture of affectionate couples varies widely. Some are shown standing close together, almost in contact, side by side, faces toward the front, and either holding hands or with an arm around a shoulder or waist. The outside hands will be clasped in front, while the inside arms will be encircling each other's waist or shoulders. Another pose places the couple face-to-face in profile to the observer, and the hand of the male deity will be exploring within the garment of the female. A variation of this allows contact between the pair by having the male advance a leg against his partner. Another type shows the couple kissing. The love play advances from hand-holding, embracing, and caressing to kissing, and finally to the sexual act.

Couples in sexual intercourse are shown either symbolically or realistically. The poses of the couple vary according to these two types. Couples may be fully clothed, partly clothed, or naked in the act of coitus, standing, sitting, squatting, or lying down. The intent and the effect of these sculptures is not erotic or pornographic but, rather, is natural, matter-of-fact, and robust. The poses and expressions of the couples show a healthy sense of humor, geniality, and earthy pleasure. The god Kunado (Come-not Place) must also have been a protector of privacy for people during their lovemaking. Sumptuary laws controlled a great deal of the poor farmer's life, but they could not be enforced after dark.

Another kind of Dosojin shows the couple in a dignified pose, in wedding dress, or clothed in many different kinds of costumes, and in a variety of postures. They usually are standing erect in full-face or three-quarters full-face, but in some cases the bride is kneeling, squatting, or sitting, or even bending backward, as if off balance, and with a rather pained expression. This last kind of Dosojin negates the principle of equality in the partnership: here the male is dominant, and for this reason the type is called the "man-first style." Many of these are dated, showing that they were made seventy to a hundred or more years ago, preceding and during the Meiji era.

One other posture which appears in numbers sufficient to be recognized as a type is that showing the couple with hands folded in prayer. They usually are standing beneath a torii or temple entrance. This type is strongly influenced by Buddhism and is said to represent a couple to whom love or happiness comes through religion.

THE PREFECTURES AND MAJOR REGIONS OF JAPAN

TOHOKU
1. Aomori
2. Akita
3. Iwate
4. Yamagata
5. Miyagi
6. Fukushima

KANTO
7. Gumma
8. Tochigi
9. Ibaraki
10. Saitama
11. Chiba
12. Tokyo
13. Kanagawa

CHUBU
14. Yamanashi
15. Nagano
16. Gifu
17. Niigata
18. Toyama
19. Ishikawa
20. Fukui

TOKAI
21. Shizuoka
22. Aichi
23. Mie
24. Wakayama

KINAI
25. Shiga
26. Kyoto
27. Hyogo
28. Osaka
29. Nara

SAN'IN
30. Tottori
31. Shimane
32. Yamaguchi (northern)

SAN'YO
32. Yamaguchi (southern)
33. Hiroshima
34. Okayama

SHIKOKU
35. Kagawa
36. Ehime
37. Tokushima
38. Kochi

KYUSHU
39. Fukuoka
40. Saga
41. Nagasaki
42. Oita
43. Kumamoto
44. Miyazaki
45. Kagoshima

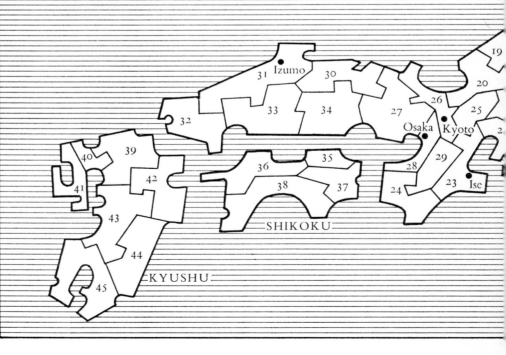

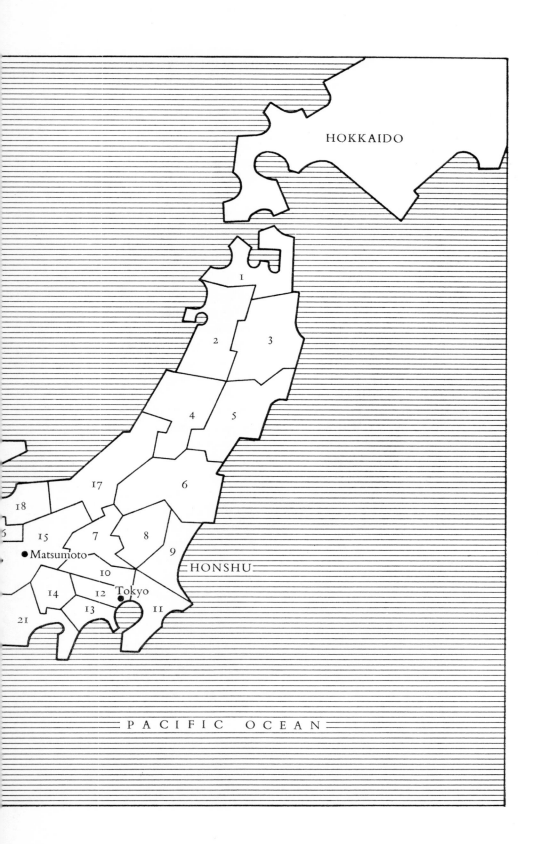

HOKKAIDO

1

2   3

4   5

17   6

18

16   15   7   8

9

●Matsumoto   10   HONSHU

14   12   Tokyo

21   13   11

PACIFIC OCEAN

Hands and Things in the Hands   The hands of the deity and the things held in the hands are significant elements that are used symbolically to express the sexuality of Dosojin. Sculptures showing the two deities engaged in sexual intercourse were subjected to controls by the government and by the Buddhist establishment. Trying to circumvent this censoriousness, the people were quick to change from a representational realism to a subtle symbolism. The sexual meaning was disguised by using a variety of devices and articles, such as showing the figures holding their hands in such a way that one suggests the vagina and the other the entering penis. Sexuality is emphasized by greatly enlarging the hand of each figure as it reaches toward the other's crotch. When in turn these relatively obvious devices were subjected to censorship, sculptors developed new forms which were much more discreet. One of these was to carve the sleeve of the female deity into a shape resembling the vulva by showing overlapping layers of several garments which cunningly suggested the labia of that organ. The male hand is shown placed over this artful site. This adaptation to need was a clever use of a symbolic form in yet another way, since it no longer required an unnatural lengthening of the arms in order to place the hands in the region of the partner's loins. The earlier designs, with their elongated arms and huge prying hands, do have a delightfully humorous quality, however, that was lost in later productions.

Objects held in the hands comprise another category of symbols used to express sexuality. The objects are male or female in character according to their shapes, and, as is only proper, each kind is held by the partner of the opposite sex. A sakè bottle or a gourd, for example, is held by the woman, and the sakè cup or dish is held by the man. Items carried by couples identified with Buddhism are such varied things as *tama* or *mani* (jewels), miniature pagoda or stupa, lotus flower, cane with ornamental head, begging bowl, and flower vase. The couple figures identified with Shinto hold such things as sakè bottle (or gourd, dipper, or jar) and sakè dish or cup, scepter and fan, sword, branch of the sacred *sakaki* tree, willow twig with *mochi* rice cakes impaled on its end, cane, spear, *gohei* (pendant paper strips, called *shide,* on a baton), *yufu* (a folded cloth), and *sambo* (a small wooden stand for holding votive offerings). The items carried by couples identified with authority, such as holders of high office, members of the imperial court, the military, and great deities, include the spear, sword, magic box, scepter, fan, scroll, and peach kernel.

The Buddhist symbols mentioned above indicate some reference to Buddhist doctrine in addition to illustrating sexuality. The tama or mani has the power of preventing all unhappy events and of purifying water. Moreover, it has the power to prolong life, insure safe delivery of babies, and answer prayers of all kinds. It is the perfect symbol of prevention and procreation. The miniature shrine, pagoda, or stupa is both a phallic symbol and one of adoration of the Buddha. The lotus flower and the flower vase are symbols of purity: the lotus rises out of mud, and the vase is a fertility symbol of plentiful yield—it is a cornucopia from which a deity may draw any kind of good thing. Dosojin posing as nun and priest often shows the male carrying a begging bowl, or a staff with its ornamental head of jingling rings. Both of these were used by traveling monks. The jingling staff was used as a support and as a defensive weapon against dogs, snakes, and hoodlums. It symbolized the truth as attained by the Buddha. It is also a phallic symbol. Often the top of the staff was modeled in the shape of a penis.

A delightful exception to the sculptures showing the gestures of hands and things held in the hand is the one that shows no hands. These are concealed in voluminous sleeves, which are held folded over the chest. The hands are suggested, and can almost be felt, within the sleeves.

The symbolic use of feet should be mentioned, since in art (and in symbolism) hands and feet are things of a kind. Most sculptures of Dosojin show a pair of feet as little more than stumps peeping out from under long robes. When the couple is wearing the bloomer-like trousers called *mompei,* the leg ends in a clumsy sort of foot, clearly visible, with all toes showing. On some sculptures there are no feet at all, the robes being carried down to the ground. But on a few statues the feet are shown enlarged and bare. The man's foot will be playing rather surreptitiously with the woman's foot. There are also some rare examples in which the couple is standing very close together, as if it were one body, with two heads and only two feet, symbolizing oneness.

Clothing and Headgear   The clothes in which the couple-deities are clad indicate their station in life, their occupation, or the activity in which they are engaged at the moment. Many are garbed in the robes of either a Shinto priest or a Buddhist priest. A favorite style is that of a high-ranking courtier of the Heian period (794–1185), while others show ordinary people in working clothes, in *yukata* (thin cotton kimono), or in kimono, either ordinary or elegant. Then there are figures garbed in a nondescript style, showing a mixture of Shinto and Buddhist priest's robes, a courtier's headdress, and things carried in hand that are not consistent with the station in life indicated by the robes. The dress of travelers is still another style: usually these figures are identified by the leggings, walking staff, and begging bowl of a Buddhist priest, and by indications of wrinkled clothing, suggesting that they have been slept in. The sculpturing of the clothing is very simplified in most cases, no patterning being shown. But in depicting courtiers, stone-carvers took great pains to show five, six, or seven layers of garments; and often the form of the headdress was executed with great precision, since it indicated the rank of the wearer.

Headgear and hair styles are of more interest than the clothing because, in addition to the fact that the forms are symbolic, often they are unusual and dramatic to Western eyes. Many of the male deities wear a kind of headdress known as *eboshi,* which in the sculptures is simplified into a conical form or into an unmistakable phallus. Eboshi, in a number of variations, were worn by courtiers, daimyo, and members of the warrior class. They appear upon the images of only a few male deities, for to represent the lordly headdress was a bold transgression for a sculptor. Many other kinds of hats are worn by the male deities; some look very much like the cloth caps of Englishmen. The "wedding type" of couple Dosojin shows the female with a so-called "fishtail hairdo." This is a very long type of ponytail arrangement, braided and decorated with ribbons, and ending in the shape of a fishtail. It denotes a court lady of very high rank. Sometimes male and female deities are shown with tall conical hats somewhat like small dunce caps. A few female figures wear no hat at all: their hair is held in place by a head band or by a folded cloth, a yufu, laid over the top of the head.

Decorative Elements and Symbols   The couple Dosojin figures are always carved against a background of some kind. It may be only the heavily textured stone itself from which the figures emerge; that is to say, the material immediately around the figures has been chiseled out and the figures project from the same face of the stone, as does the remaining border. The shape of this chiseled-out area was controlled. About forty standard shapes were used for the background and frame. Some of these are: circle, square, rectangle, bell, oval, tama (jewel), pomegranate, peach, sakè bottle, cocoon, torii, temple entrance, *shoin* window, shield, pear, lotus petal, and hut. In general, the shape of the niche enclosing the images helps to identify the figures as being Shinto or Buddhist in provenance.

Other than the background, the decorative element that appears most often is the calligraphy which identifies the village, donor, day, year, and occasion on which the stone was erected or dedicated. Sometimes the stone-carver's name also appears.

Symbolic elements appear in many forms: as clouds either under the feet or above the heads of the deities, as the sun or the moon, myrtle, pine needles, bamboo, wisteria, chrysanthemum, rooster and hen, gohei and *shimenawa* (a twisted rope of rice straw marking off a sacred Shinto area), the phallus, the lotus petal, and the Buddhist halo, all of which appear to lend meaning to the sculpture and to help establish the character of the particular Dosojin.

The Site The placement of a Dosojin sculpture was determined by a number of factors that differed with each community. Among these were the manner in which the congregation was organized, the location of the shrine of the tutelary deity of the village, and the special kind of function which that congregation wanted its Dosojin to perform.

Where Dosojin was wanted as a preventive deity, the site chosen may have been a spot along the village border, or beside a path leading down from the mountain, or at the end of a bridge. Because people believed that evil spirits descended from the mountains, Dosojin was placed facing in that direction so that he could not be taken unaware. Sometimes several small congregations from neighboring communities would join to finance one Dosojin sculpture. In this case a site would be chosen at the intersection of roads leading from all the communities, so that each congregation shared the same access to him. In a village having a tutelary deity resident in a shrine, the Dosojin sculpture often was placed as an adjunct to that deity, although housed in a small shrine of his own. Where the couple Dosojin was thought to be guarding each individual member of a congregation, and where he served as matchmaker, the image was placed at the center of the community. All members of the congregation pass through such a place and thereby Dosojin's work is made the easier. In most small villages a space is set apart adjacent to the town hall where public notices are displayed. (Today, a spindly steel fire tower is often found at this spot.) Such roadside deities as Dosojin and others occupy this site jointly. As a god of agricultural fertility, Dosojin is also located at crossroads leading to rice fields or at the edge of a rice field.

These general considerations were affected by the availability and suitability of land. Low ground would be undesirable, since it was subject to flooding. Orientation to physical and spiritual influences was also a factor. Some congregations felt that the couple Dosojin should not turn its back toward the Grand Shrines at Ise, where the sun goddess, Amaterasu Omikami, is enshrined. The same consideration might apply to some other important deity enshrined nearer by or locally. The capital city and the Imperial Palace required equal respect. Generally, it was considered taboo to allow the figure to face northeast or southeast, both inauspicious directions. Each year is supposed to have its lucky direction, as well as its lucky time, and the erecting and orienting of the sculpture was made to agree with these auspices.

Attributes of Dosojin   The worship of Dosojin reveals how widespread was the people's faith in this deity, perhaps because of the very flexible set of attributes they had given him. Either separately or at the same time, Dosojin is the guardian of travel, the watcher of the road, the defender against evil, the spirit ensuring bountiful crops, and the divinity determining the increase of mankind and the prospering of its generations. In practice, moreover, there is a great variety in the manner of worship of Dosojin, as the customs of several prefectures will illustrate.

In general, Dosojin is concerned with the basic problems of human existence, and it is in this context that Japanese regard him. "A child is born in a village, she grows to adolescence, she marries happily through the help of Dosojin, she bears a baby, and the baby grows up and marries . . . and so on. . . . This has been repeated for hundreds of years. Dosojin knows everything and every secret of the village people of the past and the present, and yet without a word he watches over the village and protects its people. Patiently, with a never–changing love, he guards, guides, and teaches the way of life to passing generations."[8]

II

THE WORSHIP OF DOSOJIN

Phallic deities in the form of roadside sculptures reached a height
of popularity in the eighteenth and nineteenth centuries. They were
regarded with affection, warmth, and familiarity, even to the point
of license. Their appeal was based upon the apparent effectiveness of
the deities they represented in solving the problems of daily life:
people prospered under them and so gave credit where it seemed to
be due. And, because people trusted and believed in phallic deities,
they devised ways of working and sharing in cooperation with one
another, so that, in time, life did seem to be easier and better. Actually
the change in the well-being of the people was due to the end of
feudal wars and to the improvements that came with agrarian
reforms. The change in the pattern of daily life was also brought
about by better systems of communication, by education, and by
advances in medicine, science, and agriculture. The problems and
crises of daily life were being met by new knowledge and new
methods.

As time went by, and religious attitudes changed slowly from
concern with spiritual values to desire for material rewards, the
phallic deities, too, changed in character. The lessening of the need
for protection and for worrying about agricultural abundance or
human fecundity was paralleled by an inevitable change in religious
ideas. In some places Dosojin became associated with the Hindu-
Buddhist Shoten, of the elephant features, and the sexual aspects of
his character were exploited by erotic cults. Other aspects of Dosojin's character were amalgamated with several other Buddhist

deities who now are considered to be good-luck divinities. They are recognized today not only in all concerns of family life but also in business and industry. Popular folk-art images of good-luck divinities appear on the family prayer shelf, and also in such places as the office filing cabinet, the bar of a drinking club, or the dashboard of a taxicab or bus. The old religious attitudes originating in animism deteriorated as a result of the popularity of the gods and the sophistication of the people. The pattern of change occurred slowly, in the course of several centuries, and at first was abetted by two forces: the families who controlled the central government, and the priests of the Buddhist establishment.

With the writing of the *Kojiki* (Record of Ancient Matters) in A.D. 712 and of the *Nihongi* (Chronicles of Japan) in 720, the ancient folk legends and the hierarchy of folk deities were fixed for both political and religious purposes. With the formalizing of this hierarchy and dogma, which together are the heart of Shinto, the rulers in power moved, as early as 789, to halt the indiscriminate addition to the pantheon of deities, whose numbers were already confusing to the populace. The reason behind this decision was twofold. First, the ruling families of the time were established in the power structure by being identified or associated with deities. Thus, by establishing relationships with officially recognized deities, other families, shut out from power, hoped to work their way into the select membership of the elite. The second reason lay in the fact that the masses of the people were using the animistic folk deities to suit their own vulgar purposes. These folk deities were competing for attention with the gods of the official Shinto pantheon, and the ruling classes felt themselves endangered thereby. The ruling classes sought to solidify their position by excluding any deity not related to their families' lines of descent from the primal ancestors. The common people, caught in this power struggle among the upper classes, tried to preserve the identity of their familiar old folk deities by associating them with Buddhist deities of more recent introduction.

Origin of the Couple Deity Mention of the worship of phallic deities represented as roadside sculptures in the couple form appeared first in *Fuso Ryakki,* a book written during the late Heian period. The following story was copied from another book on the second day of the ninth month, in the second year of Tenkei (939):

"Recently we see here and there in the capital at the point where two roads meet two wooden figures of gods placed facing each other. The male god figure is painted red and has rich hair topped by a headgear, whose ornamental strings hang down along the temples. Some pairs stand and some pairs squat. Each pair has different features, but all pairs are so arranged that two figures, one male and one female, face each other. Each figure has its sex organ carved below the belly. A small table is put before the couple with a receptacle on it. Many children gather together before the figures to worship reverently. The couple god's image is called either 'Kishin' [Mata no Kami] or 'Mitama' [Sacred Spirit]. It is not known what gods are represented by them. People think they are strange."[1]

The earliest reference to the custom of worshiping Dosojin for the purpose of matchmaking is found in a passage in *The Tale of Soga,* a picture scroll from the beginning of the Muromachi period (1336–1568): "The relationship between husband and wife, under the auspices of the deity of Izumo Road [leading from Kyoto] is far from being superficial; it is eternally unchanging. . . ."[2]

The Dosojin standing along the Izumo Road preceded by far the great deity of Izumo Shrine, Okuni-nushi-no-Mikoto (Great Land-possessor Deity), and was much more famous as far as matchmaking was concerned.[3]

In the front garden of the Tokyo National Museum stands a large upright stone that is considered to be the foremost example of the couple Dosojin. It was excavated in Ishigami, Asuka, Nara Prefecture, and is identified as belonging to the early part of the Nara period (646–794). This stone, about 5 feet 9 inches in height, is carved with the images of two clothed figures, male and female, in such a way that its entire surface is covered by the figures, each merging into the other. They stand neither side-by-side nor back-to-back but blend and flow around the whole stone, in three dimensions. The figures are primitive in appearance and the quality of the sculpturing is especially bold and simple, even crude. It is a very forceful sculpture. And it is unlike any other couple Dosojin yet found, although Eiichi Ashida has observed that the *saru-ishi,* or monkey stones, on the four corners of the tomb of Kibi-hime-no-Mikoto, who was associated with the great Prince Shotoku (574–622), and sculptures at other tomb locations have traits in common with this impressive Dosojin from the seventh century.

Dosojin: Two Meanings It is known that the characters for Dosojin first appeared in a collection of Japanese names in the *Wamyo Ruijusho,* a book compiled in the Heian period during the reign of Emperor Daigo (885–930). In that collection the characters for Doso are read "Sae-no-Kami," meaning "Preventive Deity."[4] Thus both Kunado-no-Kami (Deity Thrust-erect Come-not Place, usually shortened to Come-not Place Deity) and Sae-no-Kami (Preventive Deity), as symbols for the preventive aspects of phallicism, came to be called Dosojin. Those ancient powers were known as guardian deities of roads, and in this instance Dosojin was translated to mean "Road Ancestor Deity." However, Kunio Yanagita the anthropologist and folklorist, in a long exchange of letters with amateur scholars on this subject, discussed the differences between those deities known collectively as Sae-no-Kami, road-blocking deities, and the one known as Sai-no-Kami (Dosojin), the deity of happiness. Yanagita pointed out that images of Sai-no-Kami are found in many different kinds of places, not just along roads or at intersections, as are the Sae-no-Kami. For instance, Sai-no-Kami is found on promontories overlooking the sea, on river banks, along paths deep in the mountains, on ridges overlooking valleys, and in many other sites. Sai-no-Kami, or Dosojin, the deity of happiness, undoubtedly evolved from the phallic god Konsei Dai-Myojin (Root of Life Great Shining Deity), or Konsei-sama, who is represented by natural or carved stones in the form of male and female sex organs; or in images of the mountain deity Sanno; or in figures of monkeys with their sex organs exposed (and sometimes emphasized with red paint); or even by stone figures of men and women shown in the sexual act.[5] The attributes of these deities range from road-blocking and preventing evil to assisting in the creation of life. These are negative and positive forces, sometimes symbolically expressed separately and sometimes expressed together, as in the deity Dosojin.

In his book entitled *Gods of Doso*, Eiichi Ashida discusses the ancestral form of the ideographs for Doso in relation to calligraphic Dosojin carvings. He showed that *do* may be translated as either "road" or "earth," and that therefore Dosojin may mean "Earth Ancestor Deity" as well as "Road Ancestor Deity." This interpretation encompasses in one deity both the procreative and the preventive aspects of phallicism. As Ashida has pointed out, the procreative aspect of the character *so* is obvious in its ideograph, which definitely was meant to depict a phallus: "About 1400 B.C. in China there originated a style of pictographs on tortoise shell and bone which are thought to be the ancestors of Chinese characters as they are now known. [These pictographs were used in divinational practices.] The rudiment of the character *so*, standing for ancestor, . . . in the original tortoise-shell and bone pictographs was represented by the male sexual organ."[6] This can be seen clearly in Figure 8.

Similarly, the character for *do* in the form shown in Figure 67 unmistakably shows the female organ. Thus the appropriateness of translating *do* to mean "earth" is confirmed, since the earth is invariably referred to as being female. This explicit style of the ideographs used in writing the characters which identify Dosojin links Konsei-sama, represented by male and female organs, with Sai-no-Kami, deity of happiness.

Although most folklorists assume that the paired image of Dosojin came into being at about the middle of the Heian period, the oldest

Dosojin image discovered (excepting the Asuka stone) seems to be the one at Furumi, Asahi-mura, Nagano Prefecture, which is said to have been made in the Tensho era (1573–92). Beginning in about the mid-seventeenth century the creation of these statues flourished in two peak periods.[7] The first peak period included the eras of Genroku (1688–1704), Kyoho (1716–36), and Horeki (1751–64). The second peak period included the eras of Bunka (1804–18), Bunsei (1818–30), and Tempo (1830–44).

Two reasons are offered to explain these peaks of popularity. First, the fact that when the civil wars came to an end with the official establishment of Tokugawa rule in 1603, and the raising of great castles stopped as the long peace began, large numbers of masons were released from building fortifications and thereupon turned their talents to making gravestones and roadside sculptures. Second, at about the time of the Kambun era (1661–73) farmers began to emerge as an independent dominant class in the agricultural villages, which no longer were completely controlled by the daimyo, lords of the feudal demesnes. Thereupon the old system of political organization of farm workers into units mutually responsible for production, discipline, and collection of taxes was turned to recreational and religious purposes as well. Dosojin congregations were formed, and there was abundant production of religious and commemorative sculptures of many kinds, the largest proportion being Buddhist.

Diversity of Faith in Dosojin   The great diversity of phallic folk customs still in practice today shows that the original awe and reverence for the powers of procreation attributed to nature, to the phallus, and to phallic deities still exist, although they may not be as thoroughly understood by the people now as in former times.

As recently as a hundred years ago communication systems could not penetrate the isolation of villages and of whole districts in Japan. The religious attitudes of people in one area could be quite different from those on the other side of a mountain. Thus, the attributes of Dosojin varied in role and function according to the expectations of the people in a specific locality. Therefore the aspects which characterize each type of Dosojin image are derived in part from the history and the experiences of the people in each locality. But the worship of Dosojin was erected primarily upon the ancient two-horned potency of phallicism: the power of prevention and the power of procreation.

Dosojin as a Deity of Fecundity in Man   In certain regions of the country the custom of worshiping the Dosojin image is followed for the purposes of begetting children, finding suitable marriage partners, and attaining happiness in the sexual experience. Dosojin images scattered here and there throughout the rolling country drained by the Fuefuki River in Yamanashi Prefecture are worshiped by people to whom a child has been born recently or by people who hope to produce an heir. In olden times the sterility of a wife could be a reason for divorce. In farm and mountain villages the family could not survive without the helping hands of many workers. Children were wanted and loved. In such places many of the images are shown face-to-face in close embrace, symbolizing the sexual act. In the Dosojin festivals of such regions models of the sexual organs are made from straw and the leaves of an evergreen tree and are placed in position together. Members of the congregation bring drawings of the sexual organs on sheets of paper of uniform size, which are bound in book form and burned in the Dosojin festival fire. Barren women pray to Dosojin to grant their hope of becoming pregnant.[8]

The villages of the Lake Suwa area, 120 miles northwest of Tokyo, have long been famous for the beauty and charm of their young girls, who are of a gentle and industrious nature. They are supposed to make ideal wives. The custom is still popular among the young girls in hot-springs towns of this vicinity to smear o-hagi (a rice cake covered with sweet bean-jam) over the faces of the couple Dosojin on the morning of January 8. The first girl to do this is assured that she will marry into a very rich family.[9]

While the couple Dosojin image is found mostly out of doors, in the fields and woods or along roads, some images which are considered to be very special are kept as altar pieces in shrines. One such pair, carved in wood, is located at Tsurushi-Sakai in Yamanashi Prefecture. They represent the deities Saruta-hiko and Uzume. Saruta-hiko is a solemn bearded figure with a realistic phallus for a nose. Uzume is shown with exposed breasts, a pot belly, and an open mouth set in a pudendalike face.[10]

In Tottori Prefecture, where the worship of Dosojin is still very popular, the people revere a variety of symbols, such as standing trees, natural stones, small stone shrines, and the like, which they identify as Sai-no-Kami, the deity of happiness. The number of stone images of Dosojin appears to be limited, however. The people of this prefecture follow the custom of dedicating straw horses and straw-wrapped parcels of rice cakes to Dosojin, whom they regard as the deity of matchmaking. Young men and women visit Sai-no-Kami, beginning just after midnight on the fourteenth of December (according to the lunar calendar), the day of the annual festival. The young people compete for the chance to be the first to pay their respects to the deity and to assure themselves of a share of good luck before it runs out. Go-betweens, elders who assist young people in finding marriage partners, are called "sai-no-kami" in this region.[11]

In the area from Nagano to Iwate prefectures, Dosojin was considered a member of the family. He was represented by wooden images about twelve inches high placed on the family prayer shelf. Offerings were presented to him just as to family ancestors. Because infant mortality was very high, Dosojin was asked to protect the children from sickness and death.

Before the Dosojin festival, these images, both male and female, were taken down and dragged on the ground by a string tied around their necks. Children threw these carvings at the doors of houses or at recently married couples when they came out into the yard. In this way Dosojin's power to assist in begetting children was passed on to husband and wife. In return, the favored couple was expected to contribute money to help pay for the costs of the festival. Today, these wooden images are smaller, being made of branches of trees, one to two inches in diameter and four to eight inches tall. Faces, painted on paper with ink and colored pencils, are glued to the tops of these sticks.

Dosojin as a Preventive Deity   Smallpox was a much dreaded disease in the old days. Often enough, if the victim recovered he was marked for life with a pitted skin. The appeal to Dosojin for protection against this pestilence was widespread. In Kanagawa Prefecture, the practice was to make a ring of bamboo and cover it with red paper. The person for whom the immunity was requested, usually a child, would step on this object before offering it to Dosojin. Another practice believed to be effective for this purpose was to pour scalding water over the statue's head.[12]

In Shizuoka and Nagano prefectures, to ward off smallpox people suspended the round straw lid from a rice tub over Dosojin's head.[13]

On the Izu Peninsula there is a widespread belief that in October (which is called Kanna-zuki, the Month of No Gods) all good deities go to Izumo. Taking advantage of their absence from communities, the deities of pestilence make a round of visits to villages in order to select those people who are to be afflicted with sickness and misfortune. However, since Dosojin images are guarding the villages, standing at borders, at crossroads, and elsewhere, they confront the deities of pestilence when they come demanding the lists containing the names of all the villagers. In each village the evil deities are forced to negotiate with its Dosojin to obtain the names of his people who will be stricken during the following year. Dosojin raises objections, and withholds the list, and allows only the very minimum number of names to be recorded in the stone book he carries in his hands. At the festival of Sankuro, on January 15, he and his notebook are burned in the fire, and the names written in the book are destroyed. Thus does Dosojin protect the dwellers in his village.[14]

Dosojin as a Fertility God in Agriculture and Fishing Dosojin is identified as a phallic deity and as Earth Ancestor Deity. The phallus as a magic symbol protected rice fields from noxious insects and other natural afflictions. Dosojin images often are enshrined beside those of Yama-no-Kami (Deity of Mountains), who becomes Ta-no-Kami (Deity of Rice Fields) when he descends from his home in the mountains (*yama*) to the plowed rice fields (*ta*) in the spring. All these are earth gods, and Dosojin as Earth Ancestor Deity includes the other two.

Ashida, in *Gods of Doso,* has traced this relationship between Dosojin and Yama-no-Kami: "At Sayamoto, Takada City, Oita Prefecture, they enshrine a naturally shaped phallic stone at the stone altar of the shrine of Yama-no-Kami, and . . . on the fourteenth of January each year they hold a meeting called Oni-e to pray for rich rice crops, when they burn bamboo torches on the summit of the mountain at the back of the shrine. The villagers refer to this as the fire of Dondon-yaki. The deity called Saya-no-Kami, from which the place name Sayamoto was derived, is enshrined in this shrine of Yama-no-Kami. At Tamura, Chichibu City, they burn the pine gate decorations on the day of Sho-Shogatsu [Little New Year], and this event is called Yama-no-Kami."[15]

In the northern part of Shinshu, as Nagano Prefecture was called in earlier times, Dosojin is worshiped on the Day of the Horse, according to the lunar calendar (about February 1), when Yama-no-Kami in the form of a snake descends to the plains to become Ta-no-Kami. Offerings of straw horses loaded with packets of rice are presented to him.

The fire festival celebrated in front of Inari Shrine at Oiso in Kanagawa Prefecture on November 8 as the Fuigo Matsuri, or Bellows Festival, finds Dosojin present in the form of phallic symbols on the occasion of the return of Ta-no-Kami to the villages of the mountains as Yama-no-Kami. Furthermore, the Dosojin that is worshiped at various communities in Sannohara, Odawara, Kanagawa Prefecture, consists of a pair of male and female foxes carved in wood and painted white.[16]

According to Ito, these wooden foxes are kept in the homes of members of the congregation on a rotational basis and are brought out only on the day of the Dosojin festival. Thus the link between the fox, the original spirit of rice, and Inari (the deity of rice) on the one hand and Dosojin on the other is established. Dosojin, in this case, safeguards the production of the fields and of the sea.[17] Moreover, "the idea that the deity who grants the benefits of the five cereals is the ancestral spirit who watches over the prosperity of the villages from the top of the mountain caused the uniting of the deity of the mountains with the deity of the fields. Thus Dosojin came to be regarded as Shogatsu-sama (New Year Deity), Sorei (Ancestral Spirit), Yama-no-Kami (Deity of Mountains), Ta-no-Kami (Deity of Rice Fields), Doro-no-Kami (Deity of Roads), Fusagi (Blocking Deity), Seishin (Deity of Sex), En-musubi (Deity of Matchmaking), and Geinoshin (Deity of Entertainment Arts)."[18]

Statues of Dosojin carved in the round are peculiar to the Izu Peninsula, and the custom in the villages along the east coast, when fishing luck runs bad, is for fishermen to ask the children to throw Dosojin into the sea. Also, when friends become sick, children pray for their recovery by striking Dosojin upon the head, shouting the while, "Cure it, cure it, cure it." The Izu Dosojin often is composed of three figures squatting on separate pedestals, the center figure being the largest. Some scholars think that this triad is Ugadama, Saruta-hiko, and Uzume. Others feel that the trinity represents Musubi-no-Kami (Deity of Growth), Izanagi, and Izanami. In any event, it is still a Dosojin image.[19]

The different customs that have evolved for worshiping Dosojin show that he has many attributes and that people petition him for a variety of personal reasons in their search for happiness and well-being. The fact that Dosojin sculptures were given shapes like those of the villagers themselves made them think of him as one of their own. In the course of time his popularity spread across the mountains and through the valleys of central Japan, so that it might be said that a Dosojin culture was established there. In the western part of this central region, several different Buddhist deities usurped some of Dosojin's authority, but the erection of new Dosojin sculptures in recent years affirms both his power and the vitality of the ancient religious beliefs among the country folk.

THE FESTIVAL OF DOSOJIN

The people of farming communities and fishing villages anticipate their festival days, as all people do, with delight and excitement. The rigors of their daily existence serve to sharpen their enjoyment of the few rewards they can depend upon, among which are the festivals that are celebrated during the year. The festival of Dosojin has always been a popular one in rural communities. In some places it is held soon after the New Year, on January 14 and 15, which is the "Little New Year" or Sho-Shogatsu; but in those communities that still use the lunar calendar it is delayed by a month.[1] This regard for the old calendar is most frequently encountered in mountain hamlets and small fishing villages remote from large cities. In a sense this festival is a continuation of the ceremonies of the New Year, which begin with purification rites at the end of December.

The Joya-sai, or New Year's Eve Festival, is observed on the night of December 31, when thanks are offered to the deities for having safely brought their worshipers through another year. Each household is decorated with shimenawa, ropes of plaited rice straw, hung above gateways and doors. Other decorations are composed of ferns, lobster effigies made of papier mâché, oranges, strips of seaweed, and the white paper strips called shide. These are good-luck talismans. Mochi, or glutinous-rice cakes, and small flat cups full of sakè are placed upon the *kamidana,* the "god shelf," or household Shinto shrine. A pine branch and a bamboo stalk, representing the male and female elements, are placed on either side of the main entrance to the house.

On January 1 the emperor pays his respects to the deities enshrined at Ise—the sun goddess, the food goddess, the kami of heaven and earth—and also to the kami of several of his ancestor-emperors, such as the emperors Jimmu, Meiji, and Taisho. On January 3 the emperor participates in ceremonies dedicated to Prince Ninigi, the grandson of the sun goddess. People in general follow the emperor's example by reverencing ancestral deities within their own families, chasing evil spirits away from the house and yard, kindling a new fire, and establishing fresh relations with tutelary deities. These ceremonies take place in the first days of the new year. All obligations of the ending year must be fulfilled before the new one arrives: promises are kept, debts are paid, borrowed things are returned, and in this way the new year is started with a clean slate.

The purpose of the Dosojin festival is to welcome the spirit of Dosojin so that the people of the community may pay their respects to him for all the favors he has granted during the year. In return for their worship of Dosojin they obtain security, food, shelter, clothing, money, and material success. Happiness for individuals comes through matchmaking, marriage, lovemaking, pregnancies, the bearing and raising of children, and other forms of personal gratification. The Dosojin festival is connected with the New Year celebration, during which the tutelary deities of the village and the ancestral spirits of families and of the nation make their annual visits to their shrines. The festival is also the occasion for the departure of those ancestral spirits in the smoke of the festival fire. But the ancestral spirits of the nation, it is said, also return to visit at each change of season.

The name of the Dosojin festival varies with different communities, but, since the major rite on this occasion is the burning of a sacred tree, in most places the name is derived from a reference to the fire. Hence it is called the festival of Tondo-yaki, Dondon-yaki, Sankuro, Sagicho, and Dorokujin, as well as of Dosojin. In Kyushu it is called Onibi, Ondobuè, or Onekko, all of which are names for the tree. The general style of all these tree-burning festivals is the same, and a fun-loving spirit pervades them.

The planning and promotion of the annual Dosojin festival is the responsibility of the *kanjin-moto,* the festival-promotion group. This consists of a leader and two groups of men, one of elders and one of men under thirty-five years of age. The office of *miyamoto,* chairman of the village Dosojin association, is either hereditary or determined by election from the elder group in the kanjin-moto. The miyamoto is also the chief of ritual matters for the festival. The elder group, usually consisting of three or four men, is known as *miya sewanin;* it is responsible for arrangements relating to the Dosojin shrine, such as preparing the image or symbol of Dosojin, lighting lanterns, and erecting the hut. The younger group, consisting of five, ten, or even twenty men, is called *wakashu sewanin;* they do the more active work involved in organizing and producing the festival.[2]

On January 2 the festival-promotion group meets for its first planning session for the coming celebration. After January 7, when traditionally seven kinds of herbs are eaten, and January 11, when the initial event connected with rice planting takes place, they begin to carry out their plans. Having prepared the community by means of a general announcement, they start collecting donations for the purchase of trees, decorations, ropes, and supplies to be used during the ceremony.

The festival of Dosojin is the happiest and most carefree of the yearly celebrations because young people, and especially children, take part in it. The young people are involved in preparations for days in advance. They are divided into groups according to age or sex and go about visiting recent newlyweds and extending best wishes to the brides. They carry a kind of baton made of straw, with which they strike the young wife on the hips or buttocks. This act is supposed to bring her good luck in becoming pregnant and an easy time during childbirth. These groups of young people visit each member-family of the Dosojin congregation to receive their contributions for the promotion of the festival. They accept money, food, sakè, and materials for decorating the festival tree and for burning in the festival fire.[3]

An old custom, essentially the collection of dues, is still observed in the community of Ami-Isahiki in Odawara, Kanagawa Prefecture: families who have teen-age children contribute to the congregation four pints of sakè for each boy and two pints for each girl. A similar but smaller contribution is made when a child graduates from grammar school.[4]

On December 8 the event of Ichiban Musuko, or First Son, takes place. Young boys make the round of houses in the community, and in each yard they attempt to lift a heavy stone, which is wound around with a rope, and then pound the earth with it. The oldest boy in the group tries first, and each boy's effort is accompanied by a chant, the words of which are adapted to the occupants of the house. Thus, at a house where there is an heir or heiress the boys will chant: "May a good bride (or bridegroom) come to so-and-so, Ichiban Musuko." At a house where there is no child, they will sing: "May a good baby be granted to you, Ichiban Musuko."

Business houses are included in this visiting. The boys try to lift the stone, but only a few are able to do so. These successful ones expect to receive donations of money, which they turn over to the miyamoto. He buys *tofu,* or soybean curd, with some of this money, and distributes it to the households so that all the contributors and their families may be protected from disease. The boys are given treats for their good work.[5]

These roving bands of children are full of high spirits. They recite prayers and sing songs. Some of the songs are bawdy and affectionately insulting to those to whom they are addressed, whether they be young wives or husbands, spinsters or bachelors. People are not the only objects of this teasing attention, for all kinds of liberties are taken with Dosojin: his statue may be beaten with sticks, smeared with mud, urinated upon, and otherwise insulted. All this is done by way of showing that Dosojin is considered to be like one of the villagers.

Early in the morning of January 11, *matsu-kai,* "going out to buy pine trees," takes place. In the old days the direction to the east was thought to be auspicious, and the party sets out accordingly in search of a tree.

At Asama, in Kanagawa Prefecture, about one hundred young men from fifty or sixty families go into the hills near Hiratsuka to purchase trees. They buy two large pines, each about fifty feet tall, and thirty-five to fifty men will carry each of the trees home. They also buy one large *ombe* bamboo and two slender *shime* bamboos with which to mark the village border and from which gohei are hung.

The event of purchasing pine trees to be shared by the eight communities of Oiso is marked by pretended arguings, and is called the Quarreling Festival. On the way from Hiratsuka the men sing songs, such as: "Even iron mountains cannot beat / Such a number of men, *sora yare!*" or "Auspicious, auspicious, / Honorable Young Pine . . ."

On the way home, when the tree-carriers reach the Hanamizu River, they stop at its bank to cut willow branches upon which rice dumplings will be impaled and roasted in the festival fire before they are offered to Dosojin.[6]

Today, in most villages, trees are bought at a lot where they are being sold, much as Christmas trees are sold and bought in the United States.

The Festival Tree   Each community has a special name for the sacred tree. Generally it is called *yorishiro-gi,* deity-descending tree, or *o-shimboku,* sacred tree; or, in Nagano Prefecture, *o-hashira,* honorable pillar. When a very large tree is chosen it is called *nembashira,* gigantic pillar. Such a great tree must be propped up by two or more *kaebashi* or *ukebashira,* supporting pillars. As we shall see, the concept that the spirit of a deity dwells in a tree, or descends from upper space by way of a tree, has been handed down from very ancient times, when a shrine was simply a place deep in a primeval forest.

Different kinds of trees may be chosen as yorishiro-gi, the most popular being the cryptomeria, cypress, pine, bamboo, and willow. In Kanagawa Prefecture the congregation of the Ashigawa group selects as its sacred tree the *ombe-dake,* a green bamboo. Upon this is draped a large banner bearing huge characters in black ink which read, "In respect to Dosojin."[7]

The sacred tree is decorated with symbols of the sun and moon made of papier-mâché, arrows, five-color paper pendants, masks, fans, images of Daruma, straw sandals, shimenawa, and so on. But above all, the main decorative feature is an unmistakable phallic symbol, in the form of either a large papier-mâché cone or a *hiichi,* a triangular flat bag made of black cloth and stuffed with wadding (and representing, of course, the pudendum). This is placed high on the tree. Sometimes a large fan with the red disk of the Japanese sun painted upon it is fixed to the very top of the tree. In some villages small bamboo stalks turned upside down are tied to the sacred tree in order to make it burn better when it is set afire. New Year gate decorations, pine branches, and other flammable materials are placed at the base of the tree to feed the fire.

The tree is decorated while it is still lying upon the earth, and then is raised and fastened in position with ropes that secure it either to the ground or to nearby housetops. The lines made by these ropes are likened to the outline of a mountain, and in more ways than one they link the mountain deity with Dosojin. This mountain shape is regarded as a fertility symbol and even appears on some of the floats in Kyoto's famous Gion Festival.

A small signal fire is lighted close by the sacred tree to attract the deity spirit from afar as it approaches the village. Because spirits descend best at night, the ritual of *kami-oroshi,* calling down of the deity, takes place during the night preceding the one on which the tree is to be burned. Offerings are made to the deity of the festival throughout the night so that the tree which is his temporary abode will not be set afire prematurely.

The Seven Deities of Luck   On January 11, at about nine o'clock in the evening, the kanjin-moto group of Shimofukuzawa, in Yamanashi Prefecture, go out to visit the families which have held a wedding during the previous year and those in which the head of the house is entering upon a year of ill omen. (The forty-second year is considered an especially worrisome time for men.) The chief of the group heads the procession, followed by young men variously costumed as a lion, the Seven Gods of Luck, and Saruta-hiko (represented as Hyottoko, a funny-faced man) and Uzume (represented as Okame, a fat-faced woman). Musicians playing flutes and drums bring up the rear. As the group approach each house they plan to visit, they chant merrily:

"Oh, how auspicious, how auspicious.
The Seven Gods of Fortune are here.
Oh, how auspicious! How auspicious!"[8]

The Seven Gods and the others are welcomed by the family and invited to enter the guest room. They cheer and sing as they go in. The head of the procession occupies the seat of honor, and to his right are seated the lion and the Seven Gods of Luck in this order: Ebisu, Daikoku, Fukurokuju, Bishamon, Benten, Hotei, and Jurojin, followed by Okame and Hyottoko. To the left of the leader sit his assistants, two of whom are middle-aged married men, and the musicians. After a prayer of greeting to the deities is recited by the assembled family, the chief of the procession makes a congratulatory speech and presents to them, as a gift from Dosojin, a wooden tray bearing a phallus head made of red lacquer. The bride, who has been waiting in another room, is led in by the head of the household to join the company. The chief of the procession faces the young married couple and makes some congratulatory remarks, part sermon, part obscenity. The lion performs a dance, after which the Seven Gods of Luck get up and, with cheerful words and gestures, scatter leaves (as make-believe coins) all through the house. The spectators join in the merrymaking throughout the ceremony.

At this point the performance of *okata-uchi,* beating the bride (which is now out of fashion), used to take place, to the accompaniment of such chants as this:

"Let us say words of congratulation
To the house of the bride.
The bride in one corner of the storeroom
Has her face thickly covered with paint."[9]

The ritual of driving away evil for the sake of men who have reached the age of forty-two is performed in much the same way. The main difference is in the chief's speech, which starts: "Dosojin has come, with the company of the Seven Gods of Luck, to the house of Mr. So-and-so to drive away evil spirits from his forty-second year."

The chief advises the man to follow the example of some successful or famous person who has made a fortune in the same business as his. Then the gift of Dosojin is offered, together with this homily: "The gift which Dosojin presents to you today is made of *katsu* wood [a kind of sumac tree, presented because another word pronounced *katsu* means "to win"], which has the power of overcoming any difficulty. You must place this in the family shrine and, if you worship this morning and evening, you will be guaranteed the power to overcome all difficulties. Do you understand?"[10]

In both these ceremonies the symbol of the phallus is presented for its magical power. But Hyottoko and Okame, the characters representing Saruta-hiko and Uzume, do not participate in this phallic rite because their roles have degenerated to those of grotesque clowns. Their symbolic function has been taken over by the Seven Gods of Luck, who are lavishly endowed with sexual power and with the ability to grant sudden and great wealth.

Votive Offerings   Throughout the year, as well as at the Dosojin festival or Sankuro festival, people pray and make offerings to Dosojin. The kinds of offerings they select reveal the nature of their prayers or the problems weighing upon their minds. As an offering, rice seems to rank first. It is presented in the form of mochi cakes or dumplings, or as a paste which is smeared over the faces of the sculptured figures. Sakè, rice wine, also is presented on special occasions. Miniature wooden models of rice bales and sakè barrels are used as offerings. Even as seed planted in the earth eventually bears fruit, so does rice by the same kind of miracle change into sakè. These are fruits of the earth in the same sense, and they symbolize spiritual transformation. This may explain why "intoxicating spirits and fertility orgies were always associated with one another in the ancient world."[11]

The *shintai,* or physical manifestation, of Dosojin is a stick, representing the phallus; and any object or utensil that retains the long shape associated with the phallus may be offered, such as a spoon, water dipper, or back scratcher. A mortar and pestle is a perfect symbol representing both the male and the female. The female symbol is also represented by abalone shells, round pebbles, and flat saucers or sakè dishes. These last are piled high in front of Dosojin. Phallic objects of woven straw, the baton and the sphere, are common in Tottori Prefecture and elsewhere. The straw horse is a symbol favored by young men and boys. Vegetables and fruits are offerings indicating hope for happiness in lovemaking. Popular items for males are elongated objects, such as a forked radish, or a cucumber, squash, or eggplant; and for females they are spherical objects, such as a potato, peach, or persimmon. When the Dosojin sculpture is a free-standing statue, it is often clothed in a red cap and a red apron as a sign of sexual power. The color red signifies virility, and red beans are mixed with rice to make a symbolic dish for people to eat in order to assure good health.

Another kind of offering is the one associated with the preventing of illness or with other specific personal wishes. It takes the form of messages written on strips of paper, which are tied to branches of trees near the Dosojin stone. Messages also may be written on fans, scrolls, wooden plaques, or shaven forked sticks. The specific malady or misfortune, such as toothache, sore throat, or the alienated affection of a spouse, is presented to the god for remedy. Another preventive type of offering is the one used to drive away demons. For this purpose such things are used as sardine heads, thorny laurel twigs, dried beans, and hard peas. The first two are hung above doorways or upon gates, while the latter are scattered about the house or yard.

The stick as the shintai, or physical manifestation, of Dosojin takes on special form in a symbol called the *kezurikake*. This is a baton of elder or willow stripped of its bark, one end of which is made into a tufted head by cutting paper-thin shavings on it with a sharp knife. The stick is twenty-four to thirty inches long, and the arrangement of the shaved end takes many forms. Frequently the lower end is decorated with figures drawn in black ink, the favorite symbols being those of long life, such as the heron, tortoise, or pine, bamboo, plum, and myrtle leaves. Such a kezurikake made from the wood of a thorny tree is placed at both sides of doorways and under the eaves of a house as a talisman against evil spirits. The kezurikake is set upon family altars for the same reason. The sacred fire of Dondon-yaki is transferred to the family hearth by means of a kezurikake burning like a torch. In this way the hearth is blessed and good fortune is assured. Sticks, especially forked sticks, are shaved of their bark at the upper end, and human faces are painted upon them to represent the fertility gods Saruta-hiko and Uzume. Thus these deities are linked with the tree-fork deity, who guards the productivity of orchards.

A substitute sacrifice which can be made to Dosojin, as well as to other deities, is the *ema,* or painted wooden votive plaque upon which the intended actual offering is depicted. Just as the sacrificing of actual horses gave way to the giving of woven straw horses, so did the presentation of actual things give way to pictures of those things. Subjects or objects frequently pictured upon ema are the large white radish called *daikon,* representing a phallus; a woman embracing a phallus; the human sexual organs, male or female; the loins, symbolizing the spirit, shown locked in a vise, symbolizing lust; and the three wise monkeys with heads carved as phalli. A horse, rooster, monkey, or any other "fecund animal" can also be painted or carved upon ema. And lately, ema themselves are also pictured on pieces of paper rather than on the more expensive carved or painted wooden plaques. The latter have become collector's items for tourists.[12]

Finally, offerings are made of folk toys and decorative or utilitarian articles. These include both male and female Daruma dolls made of papier-mâché; the bodiless head of the Buddha; *kokeshi* dolls, male and female, on which sexual symbols are carved or painted; ceramic phalli; ceramic foxes with bushy tails; ceramic roosters and hens; and copulating farm animals. Many kinds of folk statues are offered to Dosojin, such as those depicting an old couple; or a priest and an old woman; or three old ladies of a dance group, exposing their buttocks; or a ceramic phallus upright in a boat; or a ceramic face of Uzume with puffed cheeks and open mouth, and one of her partner with his phallus nose. All these products of folk art are humorous, as well as mildly and delightfully obscene.

The Fire   The burning of the sacred tree is the emotional climax of the Dosojin festival: this is the big event that the villagers eagerly anticipate. The burning of the tree is the ritual purification of the village and of Dosojin, whose stone image, when it is placed in the fire, is cleansed of the contaminations it has accumulated during the year of standing guard against evil spirits.

In addition, the fire is a method of divination for an individual person. Young people who are trying to learn the art of writing *kanji,* the complex Chinese characters, burn their first efforts of the year in this fire, believing that because they do so Dosojin will give them greater skill. People of all ages cook mochi in the fire, in the belief that after they have eaten the rice cakes they will be protected against toothache, colds, and other common ailments. People bask in the heat of the fire, thinking that it will help cure rheumatism, ensure easy delivery of babies, and bring succor to other less common conditions. Hearth fires are lighted anew from the festival blaze because people believe that this will help to prevent accidents in the use of the cooking fire. The ashes of the festival fire are taken home and scattered about the yard and upon the roof of the house as protection against the entrance of snakes and centipedes. The list of such beliefs and practices is long and diverse.

At last the moment arrives for the *kami-age,* the ritual of sending off the spirit of the festival, Dosojin, and the tutelary kami of the village. These spirits leave upon the billowing smoke of the Dosojin fire.

The Shrine   Even though it may be little more than a hut, a temporary shrine is always provided for the spirit of the Dosojin festival. The kinds of shelters made by different communities vary in form and materials. They may be built of straw, bamboo, or boards, or of combinations of these. A hut may be large enough to accommodate twenty people, or only three or four, or none at all. It may cover the Dosojin image or be so small that it is only a symbol placed beside the statue. In some places the hut is beautifully designed and made. It is taken apart after the festival and stored for use year after year. Today, when a large hut is built it is evidence that the social aspects of the ritual have assumed an increased importance. The warmth within the hut lessens the need for maintaining the small signal fire during the long cold night, and it shelters the members of the committee who are guarding the tree.

For the Dosojin festival of the Kunado group in Yamanashi Prefecture, the temporary shrine is a tiny one. It is built of green bamboo, with miniature columns and beams, and its walls and roof are thatched with cryptomeria needles. A round stone is placed in the shrine. This is the shintai of Dosojin and is the dwelling place of his spirit. Often the hut and the Dosojin image are burned together in the Dondon-yaki fire.[13]

For the Dosojin festival of the Azumi group in Nagano Prefecture, the hut is a large wooden structure thatched with straw. It is known as Sankuro-*goya*, Sankuro's hut, and is used in their play by the children of the congregation. People who sleep there for the night believe that they will be protected against toothaches and colds. Apparently this group still retains some element of a rite known as *okamori*, in which the members of the congregation take part in prayer. Large straw images of the male and female sexual organs are placed facing each other at either side of the entrance to the hut. But no one remembers now whether in the past all of the ritual parts of the festival—such as the offering of prayers, the invitation to the spirit, the installation of the shintai, the presentation of offerings, and other sacred and secret details—were performed in the hut where the congregation could not see them.[14]

At Shimofukuzawa in Yamanashi Prefecture, on January 11, the villagers erect four bamboo pillars on the site where an image of Dosojin used to stand before it was stolen. Between these pillars they build an *ochoya*, a hut screened by straw mats and decorated with shimenawa. A large willow tree is erected and decorated with streamers which lead to the houses of newly married couples. These ropes are called *yobai-tsuna*, "night-crawling ropes."[15] From the eleventh to the fourteenth of January children stay in the hut and sleep there at night. Dosojin is considered to be the deity of children and has the power to protect them from sicknesses during the rest of the year. On the morning of the fourteenth, the ochoya is pulled down, and its straw mats are wrapped around the sacred tree, together with all of the village's New Year gate decorations. Sea water is sprinkled on the tree as a purification, and then sakè is poured over the part where the fire is to be started. The miyamoto starts the fire with sparks struck from flint stones and everyone cries, *"Domidonya!"* While the tree is burning, sakè and bean curd are served to all who are present. Before the burning tree collapses, the old men pull on the ropes that have been holding it in place, making it fall away from the direction of the wind so that sparks will not be carried to the roofs of nearby houses.[16]

Purification and Divination   The outward forms of purification and divination associated with the burning of the sacred tree are only slight indications of the great importance of this concern. A rich expression of ritual forms has evolved from these two religious needs. Throughout the year, rites of purification and divination are still conducted in relation to the agricultural calendar. The shared characteristic that identifies both of these ritual expressions is nakedness. In fact, these ceremonies are called *hadaka matsuri,* or naked festivals.[17] Many of these rituals are performed within the framework of the Dosojin and Sae-no-Kami festivals (and of other agricultural festivals as well), but many others are performed on separate occasions in their own right.

The purification rituals, using one or the other of the two most widespread techniques for removing defilement, rely either upon bathing or upon passing the pollution to a scapegoat through physical contact. The divinational rituals attempt to determine the god's will by means of feats which depend upon the element of chance or upon ordeals such as those of athletic contests.

In the ritual of purification with water as it is performed at Samekawa Shrine in Hokkaido on January 18, in subzero temperatures, four young men dressed only in loincloths and headbands walk from the shrine through the snow about four hundred yards to the beach. They carry the wooden images of four deities, Betto (guardian of shrines), Inari (the rice deity), Yama-no-Kami (the mountain deity), and Benten (goddess of love). The young men hold a piece of white cloth between their teeth to keep them from chattering and to prevent spittle from defiling the sacred images; and, entering the sea until it reaches their hips, they immerse the statues in the icy water. Thus purified, they retrace their steps to the shrine, where they break the ice in a font and pour bucketfuls of fresh water over themselves to complete the ordeal.[18]

The naked festival at Konomiya in Aichi Prefecture, which takes place on January 13, is the best example of a purification ritual that uses a human scapegoat. The ceremony is said to have originated about twelve hundred years ago, when the scapegoat —who is called the *shin* man, "shin" meaning "center" or "heart"—actually was an unfortunate traveler captured while passing through the village. Today, in the first part of this ceremony, the crowd of naked young men rush at the shin man to touch him and thus transfer their spiritual pollution to him. In recent years, as many as sixteen thousand men have taken part in this ceremony at Konomiya, and one can imagine the mauling the shin man gets as the multitude struggles to touch him.[19] In the second phase of the ritual, which is performed on the next night, the shin man, too, is naked except for a mud pack on his back to which a small image is fixed. He is chased three times around the shrine by his naked pursuers, who pelt him with inch-long pieces of willow wood. After that he is driven into the darkness, away from the village, and beaten with willow wands until he falls exhausted. Then the pack on his back, the symbol of pollution, is removed and buried. Thus the purification of the village and of the villagers is achieved. Another account relates that in ancient times the shin man was killed and that he was buried where he fell.[20] Today the shin man is a volunteer, and he returns home safely.

Feats and contests for determining the divine will and the luck of the village include tug-of-war, boat races, rope climbing, sumo wrestling, foot races while carrying portable shrines or floats, archery, sinking tubs of rice, and a number of similar competitions between groups or individuals.

In Kanagawa Prefecture, eight contiguous villages (Sakashita, Hamanomachi, Odomari, Komamachi, Nakajuku, Asamamachi, Okita, and Sanno) observe the Dosojin festival in much the same way, by using tug-of-war as their means of divination. In Sakashita, where about forty naked young men take part in the naked festival, the sacred tree, still burning, is pulled by ropes tied to each end, with elders and children on one team and the young men on the other. In another village, a wooden sled rather than the tree serves as the centerpiece to which the ropes are tied. The *mikoshi,* or portable shrine, is fixed to the sled, and after the shintai is removed from the little shrine, the naked young men pull toward the sea while the children and elders pull toward the land. The young men seem to be winning for a while, until they are up to their necks in the cold sea and finally are pulled back to land, thus losing the contest. Some of the elders in these villages remember when *nanatoko-mairi,* a "pilgrimage to seven shrines" undertaken in order to prevent illness, was performed by people who wore no clothing.[21]

An unusual kind of divination, called the "presenting rice tubs festival of Sakura Pond," takes place in Shizuoka Prefecture on September 23 and 24. This requires the service of twenty young men who have practiced austerities for seven days and nights in a hut at the edge of the village. On the nights of the ceremony each man in turn swims to the center of Sakura Pond with a wooden tub full of rice. While treading water, he spins the tub with a downward motion, which causes it to sink to the bottom of the pond. One hundred tubs are accounted for in this fashion. About a week later the tubs begin to rise to the surface, and people watch them as they come up to see whether they are empty of rice. Each tub is marked with its donor's family name, and if one comes up empty it means that the dragon deity of Sakura Pond has accepted the offering and will grant the family's wishes.[22]

In Chiba Prefecture, the "mud-covered festival of Noda," held on April 3, also takes place at a pond. All newly married men of the village gather to carry a mikoshi into the pond, after which a mud-throwing battle takes place between the men and the young children on the banks of the pond. Undoubtedly there is some connection between these pond festivals and the ancient legends about human immolation, when young women were sacrificed to appease the dragon deity living at the bottom of a pond.[23]

On the island of Shiga in Fukuoka Prefecture, the Hosha-sai, or Walking Archery Festival, is held on January 15. Eight young men are chosen as the principal celebrants. For two weeks they live apart from their families, undergoing abstinence and purification, and training in archery. On January 14, at low tide, they go to a point of the island and dive for a rare kind of seaweed called *garamo*. When one of the eight is successful, he rushes to a high rock and performs the "dance of garamo." On January 15 the eight young men, wearing only loincloths, assemble to shoot arrows toward the sky. This event foretells the village's fortunes for the coming year.[24]

The Character of Dosojin Reflected in Song The assorted customs relating to the Dosojin festival illustrate the variety of attitudes that people of different communities hold toward this popular and beloved deity. Especially revealing are the recitations and songs that are supposed to be bawdy and disrespectful.

This is a song popular in the villages of Gumma Prefecture:

> "The day is breaking.
> The fire of Dosojin is burning.
> Get up, young husbands and wives,
> Get up.
> You should have enjoyed *bebe**
> To your hearts' content
> During the long, long night."[25]

And here is a ditty recited by the Hatano group of Kanagawa Prefecture:

> "Find a good wife for our son.
> They say he wets the bed at night."[26]

---

*Bebe is a term in the local dialect, meaning sexual intercourse.

The Funnai group of Yamanashi Prefecture sings this earthy tribute:

> "The sex organ of Dosojin is
> Said to be one *shaku* and eight *sun** long.
> Too long for any female organ to receive it,
> He had to lay it in the fork of a tree."[27]

At Kiyakawa village along the Mogami River in Yamagata Prefecture, groups of boys about twelve or thirteen years of age invade each house through the front door, brandishing Sankuro dolls and singing:

> "We've come, we've come,
> The master of the house,
> A thousand, ten thousand *koku,***
> Five thousand koku.
> Fourteen boys,
> Thirteen girls,
> *Yaedo, yaedo,*
> *Mogudara, mogudara, kemmogudara,*
> The hind hair *bonboya,*
> The forehair *etamaka jinjima;*
> Wife *chankorome*
> Has just got drunk, the lion;
> Stinking navel, urine;
> Sai-no-Kami, sleeping and spending the night.
> No, no roast peas,
> No cooked beans,
> The wife of this house eats hairy beans.
> Who's she? Who's she?
> Crooked eyes, broken nose,
> Lame, lame,
> Good bride to marry,
> Bad bride not to marry,
> Congratulations for one thousand years."[28]

At the village of Joban in Nagano Prefecture, some people put a straw doll in front of the Kannon Hall (which is Buddhist) to get rid of a cold, and they sing:

> "The god of colds is a fool.
> Discovered by the doll,
> He ran away.
> *Supopon! Supopon!*"[29]

*The *shaku* is equivalent to about twelve inches; one shaku comprises ten *sun*.
**A *koku* is equivalent to approximately five bushels.

At Shimofukuzawa, in the valley of the Kamezawa River in Yamanashi Prefecture, people dissolve the ashes of their Sagicho festival fire in water and sprinkle that around the house on the following day, in the belief that doing so will free them of snakes and centipedes during the year. This song is recited on that occasion:

"Come what may,
Snakes and centipedes,
I am the son of a goldsmith.
Bring what you will,
Spears and swords."[30]

At Kosobe village in Nagano Prefecture, at dawn on January 15, young children tap with sticks on the veranda door and clap wooden blocks together, crying out:

"Who is going to drive away the birds today?
Taro-san and Jiro-san are going to drive them away:
Jiro, Taro are driving away the birds.
I am going to drive them away a little."[31]

The Festival Reconstructed The Dosojin festival as it is performed today still includes most of the ritual phases of the Celestial Matsuri which, as Part Four of this book will show, is so obviously its prototype. The Celestial Matsuri, according to mythology, was brought down to earth by Ninigi-no-Mikoto (Prince Ninigi) for the purpose of providing men with a new religious system so that they might live in the "Way of the Kami." Mythology, as we know, is a record of words and symbols, a crystallization of the experiences of a people or race. Thus, ancient agricultural rituals, such as the Dosojin festival, by whatever name they were called then, were certainly the source and inspiration from which the myth-makers constructed the Celestial Matsuri.

One of the very early agricultural customs in Japan was a festival which included much dancing and ended with copulation as an act meant to replenish the power of the deities of agriculture and fertility. By participating in such rituals, each individual experienced a reintegration of his spirit with that of the kami of heaven and earth, through whom the great and the ordinary events of daily life were woven together into a meaningful whole. The Dosojin festival at the commoners' level has the same purpose as does the Daijo-sai, or Great Harvest Festival, held during the investiture ceremonies, in which a new emperor seeks to experience his own spiritual reintegration with the kami of heaven and earth.

Nowadays, while the Dosojin festival has lost some of its religious quality, and some of the ritual aspects are not observed in current practice, nevertheless the typical elements of religious expression found in formal Shrine Shinto are definitely recognizable. These include purification, divination, calling down the spirit of the deity, presentation of offerings, recitation of *norito* (ancient prayers possessing great power), presence of a hut or shrine and of the shintai, sending away the deity's spirit, and eating offerings of food. Singing and dancing as offerings usually give way to indulgence in personal pleasure. The action of the Dosojin festival as it is summarized below is a composite version based on the current customs of villagers in the five prefectures of Yamanashi, Nagano, Gumma, Shizuoka, and Kanagawa.

Elements of the Festival   The preparations for the festival and the appurtenant customs having been accomplished, the festival tree stands at a purified site which is, in fact, an open-air shrine. The headman of the village serves as the ritualist. He invokes the spirit of Dosojin to descend from upper space by way of the sacred tree, to which it is attracted by a signal fire burning nearby. Descending through the tree, the spirit occupies its shintai, which is some physical object or symbol, such as a long smooth stone or a wooden phallus, placed within the shrine, or the stone image of Dosojin himself. Prayers are recited and offerings are presented by the ritualist, and the blessing and protection of Dosojin are requested for the coming year on behalf of the congregation. Individuals present their offerings and petitions throughout the day. In some communities the divination to determine the kind of luck people will have for the coming year is performed in the daytime and is a ritual in itself that does not involve the festival tree. In other places, as night falls, the tree with all its decorations and the hut with the statue of Dosojin in it are set afire. Thus, even as Dosojin is purified of last year's burdens, he is made ready to take on the troubles of a new year.

As the burning tree is consumed in the fire, the spirit of Dosojin and those of the villagers' relatives rise on the smoke and are sent off to their respective resting places. The congregation, especially the children, make merry, singing and cavorting around the fire. They toast rice cakes impaled on sticks, just as Westerners do with marshmallows. Such is the feasting after the ritual. Then, as the fire dies out, people drift away into the cold night, and the festival is over for another year.

The Dosojin festival, or the Dondon-yaki festival, although somewhat altered in form, is still an agricultural festival of thanksgiving, an invocation for prosperity and good health for the community, and a seeking for spiritual peace and unity. The robustness that is typical of agricultural fertility rites in the past still appears in many places, especially in those where nearly naked young men take part in rituals of purification and divination. The recent study of the Dosojin festival by the Agency for Cultural Affairs shows that the popularity of the Dondon-yaki festival has revived very strongly in a sizable portion of Honshu, from Aomori, Iwate, Akita, and Yamagata prefectures, along Tottori Prefecture, all the way to the Izumo area in Shimane Prefecture. The Dondon-yaki festival is observed even in places where only a few sculptures of Dosojin are present.

The folklore movement in Japan is attempting to preserve wayside sculptures through local laws or by placing these images in local museums. And it is to be hoped that an interest in preservation of such rural festivals as this one will develop throughout Japan, in the same way that concerned societies have saved folk dances from being forgotten and lost.

PART TWO

THE WORLD OF DOSOJIN:
A PHOTO-ESSAY

The author is indebted to the following for permission to reproduce their photographs in this book:

Eiichi Ashida and the Ikeda Publishing Company, Limited, Tokyo: Figures 1, 2, 3, 5, 6, 7, 8, 10, 11, 17, 18, 19, 20, 21, 22, 23, 25, 30, 31, 33, 34, 35, 36, 40, 41, 43, 44, 47, 49, 51, 53, 54, 55, 56, 57, 58, 59, 60, 64, 65, 66, 67, 68, 69, 70, 71, 72, 73, 75, 80, 81, 82, 83, 84, 88, 89, 90, 91, 92, 93, 94, 95, 96.

Sanshiro Ikeda: Figures 4, 9, 12, 14, 15, 16, 24, 26, 27, 28, 29, 32, 37, 38, 39, 42, 45, 46, 48, 50, 52, 61, 62, 74, 76, 77, 78, 85, 86, 87.

Zenjiro Ishikawa: Figure 79.

Fushimi-Inari Shrine, Kyoto: Figures 100, 101.

The photographs for Figures 13, 63, 97, 98, and 99 were provided by the author.

1. Dosojin couple, possibly travelers or Buddhist priest and nun. Gumma Prefecture.

2. Dosojin couple. Nagano Prefecture.

5. Dosojin couple in coitus, with an offering of flowers. Yamanashi Prefecture.

4. "Dancing Dosojin." Nagano Prefecture.

6 (above). Hybrid Dosojin combining calligraphy and human figures. Nagano Prefecture. See Figure 41 for detail.

7, 8. Right: calligraphic stone bearing ideographs reading "Dosojin." Opposite page: detail showing the ideograph for *so*, "ancestor," carved to resemble a phallus. Kanagawa Prefecture.

10. An unusual votive stone with a phallus carved in relief.
Dated 1832. Miyagi Prefecture. See also Figure 64.

9. Dosojin couple. The woman carries a willow branch with dumplings.
Nagano Prefecture. See also Figure 46.

11. "Night and Day Dosojin." Nagano Prefecture.

12. Dosojin guarding crossroads and rice fields. Nagano Prefecture.

13–16. Four examples of "man-first" Dosojin. Nagano Prefecture.

17. Dosojin couple depicted in mountain dress. Tottori Prefecture.

18. Dosojin with an offering of a straw horse. Tottori Prefecture.

19. Izanagi and Izanami as Dosojin. Dated 1883. Tottori Prefecture.

20. Dosojin couple in an attitude of prayer. Nagano Prefecture.

22. Dosojin couple. Yamanashi Prefecture.

24. Dosojin couple wearing court dress. Nagano Prefecture.

25. Dosojin couple. Niigata Prefecture.

26. Dour Dosojin couple with a *gohei*. Nagano Prefecture.

27. Dosojin couple standing under a *torii*. Nagano Prefecture.

28. Dosojin couple. Nagano Prefecture.

29. Dosojin couple beneath a shrine or temple roof. Nagano Prefecture.

30 (opposite page). "Gratification of the Great Wish" Dosojin. Kanagawa Prefecture.

31. Dosojin couple. Sexuality is suggested through the man's hand inserted in the woman's sleeve. Nagano Prefecture.

32. Dosojin couple with sun and moon symbols. Nagano Prefecture.

33-36 (opposite page). Clockwise from upper left: modern Dosojin, dated 1962, Nagano Prefecture; elderly couple, Nagano Prefecture; demure couple, possibly travelers or Buddhist priest and nun, Nagano Prefecture; Dosojin, dated 1961, Kanagawa Prefecture.

37. Dosojin couple. Nagano Prefecture.

38. Dosojin couple. Nagano Prefecture.

39–41 (opposite page). Clockwise from upper left: "The Lovely Couple" Dosojin, Nagano Prefecture; elderly couple, Niigata Prefecture; seated couple (detail of Figure 6) with phallic offering, Nagano Prefecture.

42. Dosojin couple under a Buddhist temple roof. Nagano Prefecture.

43. Dosojin couple. Shizuoka Prefecture.

45. Dosojin couple. Note the male figure's elongated arm. Nagano Prefecture.

46. Dosojin couple holding a willow branch with dumplings. Nagano Prefecture. See also Figure 9.

47. Dosojin couple with hands suggesting sexuality. Gumma Prefecture.

48. Dosojin couple with hands suggesting sexuality. Nagano Prefecture.

49. Dosojin couple with hands suggesting sexuality. Nagano Prefecture.

50. Dosojin couple embracing within a Buddhist temple entrance. Nagano Prefecture.

51. Dosojin couple in an intimate pose. Gumma Prefecture.

52. Dosojin couple embracing. Nagano Prefecture.

53. Highly stylized Dosojin couple, possibly Buddhist priest and nun. Nagano Prefecture.

55. Dosojin couple with offerings. Gumma Prefecture. 56 (above). "Kissing Jizo" Dosojin. Gumma Prefecture.
57 (below). Dosojin couple kissing. Nagano Prefecture.

58. "Innocence," a Dosojin couple with exposed genitals. The wooden sword is an offering. Yamanashi Prefecture.

60. Dosojin triad. Izu Peninsula, Shizuoka Prefecture.

59. Dosojin couple in coitus. Below are wooden offerings. Gumma Prefecture.

61 (above),62 (opposite page). Seated Dosojin couple kissing while
in coitus. Note the other phallic stones, Dosojin image, and straw
offerings. Genroku era (1688–1704). Nagano Prefecture.

63. Seventh-century Do-sojin excavated at Asuka, Nara Prefecture. Tokyo National Museum.

64. Pair of phalli as Doso-jin. Dated 1893. Miyagi Prefecture. See Figure 10.

65, 66 (above). Front (left) and back of a calligraphic Dosojin comprising both male and female stones. Yamanashi Prefecture.

67. Calligraphic Dosojin, partially buried, with ideographs carved to suggest genitalia. Kanagawa Prefecture.

68 (opposite page). Phallus-shaped memorial Dosojin. Dated 1894. Kanagawa Prefecture.

69. Phallus-shaped stone. Dated 1711. Iwate Prefecture. 70. Pair of phallic stones, one natural and one calligraphic. Nagano Prefecture.

71 (above). Male and female stones in a small shrine. Nagano Prefecture.

72 (below). Small male and female stones. Shizuoka Prefecture.

73 (above). Natural phallus-shaped stone worshiped as Sai-no-Kami. Miyagi Prefecture.

74 (below). Crude wooden Dosojin images used in the Dosojin festival. Nagano Prefecture.

75. Small phallic stone. Kanagawa Prefecture.

76–79 (opposite page). Small Dosojin images made for the family prayer shelf. The one at upper left is stone; the others are wood. The image at lower left is modern.

80. Straw symbols of male and female sex organs offered to Dosojin. Tottori Prefecture.

81. Male and female effigies offered to Dosojin. Nagano Prefecture.

82 (above). Dosojin with *shimenawa* and offerings. Tottori Prefecture.

83 (below). Dosojin in the form of a yang, or male, stone. Kyoto.

84. Straw horses offered to a tree as Dosojin. Tottori Prefecture.

85. Dosojin guarding a road and rice field. Nagano Prefecture.

86. Dosojin within a small shrine. Nagano Prefecture.

87. Two Dosojin images by a road overlooking rice fields. Nagano Prefecture.

88 (above). Dosojin with Mount Fuji in the background. Shizuoka Prefecture.

89. Dosojin sculpture and natural phallic stone in a temporary shrine. Kanagawa Prefecture.

93 (opposite page). Giant straw phallus made for the Dosojin festival. Makioka, Yamanashi Prefecture.

90 (left). Wooden phalli offered at a Shinto shrine. Miyagi Prefecture.

91, 92 (below). Left: statue of Jizo in a small shrine within a Buddhist temple. Right: two Dosojin in the form of phalli, hidden behind the statue. Myoan-ji, Nagoya, Aichi Prefecture.

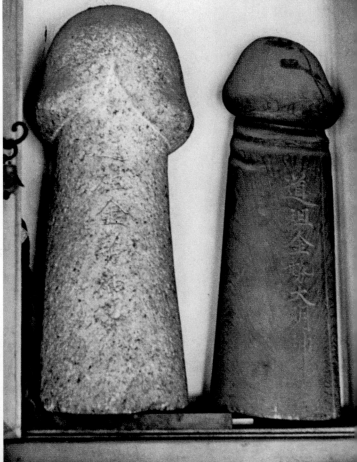

97. Main gateway to Fushimi-Inari Shrine near Kyoto.

94–96 (above). Raising the Dosojin festival tree and burning it in the festival fire. Nozawa, Nagano Prefecture.

98. Small shrine within Fushimi-Inari Shrine.

99 (above). *Miko* dancing at Fushimi-Inari Shrine.

100. Lifting a *mikoshi*, Fushimi-Inari Shrine.

101. Shinto priests transferring a deity's *shintai* to a *mikoshi*, Fushimi-Inari Shrine.

COMMENTARIES ON THE PHOTOGRAPHS

1. The heavily robed figures of this tender Dosojin couple may represent a Buddhist priest and nun dedicated to a religious life, as the book they hold between them would seem to indicate. Note that only two feet show beneath their robes. This image is in the compound of Kongo-ji temple, Miyagi, Gumma Prefecture.

2. This cheerful Dosojin couple, hand in hand and each with one arm apparently inside the robe of the other, is from Nagano Prefecture.

3. The figures on this diminutive Dosojin image in Gumma Prefecture are unusual for their facial expressions, the delicate use of the fan, and their posture of tender intimacy, the position of the woman's hand suggesting lovemaking. The canopy crowning the stone is especially finely modeled. The design on the plinth is a pot of morning glories.

4. This tiny carving, barely twelve inches high, is popularly known as "Dancing Dosojin" or "Taro, Jiro." It is the custom in this part of Nagano Prefecture in the early morning of January 15 for children to chase the birds from the newly planted rice seed by clapping together wooden blocks and crying out: "Who is going to drive away the birds today? Taro-san and Jiro-san are going to drive them away!"

5. This archaically styled Dosojin in Yamanashi Prefecture shows two naked figures kissing and engaging in intercourse. The flowering branches offered to the image indicate the affection of the villagers for their deity of lovemaking.

6. The two large ideographs on this stone read *doso*, "road ancestor," while the couple below, representing the deity, take the place of the ideograph for *jin*, "deity." This interesting hybrid stone is in Nagano Prefecture. See Figure 41 for a detail.

7, 8. The ideographs for Dosojin on this calligraphic Dosojin stone have been inscribed in a modified style of writing that expresses the phallic nature of the middle ideograph, *so*, meaning "ancestor." This stone is from Kanagawa Prefecture.

9. Dosojin's connection with the Dondon-yaki fire of the annual Dosojin festival held January 14 and 15 is indicated by the willow branch on which rice dumplings are impaled, which the female figure holds. Eating dumplings toasted in the festival fire is supposed to ensure good health for the year. This image is from Nagano Prefecture. See Figure 46 for a similar Dosojin.

10. This unusual stone is representative of a group of about twenty such stones found stacked together in a small plot near Reiyosaki Shrine at Makiyama, a small fishing village perched on a cliff a few miles east of Ishinomaki, Miyagi Prefecture. The shrine is patronized by fishermen and other seafarers, who come from far and wide to pray for safe voyages and good fishing. All the stones bear either a single phallus carved in relief, as on this stone dated 1832, or occasionally two phalli, as in Figure 64.

11. This is the "Night and Day Dosojin," the most famous sculpture of its kind in Japan, having been widely publicized in newspapers and magazines. It stands within a small wooden shrine on a hillside in Matsumoto, Nagano Prefecture, which is also occupied by two unsculpted stones, a phallus and a kteis. This sculpture shows a dignified, well-dressed, middle-aged couple standing close together in a hand and shoulder embrace. At the very top of the stone (not shown in this photograph) is the face of a scowling horned demon, and below this is the ideograph *en*, meaning "bond" or "affinity" and here referring to the marriage tie. Below the standing couple is a tiny, naked young couple copulating. Incised on one side of the young couple is the ideograph meaning "night" and on the other side that meaning "exemption."

12. This typical couple Dosojin in Nagano Prefecture is strategically placed to fulfill its functions as guardian of road, rice fields, and village at the same time.

13–16. These four couple Dosojin sculptures from Nagano Prefecture illustrate the so-called "man-first" style that became prevalent in the Meiji era (1868–1912), for the first time depicting the female as subordinate to the male. All four couples are depicted within circular frames, which is typical of this type of Dosojin. In Figure 13, the couple's dress, the man's stylized *eboshi,* and the woman's hair style indicate that the pair is of high station. The woman holds a sakè decanter and the man a sakè cup. Note that each figure has one arm inside the sleeve of the other's robe in an intimate caress. The doll-like proportions of the couple in Figure 14 result from the sculptor's effort to fit the figures into a circular frame. This pair, too, is of high rank, and the woman holds a sakè decanter, the man a sakè cup. In Figure 15, the man's authority is emphasized by the phallic staff he holds in addition to a sakè cup. The kneeling woman holds a sakè decanter. In Figure 16, the woman, holding a sakè decanter, kneels ready to serve the man, who holds a sakè cup. As with the other three couples, this one is of high station. Despite the woman's subservient posture, the clasped hands and the facial expressions of the pair indicate a tenderness and understanding between them.

17. This small sculpture from Tottori Prefecture shows the figures standing far apart in a stiff frontal posture, with downcast eyes. The costumes may be a kind of *yama-bakama* (mountain *hakama,* or divided skirt), or the lower part of the kimono have been lifted and tucked out of the way. The headdress resembles a folded cloth such as is worn by mountain women when they go to town to sell wares. The figure on the right is holding a dagger, or possibly a scepter.

18. This small, crudely carved Dosojin image, found behind a Shinto shrine in Tottori Prefecture, is crowned with a *shimenawa.* An offering of a straw horse rests against the stone. Tottori is a horse-breeding region, and offerings of straw horses are common.

19. This flat, low-relief sculpture showing Izanagi (right) and Izanami, creator deities of the islands of Japan, is typical of Saino-Kami, the deity of happiness, as depicted in Tottori Prefecture. The figures are clothed in ancient Japanese court dress. The *shimenawa* above the couple indicates their divine status. The image is dated 1883.

20. The heavy, hooded headdress of these figures, depicted standing side-by-side with hands in an attitude of prayer, suggests farm people living in a cold climate. Offerings of *o-hagi,* a confection made from glutinous rice covered with sweet red bean-jam, have been left for Dosojin. The image, located in Nagano Prefecture, is dated 1826.

21. This incised carving of Izanagi (right) and Izanami is, like Figure 19, from Tottori Prefecture and depicts Sai-no-Kami. The spear held by Izanagi relates to the myth of the creation of the islands of Japan by stirring the sea with the Heavenly Jeweled Spear.

22. This small sculpture, regarded as a deity of matchmaking, stands on a hillock overlooking a small stream deep in a forest. There are a number of similar Dosojin images in Yamanashi Prefecture. The batonlike object held by the male is thought to be a phallus.

23. Dosojin is represented in this sculpture from Nagano Prefecture as Saruta-hiko and Uzume (depicted here as cheerful, fat-cheeked Okame) standing on stylized clouds. The sculptor's skill shows in his treatment of the hair and of Saruta-hiko's beard. The braided straw canopy greatly enhances the stone.

24. The elegant attire of this couple, including the many layers of the woman's garments, her formal court hair style, and the man's *eboshi,* suggests noble birth and wealth. The woman holds a sakè decanter and the man a sakè cup. This stone is in Nagano Prefecture.

25. The figures in this Dosojin sculpture from Niigata Prefecture appear to be floating in space, their garments billowing about them. The woman holds a gourdlike sakè container, the man a sakè cup.

26. This dour couple, the woman with a sakè decanter and the man with a sakè cup, is from Nagano Prefecture. Note the Shinto *gohei,* a baton hung with strips of specially folded paper called *shide,* that frames the pair.

27. This Dosojin couple, from Nagano Prefecture, stands beneath a *torii* flanked by a fence. On either side of the *torii* is a banner inscribed with ideographs reading "Dosojin."

28. The severe expressions and rigid postures of the figures of this Dosojin sculpture in Nagano Prefecture run counter to the usually loving countenances of Dosojin. This stone is dated 1789.

29. Male and female stand far apart, though holding hands, in this Dosojin located in Nagano Prefecture. The woman holds a sakè decanter, the man a sakè cup. The rooflike element above the couple probably represents the gable of a Buddhist temple or Shinto shrine. The decorative elements of the gable include a chrysanthemum, two paulownia crests, and a thick double tassel. Below the figures is a pattern including a stylized chrysanthemum and water.

30. This Dosojin in Kanagawa Prefecture is named "Gratification of the Great Wish." The sculpture was dedicated by a woman named Oyoshi, who was enabled to marry the man of her choice through the aid of Dosojin. The female figure is biting her sleeve to contain her joy.

31. This sculpture in Nagano Prefecture is of the type in which the sexual symbolism is expressed by insertion of the man's hand into the woman's sleeve, which is rendered so as to suggest the vulva. Both figures are crowned with distinctly phallic headdresses. They stand in a recessed circular niche that protects them from the elements.

32. This Dosojin from Nagano Prefecture is unusual because of the symbols for sun and moon that appear above the heads of the couple. The sun and moon are usually associated with sculptures of Koshin (see the Appendix); on the other hand, Saruta-hiko is sometimes depicted as Koshin. The element between the couple's heads may represent silkworm cocoons. Although the man usually holds the sakè cup and the woman the container or decanter, here the attributes are reversed.

33. This image in Nagano Prefecture was made in 1962 and is molded in concrete. It appears to represent Saruta-hiko and Uzume dressed in the costumes believed to have been worn during the fifth or sixth century. The hair styles resemble those of the time of Prince Shotoku (574–622). Note the necklaces of *magatama,* comma-shaped jewels.

34. Dosojin is concerned with and represents people of all stations and of all ages, witness this elderly couple from Nagano Prefecture. The man's pillbox hat is an unusual feature.

35. The demure and loving couple in this Dosojin sculpture from Nagano Prefecture appear from their headgear to be either travelers

or Buddhist priest and nun. The only sexual symbolism is in the hands, the man holding the woman's hand within his.

36. This sculpture in Chigasaki, Kanagawa Prefecture, is inscribed with the date January 14, 1961. It is unusual because of the realistic phallic hood surmounting the composition. Each deity wears the same sweet expression and the same kind of clothing. Only the headdress suggests that the figure on the left is female.

37. The round faces and good-humored expressions of this couple from Nagano Prefecture indicate that Dosojin was often modeled on ordinary folk. The woman holds a large gourd-shaped sakè container and the man a sakè cup.

38. The figures of this tiny Dosojin sculpture in Nagano Prefecture are idealized and their forms stylized. Here the woman envelops the man's hand in hers in the gesture symbolic of sexual union.

39. This Dosojin, known locally as "The Lovely Couple," suggests idealized love. Here again the woman holds the man's hand in hers. This stone is found in Nagano Prefecture.

40. This elderly couple stand close together, with the symbolic sakè container (here held by the male figure) and sakè dish or cup partially hidden beneath their robes. What they have in common seems to be shared in secret. This Dosojin is from Niigata Prefecture.

41. This seated couple, dressed formally, is a detail of the hybrid Dosojin of Figure 6. The woman holds a sakè decanter and the man a sakè cup. Below the couple is a phallic offering.

42. This couple stands within a rectangular niche topped by an incised design representing a Buddhist temple roof. The ideograph atop the roof reads "longevity." The male figure enfolds the hand of the female figure in his, symbolizing the sex act. This Dosojin is in Nagano Prefecture.

43. The solid, peasantlike figures in this Dosojin from Shizuoka Prefecture are sculpted in high relief. The heads of the figures and the sakè container and cup are exaggerated in size. Note the rooflike detail and flowerlike medallion at the top of the stone.

44. The sculptor of this Dosojin in Gumma Prefecture has combined sensitivity and economy of expression. The close embrace and the

large hands, the man's covering the woman's, identify this pair as Sai-no-Kami, the deity of happiness.

45. This cheerful couple Dosojin in Nagano Prefecture exhibits several typical features. Male and female are indistinguishable in size, expression, and clothing, although the fall of hair on the figure to the left identifies this as the female partner. The man has one hand in the area of the woman's genitals, his arm elongated to make this possible. Each figure has one arm (also elongated) around the shoulders of the other.

46. This couple is carved out of one face of a large phallus-shaped stone. Both partners hold a willow branch on which rice dumplings are impaled (see also Figure 9). The male's other hand is suggestively positioned, opening his partner's robe. Note the bow-shaped arch above the figures. This sculpture is in Nagano Prefecture.

47. This image was found in a small grove of wild bamboo in Gumma Prefecture. Sexuality is expressed in the enlarged hands and their position on shoulder, breast, and pubic region.

48. This couple, hooded as if for a cold climate, stands within a deeply carved niche. The hands are enlarged, and one is placed over the woman's pubic region. This stone is in Nagano Prefecture.

49. In this sculpture from Nagano Prefecture, sexuality is indicated by the man (right) stepping on one of his partner's feet, and by the couple's clasped hands, which are enlarged to signify the importance of union. The left hand of the woman is greatly enlarged and is placed over her pubic area. The downcast eyes and gentle facial expressions give the sculpture a solemn dignity.

50. This embracing couple stands within a Buddhist temple entrance, signifying the religious quality or spirituality of love. The carved plaque above the couple bears the ideographs for Dosojin. This stone is from Nagano Prefecture.

51. Here Dosojin is represented by an elegantly dressed couple of aristocratic countenance. The pose is intimate, the woman with one foot advanced in front of the man. The woman bears a sakè decanter and the man a sakè cup. This stone is in Gumma Prefecture.

52. This Dosojin couple in Nagano Prefecture is shown embracing

face-to-face. The woman's hair style and trailing robe indicate aristocratic status. This sculpture dates from about the middle of the Edo period (1603–1868).

53. The sculptural treatment of this couple Dosojin from Nagano Prefecture is unusual. Carved in the round rather than in relief, it is highly stylized and appears rather modern in style. The shape of the heads, the features, and the elongated ears suggest that the figures are a Buddhist monk and nun.

54. This richly costumed couple in Niigata Prefecture probably represents celestial deities standing on clouds. The fluid, relatively sophisticated style of this sculpture contrasts with the more straightforward composition of couple Dosojin in other regions.

55. Blocks of wood inscribed with the ideographs reading "Dosojin" are offered to Dosojin in many communities. This example is from Gumma Prefecture. One offering (not shown) bears the date January 15, 1963. The inscription on the block of wood placed on the base of the image to the viewer's left reads "Female Dosojin," while that to the right of the image reads "Male Dosojin."

56. This Dosojin image is considered one of the masterpieces of Gumma Prefecture. It is called "Kissing Jizo" because the two figures appear to be dressed in the simple robes of Buddhist monks. Jizo often takes this lowly guise in serving humanity.

57. In this high-relief sculpture from Nagano Prefecture the Dosojin couple is posed somewhat stiffly in the act of kissing. The frontal embrace with interlocking legs suggests that the pair may actually be engaged in coitus. The frail legs contrast with the oversized heads.

58. This Dosojin with exposed genitals is called "Innocence" by the local villagers. The erect penis of the male deity has been mutilated. Boys offer wooden swords to this Dosojin on January 14 each year, while girls offer rice cakes. The longer of the two swords shown in this picture bears on it the name of the donor and the date (January 14, 1962). This sculpture is from Yamanashi Prefecture.

59. This Dosojin couple from Gumma Prefecture is engaged in coitus, the female deity sitting on the lap of the male. Each year the seven families of the local community dedicate a pair of carved and painted blocks of wood to this image on the eve of the Dosojin festival.

60. Many Dosojin from the Izu Peninsula, Shizuoka Prefecture, consist, like this one, of three separate figures sculpted in the round. They are always shown seated, with hands folded in prayer or holding a scepter, jewel, fan, or baton. The identities of the members of the triad are disputed. One school maintains that the central figure is Ame-no-Minaka-nushi-no-Mikoto, the firstborn celestial deity of Japanese mythology, flanked by Izanagi and Izanami. Others hold that Ugadama is the central figure, flanked by Saruta-hiko and Uzume.

61, 62. This Dosojin sculpture, located in Nagano Prefecture, is modeled in the round. The couple is kissing while engaged in coitus in a seated position. The image is believed to date from the Genroku era (1688–1704). Note the other couple Dosojin and the phallic stones in the small shrine, and the straw offerings in the foreground.

63. This Dosojin sculpture dates from the seventh century and was excavated at Asuka, Nara Prefecture. It stands about five feet, nine inches high. The male and female deities are similarly clad. The male is crowned, while the female holds a wine cup to her lips. This sculpture now stands in front of the Tokyo National Museum.

64. This stone is from the same group as that in Figure 10. The two phalli are undoubtedly intended to represent Dosojin. The stone is dated 1893.

65, 66. This Dosojin from Yamanashi Prefecture includes both a male element, the upright stone inscribed with the ideographs for Dosojin, and a female element, the spherical stone resting in a recessed base on which the male stone also stands.

67. This calligraphic Dosojin stone shows the phallic nature of the deity through the shapes of the ideographs. The top character, *do* (road), has deliberately been made to resemble a vulva. The right-hand element of the second character, *so* (ancestor), has been shaped so as to emphasize its similarity to a penis. The bottom ideograph, *jin* (deity), is almost completely buried in the earth. This stone is from Kanagawa Prefecture.

68. This phallus-shaped Dosojin in Kanagawa Prefecture is a memorial to the spirit of the nature religion of the past. It is dedicated to the wish for rich crops of the five cereals and for offspring. The inscription reads:

"Here lies Dosojin. About ten *ken* from here
there were old pine and old pasamia
woods gathered in clusters.
Now they are gone to make room for the
prefectural highway.
The road runs round the hillside,
the rain-drenched mountains surrounded by
profuse river, wind, flower, snow.
The moon, the four seasons are all good and helpful.
As God wills them, those who run and walk
write therefore on stones to inform them.
The twenty-seventh year of Meiji [1894], on the
day of Kanname-sai.
Koyo Gijuku, President, Seventh Rank
Riki Matsuoka
Dedicated by Koto Ai
Initiated by Kochu Nakamura"

69. There are many examples in Miyagi, Yamagata, and Iwate prefectures of stones naturally shaped like phalli and representing Dosojin, but very few carved stones of the size and shape of this one, which stands with two other stones in Nanasawa, Iwate Prefecture. It is dated 1711.

70. The right-hand stone is inscribed with the ideographs for Dosojin. The companion on the left is a natural stone phallus. The raised white ring near the top of the stone was formed naturally by sedimentation, and only enough carving has been done to bring it into prominence. These stones are from Nagano Prefecture.

71. This small shrine at the edge of a field in Matsumoto, Nagano Prefecture, houses a small couple Dosojin and two large stones, one female (left) and the other male. Both have been shaped somewhat by the sculptor's chisel. Such stones are most commonly found at the edge of rice or mulberry fields.

72, 75. Small stone phalli like these often appear adjacent to couple Dosojin sculptures. That in Figure 72, comprising a male and a female stone, is from Shizuoka Prefecture, while that in Figure 75 is from Kanagawa Prefecture.

73. This Dosojin consists of a natural stone projecting from a cliff above the Minami-Sakai highway a few miles north of Ishinomaki, Miyagi Prefecture. Because of the stone, this community was called

Sainokami. Ishinomaki has always been noted as a fishing port. The prostitutes of the town, together with their patrons and friends, came to worship Dosojin here in bygone days.

74. These crude wooden Dosojin images are dragged through the streets from house to house by children prior to the annual Dosojin festival in communities of Nagano Prefecture. The children throw them against the doors of houses where newly married couples live to bring the couples good luck in conceiving and bearing children. This custom accounts for the battered look of the figurines and for the remnants of rope tied around the necks of most.

76–78. Dosojin was considered to be a member of the family, and small images like these were placed on the family prayer shelf. Dosojin was expected to protect the newly born and the very young and to keep them in good health. Figure 76 is of stone, while the other two are of wood. Few such wood figures are found today, although in ancient times larger wooden sculptures were also found on the roadside. All three of these images are from Nagano Prefecture.

79. This small wooden relief sculpture of Dosojin by Yosuji Seki was mounted recently on the wall of the staircase of a house designed by architect Zenjiro Ishikawa. Dosojin is not always a lonely guardian of roads but occasionally is found in a special place of honor.

80. Seen here is an offering of a straw baton or phallus, called a *hotsutome,* and of a flattish straw object representing the female sex organ. They were found lying against a Dosojin sculpture in Tottori Prefecture.

81. Offerings of male and female effigies, called Sankuro, made from sticks with painted faces, are presented to Dosojin at the time of the Dosojin festival (also called the Sankuro festival) on January 14 and 15. This image with offerings was found in Nagano Prefecture.

82. The Dosojin relief on this stone is one of the flat designs from Tottori Prefecture like those pictured in Figures 19 and 80. It is unusual to find the profusion of offerings shown here. The sacred *shimenawa* covering the face of the stone, and hiding the carving, is especially grand. At left are several straw packets containing rice dumplings. Dangling above the stone is a pair of straw objects, the flattish oblong one representing the female sex organ and the onion-

shaped *hotsutome* the male sex organ. After a wedding, children strike the bride on her hips or buttocks with a *hotsutome* so that she may bear a healthy baby soon.

83. Stones like the one shown here are identified as *yo-seki,* or yang—that is, male—stones. They are also called *korin-seki* or *yogo.* The custom of worshiping Dosojin in this form was prevalent all along the road leading from Kyoto, where this stone is located, to Izumo in Shimane Prefecture in the early Heian period (794–1185). Travelers, as well as those interested in matchmaking, were supposed to pick up the top stone and walk around the lower stone with it while praying for a safe trip or for good fortune in matchmaking by mimicking the mannerisms of men and women. This custom was known as "stone divination."

84. Straw horses are hung from the branches of a young oak tree in Tottori Prefecture. They have been offered to the tree itself as Dosojin because the stone image that once stood there has been removed. In other cases a tree and a rock at its base are together regarded as Dosojin, the tree representing the male element and the rock the female element.

85. Here Dosojin stands beside a road in Nagano Prefecture, overlooking a rice field with its harvested crop. The couple is shown in an exploratory lovemaking pose, the female perhaps a little coy.

86. This couple Dosojin in Nagano Prefecture is sheltered within a small shrine. Offerings of straw phallic batons hang on all four sides of the hut, while more are scattered on the ground to one side.

87. These two couple Dosojin stand at the roadside, their backs to the rice fields below, in Nagano Prefecture.

88. This small weathered Dosojin sculpture is located in a village in Shizuoka Prefecture at the foot of Mount Fuji.

89. Dosojin sculptures in Kanagawa Prefecture are often found in the company of naturally phallus-shaped stones, as shown here. The sculpted stone is dated August 16, 1670. In very old sculptures like this one, there is little or no differentiation in the size and characteristics of the male and female figures. An offering of *mochi,* cakes made from glutinous rice paste, has been made to this image, and a temporary shrine has been erected over the stones on the occasion of the annual Dosojin festival.

90. The spirit honored at this Shinto shrine in Natori, Miyagi Prefecture, is the daughter of a nobleman who took her own life when her father disowned her for falling in love with and marrying the son of a merchant. The *shintai,* or physical manifestation, of the deity originally was a stone phallus, later replaced by a wooden one six feet long. A few small wooden phalli are shown offered below the sanctuary. The votive plaque, or *ema,* to the left depicts Saruta-hiko, with his phallic nose, and Uzume.

91, 92. These two photographs are eloquent testimony to the way in which phallic worship has been disguised with a Buddhist façade. On the day that these photographs were taken, Myoan-ji temple in Nagoya, Aichi Prefecture, was undergoing a general housecleaning and the priests were occupied with their tasks. The photographer was given a key to the Jizo Hall and there discovered a seated statue of the bodhisattva Jizo (Kshitigarbha) within a small shrine (Figure 91). Parting the dust-covered curtains behind the statue revealed a pair of Dosojin in the form of phalli, one of stone and the other of wood (Figure 92). The stone phallus bears ideographs reading "Doso Konsei-jin," while the inscription on the wooden phallus reads "Doso Konsei Dai-Myojin."

93. Giant straw phalli like the one shown here are a feature of the Dosojin festival in Makioka, Yamanashi Prefecture. This one is protruding from a straw hut above an opening decorated with a *shimenawa* from which white paper *shide* dangle, signifying the sacred quality of the place or the presence of a deity. The phalli are burned at the time of the tree burning.

94–96. These photographs were taken at the hot-spring town of Nozawa, Nagano Prefecture. This community has developed a spectacular form of the festival tree for the annual Dosojin festival in mid-January. The core of the structure consists of the trunks of five sturdy beech trees 50 to 75 feet in height, which have been brought down from the mountains. On this framework a platform of logs tied together with straw ropes is constructed 12 to 15 feet above the ground. Branches are piled on the platform to simulate a thatched roof and to provide fuel for the festival fire. The under-side of the platform is festooned with straw hangings. Paper lanterns and a small *mikoshi,* or portable shrine, are hung from the trees. At the culmination of the festival the tree is set afire and completely burned.

97. The main gateway to Fushimi-Inari Shrine, near Kyoto, is

guarded by two stone foxes who sit on high pedestals flanking the stairway. The female fox (left) holds in her mouth a symbolic key to the rice storehouse, while the male fox holds a ball or *tama* (jewel) symbolizing the *mitama,* or sacred spirit, of Inari, deity of rice. The large upright tails are typical of sculptured foxes.

98. This small shrine within Fushimi-Inari Shrine is surrounded by a fence of stone pillars and marked by a stone *torii* beneath which is a series of smaller wooden *torii* donated by worshipers. The stone *torii* and each fence post are inscribed with the donor's name. Six foxes are gathered here, two being within the wooden *torii*. The pair of seated stone foxes in front of the stone *torii* are depicted with *tama* (left) and key.

99. Visitors to Fushimi-Inari Shrine make contributions of money and in return young girls serving as *miko* perform rituals that include dancing and the presentation of offerings. The music, played on long harplike *koto* (seen in the background), drums, and flute, is eerie and dramatic. On Sundays this performance is repeated several times an hour.

100. A huge, heavy *mikoshi* is lifted by scores of men before setting out from Fushimi-Inari Shrine to visit a series of Shinto shrines and Buddhist temples during a festival. The *mikoshi,* bearing the *shintai* of a deity, used to be borne on men's shoulders, but modern traffic conditions have made it necessary to carry them on trucks.

101. During the Hatsu-uma-sai at Fushimi-Inari Shrine the *shintai* of each of the nine major deities of the shrine is removed from its sanctuary and paraded in a huge ornate *mikoshi*. Here Shinto priests bear the *shintai* of one of the deities to the *mikoshi*. The *shintai* is covered with white cloth, and the transfer is made in such a way that the symbol of the god itself is never exposed to view. The priests handling the sacred object wear paper masks to guard against breathing on the symbol or letting spittle fall on it. The cloth covering the *mikoshi* guards against emanations from the *mitama* of the deity, much as a lead shield guards against X-rays.

PART THREE

FOLK WORSHIP

IV

CONCEPTS OF FOLK WORSHIP

The earliest inhabitants of Japan, the hunters and the gatherers of acorns, seeds, and roots, were aware that each day's life depended upon the bounties of nature and upon the forces of the elements—earth, air, fire, and water. Their wonder at the miracle of procreation and regeneration that they saw in the animals and the plants that shared their world led them—as it did so many of the world's peoples—to worship the phenomena of nature which produced and sustained life. This religious attitude came directly from an instinctive, unquestioning acceptance of the wonders of birth and growth as being evidence of the handiwork of the gods.

Preanimism and Animism The direct worship of nature, or the worship of natural objects as being divine, represents one strand in the complicated web of development of religious concepts. This belief in magic is a relatively simple notion, and precedes animism, which is the belief that all objects have a natural life or vitality, that is, an indwelling spirit which is the force that makes things happen. The sun must have been tremendously important as an object of man's worship from earliest times, for obviously its dazzling rays warmed the receptive earth and rendered it fruitful. With this observation the recurring cycles of life and death in nature were easily assumed to be responses to divine magic. The sun, the rain, the wind, the earth, each in itself, because of its magical properties, was considered to be divine.

Before the appearance of the sun goddess, Amaterasu Omikami, in Japan, there seems to have been a male sun god, Hiruko, the firstborn and legless child of Izanagi and Izanami, the so-called "leech-child" whom they disowned. At any rate, sun cults existed in Japan in very ancient times; and the use of elaborate sun-dial arrangements apparently were related to burial ceremonies and to methods of forecasting the changes in seasons.[1]

Wondrous Deities The large number of phallic symbols and centers of the sun-dial ritual connected with burials in Jomon times (to c. 200 B.C.) indicate that the phenomena of life and death were deep and constant concerns to the people of those early times. Pre-animistic worship of natural phenomena, such as the sun, wind, fire, mountains, the phallus, and so on, is reflected both in Japanese mythology and in the earliest records. "When the deity Izanami was burned as she gave birth to her last son, Kagutsuchi, the God of Fire, her pudenda was burnt and she died . . . and lo, giving birth to Fire, her pudenda was burnt."[2]

This portion of the ritual of the festival for appeasing the fire god refers to fire and to the god of fire interchangeably and without distinction. Fire as such was considered to be a deity.

Many mountains were regarded as deities. The greatest of these is Fuji, which aroused awe and reverence in the hearts of people during the age when it was an active volcano. And the almost magical hold of its beauty upon many people today, as well as in the past, is well known. Almost as soon as they had learned to write, the Japanese people were expressing in poems their respect for Mount Fuji: "The highest peak of Mount Fuji . . . is a wondrous deity . . . and a guardian of the land of Japan."[3]

Animal Deities Genchi Kato has identified a large number of animal deities that were worshiped in ancient times in Japan. The crocodile, Sabimochi-no-Kami (Blade-possessor Deity), was among those listed in the *Kojiki* as great gods. While animals are no longer worshiped as gods, many still are considered to be messengers of the deities and therefore are regarded as being sacred. Among these Kato has listed "deer, Take-mike-tsuchi at Kasuga [Shrine] at Nara; monkey, Yama-no-kami at Hie [Hiyoshi Shrine]; dove, Hachiman; white egret, Kebi-no-miya [Shrine]; tortoise, Matsumo; crow, Kumano; sea monster [*wani*], Sea God, Koto-shiro-nushi; dragon, Takao-kami [rain god]; rat, Daikoku; pheasant, Heavenly Deities' Messenger [generally]; fox, Inari; sun-crow, Yatagarasu, formerly had a shrine in its honour; koma-inu, stone statues who stand in pairs in front of many Shinto shrines as guardians; cormorant, Kushi-ya-tama-no-kami; white deer, God of Ohoyama; snake,

Ohonamochi; centipede of the deity Kidau; wolf, Deity of Sanjo."[4]

Historians believe that, in earlier times, all these animal messengers were themselves regarded as deities, and that their original roles have been taken by the present anthropomorphic deities whom they now serve.

Spiritism   This is the belief that both natural objects and deities who assume a visible form possess an indwelling spirit and that mortals can communicate with these powerful spirits either directly or through intermediaries. Everything is seen in terms of spirits, and there are good and bad spirits who must be gratefully acknowledged or whose wrath must be appeased. Fortunately, this concept also provided that the bad spirits are few in number, whereas good deities, both more numerous and more powerful, can keep the bad ones in check. The spirit of a deity, whether its body assumes the form of a tree, a mountain, an animal, or a human being, is capable of leaving its body, traveling great distances, then returning to it. Spiritism was a refinement upon animism in both the concept of the spirit and the manner in which people related to it. Each spirit is thought to be capable of exercising its power on behalf of humanity or against it, but only when the deity's wrath is aroused by some offending action on the part of man does it become antagonistic. The deity's favor can be regained by prayers and offerings of an appropriate kind. The concept of spirit reached a very sophisticated level in Japanese thought; and the spirit as a living force possessing a wide range of characteristics is one of the fundamental concepts in Japan's native religion.

The Concept of Spirit   W. G. Aston gave special consideration to defining the Japanese concept of spirit. He wrote that the doctrine of spiritism is associated in Shinto with the word *mitama,* for which "spirit" is the nearest English equivalent. Strictly speaking, the mitama* is not the god but an emanation or effluence from him, which inhabits his temple, and is the vehicle of his action at a distance from the place where he himself resides.[5]

Ancient records use the term "kami" when referring to various deities of heaven and earth or to their mitama. "Moreover, not only human beings, but birds, beasts, plants and trees, seas and mountains, and all other things whatsoever which deserve to be dreaded and revered for the extraordinary and preeminent powers which they possess, are called *Kami*."[6]

*Aston gives the following etymology of *mitama* in a footnote on page 9 of *Shinto: The Way of the Gods:* "Mi = honorific. Tama = Jewel, something valuable, a New Year's present, something globular in shape, the sacred emanation from the God which dwells in his shrine, also the human life or soul (spirit)."

The attributes of the mitama are illustrated by its manifestations of power in a number of ways: "According to some of the old historical books it is reported that, among the ancient Japanese, there was a belief in four kinds of spirits: the *nigi-mitama* or gentle spirit, the *ara-mitama* or rough spirit, the *saki-mitama* or luck spirit, and the *kushi-mitama* or wondrous spirit."[7]

These are not four different aspects of one spirit but four separate spirits resident in one deity-body.

According to a variety of sources in mythology, the mitama can express its power in a number of ways, of which the following are only a few: (1) it can be separate from the body; (2) it can be male and female at the same time; (3) it can travel great distances, from place to place on earth or from heaven to earth, and return; (4) it can enter the human body and speak through it, delivering oracles; (5) it can communicate with humans through an intermediary, a shaman; (6) it is a living force, and is not to be confused with the soul, which is connected with death; (7) it has supernatural powers.

The first attribute, the ability of the mitama to be separate from the body, is demonstrated by the story of Onamochi, the creator or cosmic deity of the Izumo myth: "Coming at last to the province of Idzumo, he spake and said: 'This Central Land of Reed-plains had always been waste and wild. The very rocks, trees, and herbs were all given to violence. But I have now reduced them to submission, and there is none that is not compliant.' Therefore he said finally: 'It is I, and I alone, who now govern this land. Is there perchance anyone who could join me in the governing of the world!' Upon this, a divine radiance illuminated the sea, and of a sudden there was something which floated towards him and said: 'Were I not here how couldst thou subdue this land? It is because of my presence that thou hast been able to accomplish this mighty task.' 'Who art thou?' asked Ohonamochi. It replied and said: 'I am thy spirit (*tama*) of good luck, the wondrous spirit.' 'Where dost thou wish to dwell?' The spirit answered and said: 'I wish to dwell on Mount Mimoro, in the province of Yamato.' Accordingly he built a shrine in that place and made the spirit to go and dwell there. This is the God of Ohomiwa."[8]

This distinction between the deity and his spiritual double, which is so clearly indicated in this extract, is often ignored and the deity of Miwa spoken of simply as Onamochi.

The mitama's power to leave its deity-body and travel great distances, from one realm to another, from heaven to earth, from mountaintop to local shrine, and to return again enables it to perform those prodigies of intercession and protection that people must always regard as miraculous: "A person or natural object, whether animate or inanimate, was believed to be often possessed by a disembodied spirit, and animism was the natural result of this. Consequently, . . . when the Empress Jingu started on her expedition to Korea, the gentle spirit of a god attached itself to the very person of the Empress in order to protect her, while the rough spirit of the same god hovered over and guided the Imperial warships."[9]

This incident describes a version of so-called god possession, in which the spirit of a deity enters the body of a human for the purpose of delivering an oracle. Making the necessary contact between human beings and spirits required the efforts of very highly trained and skillful specialists, called *asobi-be*,[10] under whose sole care the ceremony of calling down the mitama of the deity was performed. Rituals to appease the anger of evil spirits also were conducted by the asobi-be, as well as those for breaking divine curses imposed upon human beings as punishment for their transgressions.

As Kato concluded, in his *Study of Shinto,* the asobi-be of Japan had their counterparts in "the shamans of the Mongols, the *kiton* of the Formosans, the *noro* of the Loochoo Islanders, the Korean *mudang*, the *pia atua* (god boxes) of Polynesians, etc."[11]

By whatever local names these specialists have been called, among scholars today they are known as shamans. A recognition of the part that shamans and shamanistic rituals played in the religious development of Japan's people helps greatly toward understanding the symbolism and the metaphor of many events in their mythology.

All the techniques of shamanistic practices are directed toward ascertaining the will and judgment of the spirit-deities by means of dreams, divinations, or inducing a state of superconsciousness, or ecstasy, which enables man to communicate with those deities.

The mitama or kami as defined above should not be confused with the departed souls of the dead. Souls continue to abide in their places of burial or in a heaven or an underworld, and are feared because they may return to harass the living. The concept of mitama, according to Aston, corresponds to the Jewish concept of the *sekinah*. Like the mitama, the sekinah is an emanation separate from the body. Aston is definite in not equating the mitama with the soul: "I cannot see that the Sekinah and the Mitama owe anything to the analogous doctrine of the separability of the human soul and body. The ghost is not the parent of either."[12] Today, in Shrine Shinto, the concept of the mitama is being adapted to meet modern ethical refinements.

In prehistoric Japan's folk worship, the spirit of the dead was thought to be only the ara-mitama, the rough, turbulent spirit. Everything connected with death was unclean and was feared. The

Buddhist concern for the soul is connected with death and the hope of reincarnation, whereas the mitama is a living force and reincarnation is not a consideration.

The Outdoor Shrine Ancient centers of ritual, long before people began to build shrines, were simply clearings in the remote primeval forest. The open area chosen or cleared by the devotees would have included an evergreen tree, preferably a sakaki (*Cleyera ochnacea*), growing naturally within it. This clearing would be marked off by a row of stones and with ropes of plaited straw, shimenawa. With prayers and other rites it would be purified and consecrated. Both this kind of outdoor shrine and the evergreen tree were called *himorogi*. Some sites of this kind are still used occasionally today.

In ancient times festivals were held at night, beginning about dusk and ending about dawn. The focal point of the ritual was the calling down of the kami to take up its residence temporarily in the sacrosanct place. The descent of the kami was made by way of the sacred tree, to which it was attracted by a signal fire or by the beating of drums, or both.

Later, when shrine buildings were erected, they occupied similar isolated but inspiring sites, often in rugged and unspoiled areas. With this change in custom, the shintai, the physical manifestation of the indwelling spirit, which had become the symbol of the kami, was placed in the innermost part of the building, in a small altar shrine or sanctuary. The shintai became an object of mystery, hidden from the view of all worshipers except the high priest. The custom of making offerings of weapons to the kami brought changes in the kinds of object which served as shintai. The mirror, sword, spearhead, bow and arrow, and bronze bell became the shintai of various kami. But phallic stones, among the earliest of such symbols, were never wholly superseded as sacred symbols.

Pollution and Purification Among the early Japanese, as in most other primitive societies, certain kinds of actions, behavior, or circumstances were regarded with a measure of dread. In time these were distinguished as "heavenly sins" and "earthly sins." Some of them were recorded in an ancient prayer called the Tenth Norito, which is used in the Great Purification Ceremony, Oharai Kotoba.

In those two classifications, "heavenly sins" refer to the affronts of humankind to their gods, and "earthly sins" refer to those misdeeds committed upon other men. In general, a body or object or place is polluted by any contact with blood, disease, or death. Thus, physical contact with blood shed by animals, or by women in childbirth or during menstruation, resulted in pollution. This kind of defilement is called *kegare*. When evil deeds were committed that offended the kami, the offense was ethical rather than physical, and therefore was regarded as affecting the mitama, or spirit. Such an offense against a kami is called *tsumi,* and the removal of tsumi is achieved by some form of spiritual purification.

Simple forms of purification for the body consist in washing the hands, eyes, nose, and mouth, and in reciting a simple prayer. In some fishing villages, people who have attended a funeral wade into the sea and remove defilement by immersing themselves in the salt water. More complicated forms of cleansing include such rituals as the Oharai, or Great Purification, one of the most important and most solemn ceremonies of the Shinto religion.[13] This is celebrated twice a year, on the thirtieth day of the sixth and twelfth months. In principle, the entire nation, from the emperor down to his lowliest subject, participates in these ceremonies.

The simplest form of purification is washing in clean water. Other techniques include sprinkling a place, such as the threshold, yard, house, or temple, with hallowed water, salt, rice, or pieces of paper. A sumo wrestler throws a handful of salt about the ring before his bout. Each time a housewife buys a new supply of salt, she tosses a pinch of it into the hearth fire. This is done to prevent household accidents and quarreling in the family. Washing or bathing in salt water combines two cleansing elements and is considered to be very effective. Spitting is a symbolic form of ridding oneself of contamination, just as is rinsing the mouth with water. To spit thrice is thought to have a magical effect. The custom of spitting on something for good luck is not limited to Japan.

Another method for getting rid of pollution is to "breathe on" some offering or "ransom object," and so transfer to it the pollution from one's own person. Still another way is to rub all parts of one's body, from head to foot, with a special sheet of white paper on which one's name, sex, and birth date are written. After this ritual rubbing has been performed, the paper must be returned to the shrine from which it was obtained. There it is packed with other such papers, and the lot of them are laden into little boats which are set afloat upon a stream, eventually to reach the all-cleansing sea. Farmers and other country folk used to transfer sickness or misfortune to a small paper doll, a *hito-gata,* upon which their names and wishes were written, and this was thrown either into a fire or into running water, thereby getting rid of pollution. Special offerings of cloth made to deities are a kind of *agamono,* or ransom, which is supposed to be effective in removing guilt resulting from having offended a deity.

By far the most potent device used in purification rituals is the gohei, the wand ornamented with strips of white paper which is waved over an object being purified. Pestilences are scattered to the four winds when the gohei is brandished. Its symbolic power ostensibly is based upon the phallus. The regimen of fasting purifies the body by withholding anything that might be contaminating. And, finally, the drinking of pure water washes out the impurities that have been polluting the offending body.

Ancestor Worship This is the belief that a few rare people are superior to all others because they possess qualities or attributes of a divine nature, and so deserve to be deified. Such individuals may be worshiped as deities while they are alive, as in the case of an emperor. Some individuals are deified only after death, when their greatness is more readily recognized or because they have become the subjects of legends. Leaders of clans, heads of villages, certain classes of men, and even institutions and symbols, such as temples and mirrors, have been and still are deified.

Nature deities were called kami in Japan, and the worship of these divinities, including deified men, was known as *Kami no Michi,* the Way of the Spirits. There is no equivalent in English to express the concept of kami. The use of the word "god" or even "deity" is very misleading, because kami does not signify spiritual quality or saintliness but simply identifies those forces of man and nature that are above the ordinary level. We might think of Babe Ruth, George Washington, Paul Bunyan, Greta Garbo, Charles Lindbergh, and others like them as kami. Japan has its own heroes and "giants" who are so regarded. Each locality has its tutelary kami, and the more far-reaching his reputation is, the more eager people are to gain his patronage and protection.

The human beings who were deified gave rise to the system of ancestor worship practiced in Japan. They include many mythological heroes who were believed to be ancestors of the emperors and, through them, of the whole Japanese nation.

A mistaken notion about Japanese ancestor worship maintains that all ancestors of a family are worshiped. This is not true. A family's ancestral deities, relatively few in number, are worshiped because they are regarded as being divine, or as possessing the divine spirit, not because they happen to be ancestors. Ordinary ancestors are revered but not worshiped. This distinction is important. And it shows how very different is the Japanese practice from the Chinese, in which all deceased members of a family are worshiped. The Chinese practice made a cult of the family, while the Japanese belief served the nation, a sector of a religious system.

Among the kami acknowledged as ancestors of the imperial family is the first emperor, the legendary Jimmu Tenno, who was a great-grandson of Prince Ninigi, himself a grandson of the sun goddess, Amaterasu. All three of these are regarded as ancestor-deities of the family that has produced Japan's emperors for more than twenty-four hundred years.

Women as Religious Leaders It is certain that in agricultural communities dependent upon rice the annual ceremonies to assure bountiful harvests required the participation of all the members of the village. Usually the headman was responsible for conducting rituals connected with sowing the seed, transplanting the seedlings, and harvesting the grain. Where the leadership of the village council was filled on a rotational basis, so that unpleasant tasks, such as burials and punishments, were not imposed upon one man or family, the office of religious leader fell upon that individual deemed to be most suited for the position by popular choice or singled out for it by some apparent expression of divine will. As agriculture became more highly specialized and increasing administrative tasks absorbed the energies of the men, women often assumed the responsibility for religious ceremonies. Some women became shamans. Eventually the role of religious leader was assigned to a woman more or less permanently for the course of her life; and in some places this priestly function became hereditary, being transmitted through the female line.[14]

In those early times there were heroines, too, such as the Empress Jingu, who led an army to Korea. In an even earlier age, the sun goddess, Amaterasu, could have been a female shaman involved in a political or religious career connected with solar cycles or religious functions. In view of the part that women played in the social structure of that distant era, the claim that they also must have served as shamans is not farfetched. Certainly, female shamans must have prepared the people to accept a female in the paramount position of sun goddess. In other words, Amaterasu herself may have been an eminent sovereign or a shaman from a ruling family who was deified because of her dominant role in the religious life of her time.

Clan Leaders as Deities In small communities and villages, certain individuals were chosen for positions of leadership because of their superior abilities and character. With the passage of time, such leaders became identified as a class and were called *uji* (as also were the heads of families). The term uji, meaning chief or headman, was an official designation, whether it applied to court officials, village headmen or elders, or guild members. The chief of the uji was termed *uji-no-kami*: the superior of the uji, or chief of chiefs. The guardian kami, or *uji-gami,* of such a special class of uji was considered to be more powerful than the kami representing an ordinary village. There were several kinds of village kami: those who had power over one's place of birth; the protectors of particular localities or regions; the protectors of fields and crops; the protectors of the oceans (which were the fields of fishermen); the protectors of roads, front yards of houses, the hearth, the fire, the water supply, and so on. There is a kami for nearly everything under heaven.

In ancient times, the head of a family was both father and priest, and he conducted the rituals of worship for the family or clan. In this role, he was known as the uji-no-kami, the family chief. Long after he died, he might become an uji-gami, the guardian spirit of the family, and the family would depend upon his spirit for guidance, help, and protection. By far the majority of such family leaders did not achieve the higher status of kami. But those few who did rise above the ordinary level in life and who distinguished themselves in service to the family, community, or nation may have become kami. Farmers often revere the founder of a family and of the family's estate as a kami because they regard as a divine gift the land which he acquired and which ever since that time has secured the livelihood of the family. Naturally, farmers would be more dedicated in the reverence they offer such ancestral spirits: they are kami by deed, and not merely by blood.

Ancestral spirits are believed to return to their family homes once a year for a period of three days. The house is specially cleaned and prepared for the occasion. The spirit is invoked to descend and, when it does, occupies a miniature shrine placed near the household prayer shelf. Offerings of rice cakes, sakè, fruits, flowers, and the like are made to it. Prayers and eulogies are recited daily. At the end of the third day it is sent off in a "spirit-departing" ceremony.

Shintoists believe that infants do not have spirits until they are endowed with one by the guardian kami of a shrine. At that time, the young child also acquires a personal guardian deity who will protect him for the rest of his life. All true Shintoists accept the fact of death, and may not show their grief upon the death of a loved one. Natural death, that is, death itself, was not regarded as physical or spiritual pollution, but rather as a misfortune or a calamity. However, since uncleanliness was abhorred, a decaying corpse was regarded with horror. In ancient times, a corpse might lie around for a couple of months before some act of divination revealed how to dispose of it properly. Buddhism managed to deal with this problem speedily and efficiently. Shinto funerals are never conducted at shrines because these are dedicated to kami who minister to the living and their happiness. Funerals are conducted at home or at public funeral parlors in accordance with Shinto rites. In farm villages, neighbors are organized into groups, on a rotating basis, to take care of funerals and other such emergencies.

Cycle of the Spirit Having acquired a spirit soon after birth, by the grace of a kami, each person goes through life under the guidance of his divine guardian spirit. When a person dies, his body, which was produced by the earth spirit, returns to the earth. However, inasmuch as his mitama was produced by the divine spirit, that will return to the divine world. Moreover, since it was produced by a kami, the mitama of any dead person has the potential of becoming a kami. Yet, because Okuni-nushi (Great Land-possessor Deity) is the ruler of the hidden world, all spirits must return to him to be governed. He is the one who decides whether each spirit has attained its divine character and may rise to the status of kami. According to the record of their virtues and vices during this life, some spirits ascend to the realm of the sky, others remain on earth, and still others follow the path to the Land of Yomi, the nether world.[15]

Mythology speaks of the retirement of the Izumo deity, Okuni-nushi, to rule over the mysterious affairs of the hidden world. The funeral rites of the Izumo Taisha (Great Shrine) sect spell out the powers of Okuni-nushi as the creator of kami and regulator of the status of spirits. It is for this reason that "in October of every year *kami* from all over Japan journey to Idzumo to pay their respects to O-honamochi-no-Kami (O-Ho-Kuni-Nushi-no-Kami) by whose favor they were raised from the status of spirits to that of *kami*. At any other time of the year *kami* may make this same journey to confer with O-honamochi to discuss the state of affairs under their local jurisdiction."[16]

The great majority of spirits are destined to continue their existence on earth, where they hover about indefinitely in some nearby place, such as a mountain or a neighboring grove. However, if the relatives can arrange to do so, a spirit may be accommodated in a "spirit shrine," where its happiness will be assured through association with the guardian kami of the shrine.

Social Structure and Folk Worship Fraternal organizations or religious societies which have limited objectives are referred to as *ko*. The ko system integrates all members of a family into a patriarchal hierarchy dedicated to an ancestral spirit, or uji-gami. The smallest unit of the ko system is the *dozoku,* or family unit. The members of such a unit offer mutual aid in such matters as building or thatching a house or sinking a well, and at times of birth, marriage, and death. However, not all ko are family-oriented, for there is a second kind of orientation, the *hito-gami,* or man-deity, system, which is based upon the close relationship of an individual kami with a religious specialist, such as a shaman or a medicine man. The social organization of this second type involves a wide circle of believers who are drawn together by the power of the kami or the charisma of the religious leader rather than by blood ties. Members of hito-gami ko practice austerities of one kind or another, while those of uji-gami ko do not. In addition to taking care of the family or village shrine, members of uji-gami ko worship such spirits as Ta-no-Kami, deity of rice fields, and Yama-no-Kami, deity of mountains, and gather for such purposes as admiring the rising sun or the full moon, making pilgrimages to the Grand Shrines at Ise, viewing cherry blossoms, and laying flowers upon soldiers' graves.

Members of hito-gami ko practice austerities, such as climbing mountains, bathing under waterfalls, and purification by fire. They are led by an ascetic called a *yamabushi,* "one who sleeps among the mountains." This kind of belief is known as Shugendo (from *shu* = perform austerities; *gen* = effect, power; *do* = way). The worship of mountains is an old Shinto tradition, which was appropriated by Buddhist monks of the esoteric Shingon and Tendai sects, who traveled through the mountains ministering to people. Through them these beliefs of mountain-dwellers came to be known as Shugendo.[17]

Cults Related to Organized Religions Indigenous folk beliefs in Japan came under the influence of Buddhism soon after its introduction about A.D. 552. The period from the ninth through the twelfth century saw the establishment of many cults that were mixtures of Shinto, Buddhism, Taoism, animism, shamanism, and magic. Three such cults that are active today are the Nembutsu, Shugendo, and Ommyodo sects.

The Nembutsu Sect People believed that the spirits of men who had been illustrious or powerful in life, but who had been maligned or persecuted, could return as malevolent spirits to wreak their vengeance by causing epidemics, famines, plagues, and other such disasters. This belief in the angry man-god, or hito-gami, was the creed of *goryo.* In order to soothe such revengeful and angry evil spirits, there was a reburial of their remains, a posthumous award of honorific name and court rank, and Shinto, Yin-yang, and Buddhist services. Buddhism promotes the idea of life in the hereafter; and it influenced the goryo beliefs by teaching that the spirit of a dead person could be led to salvation through the merciful intervention of the Buddha Amida. This intercession could be gained by means of prayers from the living and by chanting the sacred phrase *Namu Amida Butsu,* "I put my faith in the Buddha of boundless compassion and wisdom."[18]

The Shugendo Sect The origins of Shugendo are found in the beliefs of mountain people, who regarded mountain peaks, volcanoes, waterfalls, watersheds, and special trees as being divine. Mountains have a very strong cosmological significance, and the mountain is one of the shaman's ladders to heaven. Kami are said to descend to mountain peaks before continuing to their destinations on earth, and spirits of the dead are said to dwell upon mountains. Shugendo practices show strong influences of shamanism, Yin-yang beliefs, Taoist magic, Confucian ethics, and Mantrayana Buddhism.[19] The Shugendo philosophy is positive, and members of the sect believe that they acquire spiritual power by practicing austerities.

"The Yamabushi is essentially a figure who acts as a bridge between two worlds. He is a link between the ordinary human world and the 'sacred world' of supernatural beings to which ordinary men and women have no access. By dint of austerities performed in mountains, he is able to reach into the 'other world' and return armed with certain superhuman powers which he can then use for the benefit of the human community on the flat land below. He has the powers of healing and exorcism, power to vanquish the evil possessing beings that cause sickness and disaster, power to subdue fire, power of clairvoyance, and the power to fly."[20]

From this description it would appear that the yamabushi is a shaman. In fact, however, he is more a magician, a medicine man, and a clairvoyant. The yamabushi gains spiritual power by restoring his "buddha-nature" through performing austerities known collectively as "entering the mountain." These include fasting, bathing in icy waterfalls, walking on fire, scaling dizzying heights, and performing a ritual of rebirth. At the end of such preparations, a group of yamabushi will hold a ceremony in which they feast and, by performing magical feats, display competitively the powers each has gained from the mountain.

A yamabushi purification ceremony witnessed by the writer in the mountains northeast of Kyoto was attended by three or four hundred townspeople, well dressed and mostly in Western clothes. The yamabushi participating in the ritual wore a costume which featured a black lacquered eboshi headdress, a white long-sleeved shirt, a white broad-shouldered vest, white voluminous pantaloons, and white footgear and gloves. Each of the forty or fifty young men wore an animal skin, either of fox or badger, hanging from the waist over the buttocks. The leader of the group wore a regal yellow-orange cape or robe, and a peak-shaped cloth hat, and always he sat or walked under a huge red-orange umbrella. The fire ceremony took place at the center of a rectangle of ground, about 50 feet wide and 150 feet long, covered with white sand. The eerie music was made with a conch shell, flute, and drum. The huge bonfire, enclosed within a rail fence, was fed bundles of smoothly planed wooden prayer sticks. These were tossed into the blaze by each member of the group in turn. It was very difficult to get close enough to the fire to throw the bundles into the blaze. Many eyebrows and eyelashes must have been singed in the effort. The recessional at the end of the ceremony was especially impressive, because the escorting party included several townsmen dressed in pin-striped trousers and morning coats, while the sounds of the conch gave a primitive air to the scene.

The Ommyodo Sect (Yin-yang) The popular beliefs and practices of this sect are similar to those of both Shugendo and Nembutsu, in that its priests and magicians travel from village to village in order to minister to the needs of the people. These priests "practice religious magical invocations for good harvests, good weather, purification, and good fortune; in addition, they engage in such matters as divination and fortune-telling."[21] They appease the fears of people of the lower classes by making an annual visit to each house, at which time they purify the premises and distribute talismans, amulets, and astrological calendars related to farming. They also perform rituals to drive evil spirits from the village. They are in great demand at New Year time because all Japanese try to fulfill old obligations and begin the new year with a clean slate.

Folk Worship and Shinto Among the early Japanese people, every aspect of daily life was interwoven with religious acts or thoughts, culminating in the worship of particular deities and guardian spirits who could make crops grow, cure sickness, ease childbirth, and bring good luck and success and happiness. There was a guardian deity for everything, and everyone had his own guardian deity.

Eventually there came a time when this complex structure of beliefs, derived from several sources and influenced by numerous personalities, was combined and reconciled, to form the product that now is called Shinto. In this slow and patient way, Shinto became a national faith with a leadership, a system of shrines, and a priesthood, all coupled with great social and political forces. The founding of the Japanese state could be completed only when its rulers recognized that the country could be unified only if the fundamental attitudes and beliefs of the people—the religious system of the masses—were incorporated within the administrative procedures of the government.

THE PHALLIC ROOTS
OF FOLK WORSHIP

The myths, customs, and religious rites of the ancient Japanese that have been recorded in old documents reveal that the earliest forms of nature worship were rooted in phallicism. This is consistent with the fact that all religions throughout the world appear to have begun in phallicism, and that sex worship is found regularly in early stages of the development of primitive peoples. Man's awe at the miracle of procreation and regeneration led him to worship the agents he thought were responsible for the creating of life—the sexual organs. Phallic monuments, emblems, festivals, and decorative motifs are found in all parts of the world, and mythologies of all races have elements which are sometimes symbolically and sometimes quite literally phallic in content.

The magic in the power to generate life was in a very real sense a safeguard against death, and therefore men fashioned images of the organs of procreation which they worshiped as powerful protectors against death and destruction. When rocks and objects in nature were found which resembled those organs, often they were considered to be manifestations of the gods themselves and therefore were especially revered. These were placed at the edges of fields to insure their fertility and as protection against crop diseases or failure. They were also placed beside roadways, and as boundary markers between fields.

In early agricultural and nature-oriented societies, myths were created to explain the seasons of the year, and the reproductive functions of the deities were dramatized in rituals and honored with

161

festivals. As their cultures advanced, the phallic elements in the religious celebrations of most societies became more and more hidden, disguised by a symbolism which was understood only by the initiate, or in some societies were suppressed even to the point of being quite inadmissible.

In his *Study in the Development of Religious Ideas Among the Japanese People as Illustrated by Japanese Phallicism,* Genchi Kato wrote: "As is well known to occidental students of things Japanese, the ancient Japanese had myths, customs, and religious rites of a sexual character. Their ancient documents, for example the *Kojiki,* or 'Records of Ancient Matters,' the *Nihongi,* or 'Chronicles of Japan,' and the *Kogoshui,* or 'Gleanings from Ancient Stories,' are full of examples."[1]

Kato also quoted Sato Shinen, a celebrated scholar of the Edo period, with his refreshingly unembarrassed explanation of the meaning of phallicism in the early myths: "The Ame-no-Nubo-ko, or 'Heavenly-Jewel-Spear,' which the Ancestral Deities in Heaven bestowed upon Izanagi and Izanami, had the shape of a phallus, so that the divine couple got a suggestion through it and were overjoyed in their nuptial union, begetting different gods successively. These are marvellous divine affairs indeed, minutely described in our old records, to which one may well refer.

"The phallus is otherwise called the 'Heavenly Root' or 'Coelestis Penis.' In different parts of the Japanese Empire in olden times shrines were very often erected to it.

"For the Jewel Spear is the Root of Heaven and Earth. Without a male and female principle, nothing on earth can be born and grow. This is the necessary course of Nature, and we see this universal and fundamental truth not only in the animal kingdom but also in the vegetable world. So it is quite natural and reasonable, thanks to the unseen protection of the August Producing Divinity, that all sentient beings are sexually connected and leave behind their offspring from generation to generation without interruption and cessation."[2]

There is a close connection between phallicism and stones, probably because natural stones often are found with phallic shapes. In Greece, the *hermae* can still be seen, upright stones indicating boundaries but whose origins and uses were phallic. Also in Greece at a later time, statues of the god Hermes, with phallus prominent, were placed at crossroads. It is interesting to note that etymologically the name Hermes is related to the word for "stone" or "rock," and also to the verb which means "to protect."[3]

Japan abounds in stones, and the early people's belief in their magical powers is recorded in the *Kojiki,* which relates how Izanagi blocked the entrance to the Land of Yomi with a huge boulder to keep the dead Izanami from following him (see pages 201–2). There is, too, the story of the Empress Jingu, who, finding that she was pregnant while on her way to war in Korea, took along a stone (or possibly two stones) to delay the birth of her child. This was called a *chinkai seki,* meaning "guardian stone." Thus, to stones, and particularly to phallic stones, was ascribed the magical power to delay or prevent evil. Their placement along roads served not only to protect a traveler but also to prevent the entry of misfortune into a community from beyond its borders.

The dualism implicit in phallicism is certainly its most important attribute. And this magic is considered to be most powerful when the male and the female principles are represented in conjunction with each other, symbolizing to the ultimate degree the great source of life. As Buckley has written: "This dualism shows itself in the *usual juxtaposition* in India of the linga [*sic*] and yoni, in Syria of the masseba and ashera, . . . in Greece of the phallos and kteis, . . . in Egypt of the cross and ring combined into the cruxansata, in China of the yang and yin . . . and finally in Japan of the yoseki and inseki."[4]

Stones representing the phallic *yoseki* and the ktenic *inseki* are often seen beside shrines in Japan and particularly near Dosojin images. Usually the stones are placed near each other or in positions suggesting coition. Deities embodying the male and the female principles are paired in many mythologies: in Hinduism, Shiva, the god of the lingam, is coupled with Parvati (or sometimes with Kali or some other goddess, but always with one representing *shakti,* the female principle);[5] in Syria they were Baal with Astarte; in Egypt, Osiris and Isis; in Greece, Dionysus and Demeter, Zeus and Hera, or Uranus and Gaia; in China, T'ien and Ti or Yang and Yin; in Tibet, Yab and Yum; and in Japan, Izanagi and Izanami, the Male Who Invites and the Female Who Invites.

Procreative Aspect This aspect of phallicism recognizes the biological fact that procreation involves both man and woman, and more correctly should be called phalloktenism. But just as the term "man" is used to denote mankind, so is the term "phallicism" used to identify phalloktenism.[6] Bringing life into being is the *procreative* aspect of phallicism. This is simply another way of expressing the concept of the great universal creative impulse that is illustrated in those dual deities related as man and wife or simply by the symbol of the stone phallus. These are personalized expressions of corresponding transpersonal symbols for the principles of creation.

Preventive Aspect The other function of phallicism, the use of the phallic symbol for its *preventive* magic, is less obvious. It is based upon the belief that life itself is the best antidote for death—or, to put the idea into the style of sportswriters, that the best defense is a good offense. Thus, among most people, even now, sexual robustness is considered to be an indication that sickness, debility, or impotence has been avoided or prevented.

Phallicism in Prehistory   Recent archaeological discoveries support the theory that phallicism was indigenous to Japan and existed there for at least two or three thousand years before the coming of Buddhism. Some of the oldest phallic symbols yet found have been dated as belonging to the prehistoric Jomon times (that is, before 200 B.C.). These symbols are of several kinds: stone and clay rods about thirty centimeters long, with or without mushroom-shaped heads, and either plain or decorated; simple, abstract clay figurines of the human body, having only slight indications of head, breasts, and belly; oval clay plaques with overall decorations; and different kinds of pottery utensils, such as ewers with phallic spouts. The most ancient of these artifacts were found at the Hanawadai shell mound in Ibaraki Prefecture, and by the C^{14} process were dated very conservatively at about 5000 B.C., or very early in the Jomon period.[7] Additional finds of rods and figurines were made at Togari-ishi (in Chino, Nagano Prefecture) and elsewhere in excavations of prehistoric houses, some of which had small stone altars upon which images were placed.[8] By the Middle Jomon period (3000–2000 B.C.) great numbers of these images appeared in the Kanto area (around modern Tokyo) and in the regions of Tohoku (northeast of Tokyo), Chubu (west and south of Tokyo), and Hokuriku (along the Japan Sea).[9]

The appearance of stone phallic symbols in such quantity and variety during that period indicates that the aboriginal inhabitants of Japan had begun to broaden their knowledge not only of human fertility but also of gaining more generous sustenance from nature. The gradual change from a hunting to a planting culture was just beginning, and, as part of man's concern with the problems of sustaining life, he began to direct his thoughts and actions toward making the earth systematically productive.

"A planting rite was both a return to the soil of its yield and an invitation to Mother Earth to repeat this yield. Death and burial rituals came to be associated with all forms of increase, and the fading of vegetation in the winter followed by its re-emergence in the spring doubtless greatly encouraged the notion of an after-life with accompanying attempts at preserving the human remains."[10]

When the cultivation of rice was established in Yayoi times, tribal leaders seem to have rejected bronze weapons as tools of war and used them instead as religious symbols. Their preoccupation was with the fertility of the land. The spearhead soon became large, flat, and wide, replacing as a symbol of creation the upright stones of phallic form that had been used in the Jomon period.[11] Shields and spears, placed in boxes, were buried in strategic places on hills along frontiers to insure their protection. Eventually, however, the more durable stone symbols regained their original popularity and have continued in use until the present day.

The development of many kinds of sacred objects and their uses in diverse ritual practices indicate that phallicism as an early form of nature worship had developed its main ideas, symbols, rites, and ceremonies long before its myths and legends were collected and committed to writing in such sacred books as the *Kojiki*. The period during which the customs and traditions evolved that later were preserved in Japanese mythology lasted some fifteen hundred years.

Phallicism in Agriculture Following the introduction of rice cultivation in Yayoi times, or perhaps earlier, agricultural techniques became highly specialized, not simply in the matter of irrigation, construction of paddies, development of tools, and other technical matters. The performance of the sequence of work also became so specialized that in itself it became ritualistic. Certain rituals were performed at the time of seed planting, during the growing season, at harvest time, and in recognition of the beginnings and ends of seasons. Women performed a key role in agriculture, not only as members of the labor force but also in the rituals dedicated to it. As Mircea Eliade concluded: "The mystical connection between the fertility of the soil and the creative force of woman is one of the basic institutions of what one may call the agricultural mentality."[12]

The earth is commonly regarded as female: it has the capacity to bear fruit as if it were a mother, and so it is called Mother Earth. In the ancient agricultural milieu, therefore, "woman, fertility, sexuality and nudity [were] so many centers of sacred power, so many starting points for ceremonial drama."[13] The presence of any combination of these elements is an indication that a particular ritual may be connected with agricultural production. In this context, women often took the role of shamans and thus conducted religious ceremonies. This may be the basis for the fact that for many centuries in Japan the eldest daughter of the emperor has been designated as the high priest of the Grand Shrines at Ise.

Since time immemorial, women have participated in rice-planting ceremonies all over Japan, both as dancers and as planters of the young seedlings. The ceremony at Sumiyoshi Shrine in Osaka is said to go back to the very first introduction of rice cultivation by the legendary Empress Jingu. In such ceremonies and dances women never display any nudity, whereas in many divinational ceremonies and the so-called naked festivals, nearly naked men participate. In

Japan the deities of the sun, food, and sexual attraction are all female.* Therefore, it seems appropriate to reverse the relationship that is usual in other countries, in which the most beautiful maidens of a village dance before a male deity of fertility and in Japan's case to substitute young men dancing before a goddess. Also a possible factor is the Shinto dread of pollution, especially of menstrual blood and the ejecta of childbirth. The female body is considered to possess less mana than does the male. To be sure, however, the role of young men in rituals where they appear naked is not peculiar to Japan: "we may also remember the excesses that took place during certain ancient feasts of vegetation, such as the Romans' Floralia, when young men paraded naked along the streets, or the Lupercalia, when young men used to touch women to make them fertile, or the Holi, the chief Indian vegetation feast, when anything might happen."[14]

The Curse of the Harvest Deity One of the earliest references to phallicism or actual phallic rites in Japanese literature is an account in the *Kogoshui,* or "Gleanings from Ancient Stories," which tells of the magic power of the phallus to prevent disaster in an agricultural situation:

"Of yore, in the age of the Gods, Oho-toko-nushi-no-kami (Great-earth-master-deity), on a day that he was cultivating a rice field, gave his labourers the flesh of oxen to eat. At this time the child of Mi-toshi-no-kami (August-harvest-god) went to that rice field and spat upon the food, after which he returned and reported the matter to his father, who was wroth and let loose locusts on that field, so that the leaves of the young rice suddenly withered away and it became like dwarf bamboos. Upon this Oho-toko-nushi-no-kami caused the diviners to ascertain by their art the reason of this. They replied that it was owing to a curse sent by Mi-toshi-no-kami, and advised him to offer a white pig, a white horse, and a white cock in order to dispel anger. When amends had been made to Mi-toshi-no-kami in the manner directed, the latter replied, 'Truly, it was my doing. Take bare stalks of hemp and make of them a reel with which to reel it, take the leaves and sweep it therewith, take 'push-grass' of heaven and push it therewith. Take, moreover, crow-fan and fan it, and if then the locusts do not depart, take ox-flesh and place it in the runnels, adding to it shapes of the male stem (phallus). Moreover, strew the banks of earth between the fields with waterlily seeds, ginger, walnut leaves and salt.' When these instructions were carried out the leaves of the young rice became thick

*Toyo-uke-no-Kami, one of several food deities, is sometimes identified as a male.

again, and the harvest was a plentiful one. This is the reason why at the present day the Department of Religion worships Mi-toshi-no-kami with offerings of a white pig, a white horse, and a white cock."[15]

Mitoshi-no-Kami probably was outraged over the appearance of ox flesh in the Heavenly Rice Fields because any contact with death, blood, or excrement was a defilement. The sacred rice fields became polluted by blood when animals were killed in them. In addition, it must be remembered that some animals and birds were held sacred: "The flesh of certain animals was prohibited as food (the ox, the horse, the dog, the monkey, the fowl) but much was not (for example, the flesh of the deer, the rabbit, the pig)."[16]

Mitoshi-no-Kami's instructions to restore the productivity of the fields were complicated, to say the least, but not obscure to those who knew how to interpret them. First the fields were swept and purified by several means, and then they were fertilized—that is, impregnated with life-producing power—by means of ox flesh laid in the furrows and by the display of phallic symbols both in and around the fields. Through these magical acts the power of such gods as Ta-no-Kami, Saruta-hiko, Yama-no-Kami, Sanno, and other earth deities was invoked to make the fields productive. The symbol associated with these deities, especially with Saruta-hiko, was a phallus made of stone or of wood.

Phallicism in the Kojiki   At least ten myths in the first book of the *Kojiki* refer to events that are based on phallicism. In some cases the language is explicit; in others it is symbolic. These events include sexual intercourse, seduction, acts of creation, prevention, and killing, and death. In addition, there are numerous passing references to phallic symbols, rituals, and deities. One of the first stories tells of the creation of the islands of Japan by means of a magical jeweled spear. The drippings from the spear as it stirred the ocean water became an island. Izanagi and Izanami descended to this island and courted each other around a phallic column, engaged in sexual intercourse, and created further islands and children who were deities resembling their parents. When Izanami died while giving birth to the god of fire, Izanagi slew the young god, his own child, from whose body new deities were born. The birth of phallic deities from a stick, a stone, and a tree crotch are also described. There is the story of the delaying of the birth of a future emperor by means of stone tied to the body of Empress Jingu. There are accounts of phallic deities who participated in rituals that included the highest deities of the Shinto pantheon. Through these myths, phallicism is shown to be one of the primary sources of Shinto.

Some of these myths, the plots of which can only be suggested here, are discussed in greater detail in Part Four of this book.

Reforms Against Phallic Worship   Old records speak of the numbers of Dosojin images set up along roads and of the satisfaction and protection they gave to many passers-by. But the images also elicited a negative reaction. Hayashi Razan, a famous scholar of Chinese classics and Confucian ethics in the seventeenth century, wrote in the *Honcho Jinji-ko,* or "Notes on the Shinto Shrines of Japan," a criticism of phallic worship as being a nasty practice injurious to public morality.[17] Also, the *Nihon Montoku Tenno Jitsuroku,* or "The Authentic Japanese History of the Reign of the Emperor Montoku" (reigned 850–58), recorded that "two large awful rocks" appeared nightly in the light of fires on the shores of Hitachi.[18] It wasn't the sight of sculptured stones or of natural stones resembling the phallus that upset the propriety of aristocrats and government officials; they were disturbed by the festivals held around those stones, in which phallic rites were carried out in "a boisterous spirit," thereby vulgarizing their religious purpose. The customs in those "night festivals" included dancing, and ended with the disappearance of couples into the darkness. Therefore, all festivals of a phallic nature, in which images of the phallus or of the sexual act were exhibited, were banned from public view for a while.

Various reforms were instituted during subsequent years. The first of the government measures in recent times that was generally successful in suppressing some of these customs came in 1841, when Mizuno Tadakuni introduced the so-called Tempo reforms, "prohibiting all exhibitions of immoral character and the use of decorations and other devices of questionable taste."[19] The police actually searched the countryside and succeeded in either destroying many phallic images or persuading villagers to hide them away in obscure places or within temples. Countryfolk found it expedient to disguise the phallic character of all stones they had been reverencing, especially of Dosojin sculptures that showed the couple in sexual embrace.

The next wide-sweeping reform came in 1872, the fifth year of the Meiji era,[20] and was leveled not so much at the spontaneous worship of folk deities as at the erotic sexual cults that had been flourishing in Shinto shrines and Buddhist temples. The order abolished all images and practices of extreme naturalism, such as those held at Yaegaki Shrine at Izumo and at the shrine of Kumano Gongen at Ota in Chiba Prefecture. The government's most recent ban, in 1953, was directed against phallic roadside deities.[21]

Buddhist Censorship   The Buddhist effort to eradicate native folk deities covers the same period of about twelve hundred years, although it was not as direct as the government's. Buddhism could not censure the animistic deities of the native religion, with which it had to compete, but tried instead to absorb them or to substitute its own deities for those of folk Shinto. Official Buddhist doctrine held the conviction that Japan's Shinto gods and folk deities were but humbler manifestations of the celestial Buddhas of endless light in all ages. According to the *Konjaku Monogatari,* or "Former Stories Now Narrated," the phallic deity Dosojin attained salvation by virtue of hearing the Buddhist priest Doko recite the Lotus Sutra. And thereby Dosojin as Saruta-hiko, a phallic deity of considerable popularity, was raised to the rank of a preacher of moral law instead of remaining only a deity of a nature religion, as the *Kojiki* made him.[22]

Another successful substitution was achieved when the Buddhist Jizo (the bodhisattva Kshitigarbha) replaced Dosojin as the protector of children from sickness and harm. In accepting Jizo, people gave him the same attributes that they had given Dosojin; and (no doubt to his surprise) Jizo served them as a phallic deity, as well. Sometimes Jizo is found carved on old phallic stones that everyone knew to be Dosojin. Jizo also was carved, in very elongated proportions, as lying within the hull of a boat—another old phallic symbol, which represents both the male and the female principles. The ease with which those older deities were fitted into the newer framework simply meant that people quickly learned how they could worship them more conveniently in their own way, while pretending to conform with the changing decrees.

Shrines Dedicated to Phallic Deities   In general, such phallic deities as the Sae-no-Kami, the preventive or road-blocking deities, were worshiped (as they still are) out of doors, from day to day, but especially at the time of the Michiae-no-Matsuri, the Festival of the Crossroads, during the sixth and twelfth months of the year. Worship of phallic gods was not restricted to the agricultural environment alone, of course, but was accepted and supported by formal religious institutions of the highest order, such as Fushimi-Inari Shrine near Kyoto. Although many symbols and effigies stood in the open, both temporary and permanent shrines, or *miya,* were built to shelter phallic deities. One such miya constructed at Kasa-shime, fifteen miles south of Sendai, is said to have been founded about A.D. 330 by Yamato-Takeru-no-Mikoto. The deity worshiped there was Saruta-hiko-no-Mikoto. At one time, fifteen priests and their families and households served this temple. Now only a trace of it remains. "To the same imposing class belonged a temple at

Makiborimura in Iwate Prefecture. The deities there were Izanagi, Izanami, and Saruta-hiko, which three are associated with Konsei Dai-Myojin, Root of Life Great Shining Deity."[23]

D. C. Holtom identified certain phallic deities and shrines as being a part of official Shinto: "the Ebishima Shrine near Ishikoshi, north of Sendai, the Shrine of the 'Road-Ancestor-God' [Dosojin] of Wakayanagi, also near Ishikoshi at Kashima, and at Aikomura in Rikuzen, the Iwate Shrine of Shikoku, also shrines of phallic kami at Miyanoura and elsewhere in the Inland Sea. Japanese kami under more than eighty different names have been identified as associated with phallicism. A plain forked stick may sometimes be found thrown in at phallic shrines along with emblems of the phallus and kteis. A phallic deity is sometimes called Mata-no-kami or Chimata-no-kami, 'Crotch-kami' or 'Fork-kami.' All this is a part of the cult of the shrines."[24]

A shrine rivaling in importance the one at Kasashime is that of Fushimi-Inari near Kyoto, founded in 711, in which a triad of phallic deities, Ugadama, Saruta-hiko, and Uzume, is still established.

A rather insignificant shrine in physical terms, but placed in a most honored location, is the one at Ise-Yamada, "outside the north-west corner of the famous Naiku San—the Ise shrine to Amaterasu, the Heaven-Shiner, regent of the Shinto pantheon; and between two temples, one to Oho-yama-tsumi-no-kami (Deity great-mountain-possessor) and the other to his daughter, Kono-hana-sakuya-hime (Princess-blossoming-brilliantly-like-the-flowers-of-the-trees), who presides over Mt. Fuji. The shrine frames a typical phallos and kteis side-by-side."[25]

These temporary shrines, which are small wooden structures, often only four feet by six feet in area and not more than five feet high, covering natural phallic stones, are still found by the thousands in the northeast region of Japan. Some stones and sculptures are adjacent to Shinto shrines and Buddhist temples, where they have been moved for protection against vandalism, but most are still standing at the edges of rice fields, just where their original function of insuring bountiful crops placed them.

It is not uncommon for several deities to be enshrined in the same place. Saruta-hiko shares shrines with many other gods, a fact which helps to account, perhaps, for the broad base of his popularity.

"Saruta-hiko himself is undoubtedly one of the most popular Kami in Japan, both officially and still more so in popular belief. A number of temples, big and small, count him among the deities enshrined. . . . We find him enshrined in the Ise Saruta-hiko-jinja, the Tsubaki-jinja, the Okazaki Rokusho Jinja, and the Matsue-Sada-jinja, as well as in many subsidiary shrines."[26]

Thus, phallicism is recognized in effect, if not in name, in literature, ritual, and doctrine; and its deities are housed in all kinds of shelters, ranging from crude wayside huts to the grand national Shinto shrines and great Buddhist temples.

Origins of the Preventive Festivals In different parts of the country certain names are connected with the images of Dosojin, the Dosojin festival, the fire of that festival, or with the festival of Dosojin in his capacity as the deity of roads. These names are derived from ancient phallic rituals that were originally designed to seek the help of deities in protecting the people against epidemic diseases. At least three ancient festivals were established whose function was to entreat the gods for protection from harm for the people and their villages, as well as for the roads they traveled. They are Michiae-no-Matsuri (Festival of the Crossroads), the Goryo-sai, and the Sagicho Matsuri. The Dosojin festival, which has been discussed in an earlier chapter, is similar to these three preventive festivals but differs in that it is also a harvest fertility celebration and thus incorporates the two aspects of phallicism, the procreative and the preventive. It follows, then, that in some places the Dosojin festival could be called by the names of these three other festivals or by the names of rituals which they include.

Michiae-no-Matsuri: Festival of the Road Deities This Festival of the Crossroads takes place during the sixth and twelfth months of each year throughout much of Japan. Nowadays, however, it is performed with rites that have been modified from those originally used, when the ceremony consisted of placing food offerings at the crossroads outside the capital city to ward off evil spirits. The deities who are worshiped on this occasion are the Sae-no-Kami, or preventive deities. They are known individually as Yachimata-hiko (Eight Crossroads Prince), Yachimata-hime (Eight Crossroads Princess), and Kunado-no-Kami (Come-not Place Deity). These deities are equated with the preventive aspect of Dosojin, and on this occasion the appeal is made to Dosojin as protector.

The invocation recited during the ceremony is the Thirteenth Norito, which begins in this manner: "I humbly declare in the presence of the Sovran Gods, whose functions first began in the Plain of High Heaven, when they fulfilled the praises of the Sovran Grandchild by guarding the great eight road-forks like a multitudinous assemblage of rocks.

"Naming your honored names, to wit, Yachimata-hiko, Yachimata-hime, and Kunado, I fulfill your praises. Whenever from the Root-country, the Bottom-country, there may come savage and unfriendly beings, consort not and parley not with them, but if they go below, keep watch below, if they go above, keep watch above, protecting us against pollution with a night guarding and with a day guarding."[27]

The norito goes on to specify offerings of four kinds of cloth, sakè, and things of sea and land.

At the present time, people who celebrate this festival have extended their concerns to include protection of the house or shrine where the ritual is held and to the welfare of the people who make the offerings and prayers. They also remember its original purpose of preventing pestilences and prohibiting evil spirits from invading the community.

The Sae-no-Kami were extremely popular in ancient Japan. Appeals were addressed to them in divinations, and most travelers prayed to them before starting on a journey. Moreover, a ceremony in honor of these deities was performed two days before the arrival of foreign envoys in the capital in order to guard against the danger of their bringing infection, evil influences, or demons from abroad.[28]

Many a traveler carried a little cloth bag, hung from his sash, which contained rice, pebbles, or bits of dried hemp leaves. Whenever he came to a roadside image, he placed before it a small offering from the bag. Disaster or illness that might befall him during the journey was attributed to his negligence in honoring these deities.[29]

Goryo-sai: Festival for the Plague Deities This festival dates back to 869, during the reign of Emperor Seiwa (858–76), when a terrible pestilence ravaged the whole country. The emperor requested that services be offered to the "plague gods" so that the capital, at that time Kyoto, would be spared. The ritual devised for that occasion became an annual affair and is continued today in Kyoto as the Gion Matsuri. The procession for this festival features the spectacular *yama* (mountain) and *hoko* (halberd) floats. The former are carried on the shoulders of men; the latter, three or four stories high, roll along on huge wooden wheels. For the original occasion, sixty-six halberds, one for each of the nation's provinces, were erected at the site of the ceremony, and offerings were made by each province. A procession of elaborate floats invoked the protection of the kami. The halberds carried on that occasion were substitutes for the older phallic symbols. For us they are a clue to the fact that, in the beginning, the Goryo festival was dedicated to the Sae-no-Kami, the deities who prevent pestilences. This meaning seems to have been lost in the modern survival of the Goryo festival, at least as it is exemplified in Kyoto's Gion Matsuri.[30]

The Deity of the Goryo Festival The god identified with the Goryo-sai appears to be different in different places. The deity of the festival as it was performed under the auspices of Emperor Seiwa represented the vengeful spirits of five courtiers who had died in dishonored obscurity. But according to Yanagita, it is likely that there was an earlier Goryo deity because the ceremonies of Sagicho (which are associated with Dosojin) were performed in the same imperial courtyard before Emperor Seiwa's placatory Goryo-e was held there. In that earlier time mentioned by Yanagita, the deity of Goryo was identical with Kunado-no-Kami and functioned in the same way as did the deities of Yachimata-no-Matsuri and Michiae-no-Matsuri.[31] The deities of the Goryo festival as it is performed in Kyoto at the present time are those honored at Yasaka Shrine: Susano-o-no-Mikoto, Yasaka-no-Sume-no-Kami, and Inada-hime-no-Mikoto.[32] (Inada-hime-no-Mikoto is the wife of Susano-o; he saved her from death by killing the eight-headed dragon that had devoured her seven older sisters.)

The identity of the Goryo deity became further confused during the years before Emperor Seiwa's time simply through public support of the beliefs in Goryo. "By 863 there had already come into existence five major *goryo-shin* deities: the spirits of two disenthroned crown princes, the real mother of one of these princes, and two ministers who had suffered martyrdom."[33]

The spirits of many other nobles, in addition to the five named above, were manipulated by ruthless Buddhist and Yin-yang priests. Working in collusion, these priests controlled and destroyed the lives of men so that they might later, at an opportune time, establish the angry spirits of those men as *goryo* spirits responsible for recent calamities. The control of such spirits, through propitiation by enshrinement or with posthumous awards, redounded to the power and prestige and wealth of the calculating priests. In spite of that, the shrines dedicated to the spirits of illustrious men are few in number. "As the belief in *goryo* became more and more widespread, the possibility of becoming a *goryo* or a deified spirit was gradually extended to even the common people."[34]

In general, such deified spirits of men are called *arahito-gami* (rough man-god), and the brave warriors of many provinces, as well as the great men of the nation, have been enshrined as arahito-gami. For this reason, the goryo, or "august spirit," which is honored in a local shrine is likely to be that of a neighborhood hero, and he works on behalf of the people to drive away evil spirits in the same way as did his original counterpart, Kunado-no-Kami.

Sagicho Matsuri This festival is celebrated in some places, including Himure Hachiman-gu shrine, on April 14 and 15. It is a purificatory ritual, during which huge torches are burned while being carried in a spectacular procession. A great drum is borne by a group of helmeted young men at the end of the procession as a sort of rear-guard unit.

An old book, entitled *Wakan Sansei Zu-e,* published in 1713, described the Sagicho festival as it was performed on the grounds of the Imperial Palace in Kyoto: "On the fifteenth day of the first month green bamboos are burnt in the courtyard of the Seiryoden, and happy reports sent up to Heaven therewith. On the eighteenth also, bamboos are dressed up with fans attached to them, which are burnt at the same place. There is a reader of spells called Daikoku Matsudaiyu, who has four followers, two old men and two old women. These wear devil-masks and 'red-bear' wigs. These two old women carry drums, and the two old men run after them trying to beat the drums. There are two boys without masks, but with 'red-bear' wigs, who beat double cymbals. Moreover, there are five men in dress of ceremony who stand in a row and join in with cries of 'dondoya,' while one, costumed somewhat differently, calls out 'Ha!' "[35]

Yanagita believed that the Sagicho Matsuri was very old and that possibly it came from China: "Sagicho and Goryo-e must be related, sharing the same mountainlike objects and their association with Shinsen-en. In some districts, the 'mountain' of the festival is called Danjiri. The 'dan' of Danjiri alludes to the stage of Taoism and esoteric Buddhism, and corresponds to 'tsuka' [mounds]. It is strange that people build mountains or mounds for the festival and drag them about, but formerly they built stages or altars for the festival, carried them to the suburbs, and burned them after the festival. In later years, they elaborated the processions rather than these things [symbols]. Therefore, Sagicho and the festival of Dosojin are more like the original—but not so the Goryo festival."[36]

There is a distinct similarity among these three festivals, the Michiae, the Goryo, and the Sagicho: all are concerned with sending away evil spirits by invoking the help either of phallic deities or of the spirits of great men who have become kami.

Phallic Festivals   Phallic deities often are enshrined together with local tutelary deities, and when that happens the worship of such phallic deities is made inconspicuous. However, during the latter part of the nineteenth century, in big cities like Osaka, Nagoya, and Tokyo, phallic festivals took place in which enormous floats were exhibited. These carried actors impersonating phallic deities who performed rituals simulating coition. At several of these festivals, a surging mass of nearly naked young men carried a gigantic papier-mâché phallus, sometimes forty feet long.

Tagata Shrine near Nagoya in Aichi Prefecture conducts a ceremony on the first and fifteenth day of each month during which joyous celebrants, carrying huge vertical banners displaying grotesque ten-foot drawings of a phallus, lead the procession around the shrine. These are followed by a dozen costumed men who carry a gigantic wooden phallus mounted on a platform.

On January 15, the date of the Dosojin festival, the annual celebration of the Kinen-sai, or Festival for a Rich Harvest, takes place in the same community. On this occasion the procession passes through the neighboring rice fields, and horizontal banners are made to pass over the growing rice in order to assure a good crop. The talisman sold by Tagata Shrine at this festival is a small brass phallus, together with small pieces of paper upon which the name of the female deity Tama-hime-no-Mikoto is printed.

Many phallic festivals of this kind are still observed throughout Japan, and there has been a revival of popularity in those having a degree of competitiveness, such as the rituals of divination and purification in which young men appear all but naked.

Night Festivals Another kind of festival founded on sexuality took place at night and featured either a procession or dancing in which both boys and girls took part. This type of occasion allowed young people to meet under very free circumstances. Sometimes a tug-of-war was the main event, with girls on one side and boys on the other. The names of some of these "dark festivals" suggest their character. At the Kadake Matsuri, for example, the boys were supposed to *seri ni iku,* "go to push," the girls. Nare-ai Matsuri means, literally, "fornication festival." Another festival offered the boys and girls an opportunity for a little exercise known as "night-creeping."[37]

One such famous night dance is still performed on a grand scale in the farm villages near Nikko. The dancers form in great concentric rings, the boys in one, the girls in the next, moving in opposite directions. The dance is performed to a slow, throbbing rhythm sounded by flute and drums, and the movements involve a swinging of the hips, first to one side and then to the other, which is not especially suggestive except when done by young men who have drunk a little too much sakè. As the evening progresses, couples slip away from the circles of dancers and disappear into the night, eventually to find their way home.

Countless harvest matsuri, similar to those celebrated in spring, are held all over Japan. In these, too, the phallic character has been so subdued that the original religious purpose is recognizable only in the names of the festivals.

Ritual Rebirth The mountain ascetic, or yamabushi, represents one of the most successful blendings of beliefs derived from Buddhism and folk-cult practices based upon phallicism. The austerities by means of which yamabushi acquire the magic powers of their profession are not as rigorous today as they were in the Nara (646–794) and Heian periods. The common requirement today is the ascent of a holy mountain, during which time the yamabushi undergoes a week-long retreat to enable him to realize his buddha-nature. He enters the precincts of the magic mountain as an ordinary man, and he returns as a holy disciple empowered to perform magic deeds. During the complicated week-long process, he acts out this transformation in rites symbolic of conception, gestation, and birth. On the night before he goes to the mountain, the disciple eats white rice dumplings (such as usually are presented to the dead), thereby symbolizing the death of his former self. On the first day of the climb, at a shrine which marks the entrance to the mountain path, a ritual of conception is performed, when a long pole is thrust into the mouth of a cave. The phallic deity Kunado is symbolized by the staff or pole, while the cave represents Mother Earth. After this, the disciple enacts the part of an embryo in the womb. As the week goes by, rituals are performed which show the growth and the changing positions of the fetus in the womb. At the end of the week, the disciple descends to the foot of the mountain, where, in a final rite, he jumps over a bonfire, uttering a loud cry, as does a newborn child. The birth of this purified "child" represents the removal of old pollutions and a return to the sacred state where the powers so desired by the yamabushi may be attained.[38]

Phallic Symbols   The form, shape, size, and materials of phallic symbols have been indicated to some extent earlier in this study. However, the variety is so great that a summary review of the different kinds of male and female objects adopted for use as symbols will be of value:

1. *Seki-bo:* stone clubs of a pestle shape, ranging in size from very small to five feet; stone and clay figurines; oval and round plaques.
2. Clay effigies, each with a large protruding penis.
3. Spears, swords, bronze bells.
4. Stone, papier-mâché, clay, or metal phalli; bamboo-grass posies; bellows, drums, cowrie shells.
5. Kezurikake and *ino-a,* wands of elder, willow, or *tara* (a thorn tree) with tufted shavings at the tip.
6. Straw horses with a large phallus, straw male and female objects (club and ball), rings of plaited straw or of stone, stuffed triangular pillows.
7. Mortar and pestle, ewer and cup, sakè bottle and dish.
8. Stone boat, *biwa* (lute), kokeshi dolls, ceramic animals in coitus,

figures of humans with private parts exposed in varying degree, ceramic mandarin ducks (known for lifelong mating).

9. Ema, drawings or paintings of phallic objects on paper or wood.
10. Certain fruits and vegetables: male—daikon, bamboo shoot, carrot, asparagus; female—peach, plum, apricot, grape, persimmon, pumpkin, squash, and others of similar shape.

Erotic Cults and Symbols   There are many other symbols of an erotic kind. These include the Shoten images—human bodies with elephant heads, standing like humans and copulating—which belong to erotic cultism influenced by Tantric Buddhism from India by way of China.

Shoten—or Kangiten (Sanskrit, Ganesha), to use his other name—was the son of Shiva and Parvati, who conceived him after they had changed themselves into elephants. "Kangi" means "joy-giving," and his name in itself identifies the character of the cults he symbolizes.

The main sexual cult of Japan, the Tachikawa-ryu, began as a subsect of Shingon Buddhism in Kyoto about 1114, under the stimulus of a priest named Ninkan. This heretical subsect held that "the fulfillment of human (specifically sexual) desire would lead to an awakening of the spirit, that the loss of self during the act was indeed a prerequisite for the beatitude to follow."[39]

Although it was extremely popular for a while, apparently this indulgent faith was destined to degenerate and end in corruption. But it lasted for more than two hundred years, and some people say that an underground practice still continues. There are Shoten images and/or manuscripts kept in hiding— "at Hozan-ji on Mt. Ikoma near Nara, at the nearby Uguisu-no-Taki, several in Sendai, and in the Yokohama Komei-ji Temple. . . . [and] in the monasteries of Mt. Koya, not far from Osaka."[40]

Similar religious activity on a smaller scale, but occurring even earlier than that of the Tachikawa-ryu, characterized the cult of Asama Shinko, officially begun in 843. It was centered in the region of Mount Fuji and was superseded by the belief known as Fuji-ko in the sixteenth century. It started out as a simple, dignified religion, developing from agricultural beliefs that taught the sacredness of sex. But gradually it became corrupted because people exploited it for pleasure and profit, and finally it succumbed in spite of later reforms. Now it has disguised emblems and symbols, and is said to exist still in small hamlets on the far side of Mount Fuji.

While supposedly thesetwo erotic cults have waned into insignificance, discussion of this aspect of phallicism would not be complete without mentioning such Buddhist deities as Dairoku-ten. He is "one of the devil kings worshiped in Buddhism and lives in the palace standing in the highest place of the sixth world of desires, that is the Heavenly King of the World of Desires. He is two Japanese miles tall and his life span is 16,000 years (counting 1,600 years of the human being as one day). He has the power of making men and women have free sexual intercourse and making women pregnant. He is also capable of turning others' pleasures into his own at will, so he is properly called Take-jizai-ten (Deity turning others freely)."[41]

Some Japanese writers upon the subject of phallicism, such as Kenkichi Ito, feel that the Buddhist image of Shoten inspired the Japanese to create a Shinto folk deity of their own, in imitation of the imported form. There does not seem to be any real evidence to support this theory, however, even though some Dosojin sculptures do show the couple in intimate embrace. The "Kissing Jizo" sculpture shows two stiffly standing human figures embracing. This is the closest resemblance found so far to the image of Kangiten. Although Buddhist priests made determined efforts to replace indigenous Shinto gods with buddhas and bodhisattvas, the Shinto deities persisted in their original character. As far as is known, the elephant never appears upon roadside sculptures in Japan, even as a minor ornamental detail placed at the base of such deities as Koshin and others who are amalgamations of Buddhist, Taoist, and Shinto divinities. We find the boar, dolphin, monkey, snake, badger, cock and hen, fox, and horse in roadside sculptures, but never the elephant or the elephant-headed human being.

The erotic sexual sculptures relating to Shoten-Kangiten are concerned with sexual pleasure only, or with spiritual enlightenment achieved through sexual pleasure. This is a very different concept from the Japanese belief in the generative power that creates life, wards off evil, and produces food. Finally, as far as the images themselves are concerned, there is no stylistic or technical similarity between these two kinds of sculptures. Most Dosojin statues are carved in relief on stone, and the stones cannot be readily moved about. The Kangiten images are made of wood, copper, clay, and occasionally gold or other precious metals. And they are small in size, ranging in height from four inches to as many as twelve inches, including the base or pedestal. They exist only in the collections of individuals and cult groups.

Furthermore, although colossal sculptures of the Buddhist deities have been carved into cliffs in Japan, as they were in China and India, erotic sculptures are not found among them.

Summary Phallicism as an early form of nature worship in prehistoric times was the dominant religious concept among the people of Japan, as it was among the people in most other parts of the world. It had its roots in prehistory and developed its beliefs through practices in agriculture which required the ritual fertilizing of the fields with living sacrifices and other symbolic acts performed to please the deities of fertility. Historical evidence gathered by anthropologists and archaeologists points to an indigenous growth of rituals and myths rather than to importation of full-fledged religious attitudes from Korea and the continent.

The phallus and kteis were regarded as a deity responsible for the principle of creativity, the giver of bountiful crops and human increase. Phallic worship became inseparably connected with farm life, and phallic effigies were set up in rice fields and at roadsides and crossroads, and were employed in harvest festivals. Through continued use and extension, the powers attributed to phallic deities proliferated to include a variety of special purposes. But the basic concept of the two aspects of phallicism remained remarkably constant: its power could be applied to the prevention of disease and death, and to the creation of new life. Religious leaders of pre-Shinto times recognized the profound hold that phallic worship had on the people, and they institutionalized those practices by recording them in the myths and legends of their sacred books.

Phallic worship in the twelfth century A.D. was diverted from its agricultural applications and, under erotic Tantric Buddhist influences, was promoted for other uses, as well as for religious purposes. Such erotic cults flourished for two or three hundred years, and sometimes remains of their practices are confused with agricultural phallicism. However, the ancient agricultural concepts of phallicism continue in practice in Japan today, as is indicated by the continuous construction of outdoor shrines and sculptures, the presence of phallic deities in both ordinary and prominent Shinto shrines, the abundant evidence of a large variety of offerings presented to phallic images, and the conduct of phallic or fertility festivals at times of seed planting, harvesting, and the changing of seasons.

SHAMANISM: CONCEPTS
AND RITUALS

The Cosmos The very first stories of Japanese mythology to be recorded establish the belief of Japan's aboriginal people in the existence of deities, men, and all living things upon three separate but neighboring planes. The first of these was the Plain of High Heaven, or the realm of the sky, home of the deities who gave birth to all things in nature, who controlled nature's many moods, and who came down to earth to pacify and rule it with kindness and grace. Below heaven lay the Central Land of Reed Plains, or the Land of the Eight Great Islands, created as a benign dominion and an estate for the offspring of celestial deities. This is the country we know as Japan, whose sovereigns have claimed that ancient divine ancestry. And on the lowest level was Yomi, the nether land or land of darkness, the abode of unfulfilled spirits of the dead, reached through a cave leading to the Even Pass, and descending to gloomy depths in the bowels of the earth. In the West this place is known as Hades.

The Plain of High Heaven was ruled by eight *musubi,* or creator deities. The chief of this group was the sun goddess, Amaterasu Omikami. Associated with her as a consort in governing was Takami-musubi, the High Integrating Deity. Some gods descended to earth, married mortal women, and produced children who themselves were deities in consequence. From among these came the line of emperors whose divine destiny was to rule Japan. Some deities were doomed to a short and tragic existence. Such a one was Izanami, wife of Izanagi, who died in giving birth to the god of fire and was sent to the realm of Yomi.

The Japanese concept of these cosmic regions is very similar to that of the people of central Asia, and of people in other continents as well. This concept is identified with the schematics of the typical shamanistic mind, which maintains that it holds the key to the mysteries of communication among cosmic zones. This communication is made possible because of the very structure of that universe in which the three levels, sky, earth, and underworld, are connected by a central axis, along which the spirits of both deities and men may travel back and forth.

The Heavenly Pillar   In Japanese mythology, the central axis is recognized as the August Heavenly Pillar, the symbolic phallus around which Izanagi and Izanami circled in courtship. It is the central pillar of the Hall of Eight Fathoms, which is identified as the parturition house in this same courtship myth.

The pillar is one form of the central axis that connects the three cosmic realms, and its core is visualized as an opening or tube through which the spirit of a deity is able to travel from sky to earth and to the subterranean region of Yomi.[1] Through this same opening, the spirit of the shaman in a state of ecstasy can fly up to heaven to communicate with celestial deities and return again to earth with its oracles. This central pillar takes many varied forms among different peoples, and often is identified with the pole at the center of primitive dwellings or tents. It is regarded as sacred and godlike. At the foot of such poles or pillars a stone slab or altar is usually placed, upon which offerings of food are laid. In ancient ceremonial structures, prayers were offered and blood sacrifices were made at the base of this pillar. In Japanese mythology, several devices in addition to the pillar served as a means of communication between heaven and earth. Among these are the Floating Bridge of Heaven, the Eight Crossroads of Heaven, and the Heavenly Rock Boat.

Symbolism of the Tree   The place of the mountain and of the tree in this view of cosmological structure is similar to that of the pillar. The tree connects the three cosmic regions, its branches reaching to the sky and its roots going down to the underworld. The branches are steps, celestial levels in the ladder ascending to heaven, which the shaman must climb symbolically in order to communicate with the gods. The tree also represents the universe in a process of continual regeneration. It is a symbol of fertility, creation, and recurrent life and immortality—thus it is veritably the Tree of Life.[2]

Trees as Deities   Trees play an important role in kami worship, either as deities in themselves or as shrines in which the mitama, or spirit, of the deity dwells. Trees serve as devices which attract the deity's spirit and by means of which the spirit descends to its shrine. Near Myobu Shrine at Fushimi-Inari near Kyoto, for example, is a pine tree whose two main roots have grown in a shape very suggestive of the kteis. Worship is paid to this tree deity, mostly by women; and the name Sho-ichi Kimyo Dai-Myojin, First-class Marvelous Great Enlightened Deity, has been given to it.[3]

Another example of trees that were worshiped as deities in themselves is the one to be found on the former estate of Nagano Eisuke, at Miyaginohara in Sendai. It is a gingko, one hundred feet tall and twenty-two feet in circumference. Pendulous saclike growths hang from the places where branches join the trunk, for which reason the tree is known as the nurse goddess, Uba-gami. This tree, which is about twelve hundred years old, is a shrine to which expectant mothers come seeking aid in nursing their children.[4]

The distinctive sacred tree of Shinto is the sakaki, a kind of evergreen which grows to a height of about eighteen to twenty-four feet. Often it is found in the position of the shintai, or divine symbol, of a shrine. A small branch hung with paper pendants frequently serves as the shintai in various kinds of ceremonies. The shintai in this form is called the *tamagushi*. The sacred trees of shrines that are set apart as shintai usually are protected by shimenawa, ropes of rice straw. Such a rope shows that a taboo has been placed upon the tree because of the presence of divinity within.

Role of the Shaman The power to achieve communication between mankind and the heavenly deities was reserved for the shaman alone, who performed on behalf of the rest of his people. Ordinary folk had only a secondary contact with the deities by making offerings and reciting prayers. But the shaman had the power to "fly" and to reach the Plain of High Heaven through the "central opening" of the pillar. The shaman had retained this magic power, soon lost to the masses, from an earlier time, when all men were on equally intimate terms with the gods. The shaman's privileged status was due to his extraordinary capacities for attaining ecstatic experiences. The origin of the beliefs and the structure of religious practice with which shamans were associated belonged to the people as a whole and were not devised by shamans as a special class. Shamanism presupposes that an elemental force is present in all objects, and that this can be dominated by a greater force, namely that of the magician who is capable of subduing everything with the power of his incantations or conjurations.

Usually the role of the shaman was hereditary, handed down through either the paternal or the maternal line. A call to the vocation might be spontaneous, however; in such cases, the call was declared in a dream or vision, or through a divine sign from the gods or from the guardian deity of the shaman's family. The postulant had to subject himself to a critical initiation, during which he attained his first ecstatic experience. Following this success, the community accepted him as a qualified candidate and he continued his study under a practicing shaman for a long period, during which he learned the clan genealogy and traditions, and the shamanic mythology and vocabulary. When he had mastered the technique of inducing the ecstatic state and had demonstrated his magico-religious powers, the powers of his guardian deities, then he was allowed to practice as a full-fledged shaman.[5]

Being a shaman was a precarious job. Having been accepted by the community because of some talent he might have demonstrated, he held an enviable position only as long as his efforts brought the desired results. But if something went wrong, and the will of the kami did not work for the good of the community, he was subject to the wrath of his constituents—who knew that nature in its destructive moods was proving that he had broken his vows and lost his purity.

The ceremonies associated with the dead were especially worrisome, and required the removal of impurities acquired from the deceased. Only then could the advisability of proceeding with certain projects be determined.

Burial Practices During the third and fourth centuries A.D., increases in population and an attendant prosperity led to changes in burial practices. In the case of great personages, at least, interment in trenches or in clay jars gave way to burial in mounds, some of which were gigantic. For example, near present-day Osaka the tomb of Emperor Nintoku (c. 313–99) occupies about 458 acres and is 540 yards in length, not counting the width of the triple moat that surrounds it. Near centers of population and political power, smaller tombs numbered in the thousands.

The following tale illustrates the cruel and grotesque character of some burial practices that apparently were customary at one time in Japan. The story may be a rationalization of the clay figures, called *haniwa,* which were placed in level rows around a tomb to support the steep sides, and which also served as rather decorative status symbols for the deceased. Nonetheless, it is difficult to say whether or not the legend explains the haniwa.

The tale deals with Yamato-hiko, brother of Emperor Suinen, who was buried at some time between 3 B.C. and A.D. 270, according to the way in which the records are interpreted. "Yamato-hiko was buried at Tsukizaka in Musa. Thereupon his personal attendants were assembled and were buried alive and upright in the precinct of the misasagi [burial mound]. For several days they died not, but wept and wailed day and night. At last they died and rotted. Dogs and crows gathered and ate them.

"The Emperor, hearing the sound of their weeping and wailing, was grieved in heart, and commanded his high officers, saying: 'It is a very painful thing to force those whom one has loved in life to follow him in death. Though it is an ancient custom, why follow it if it is bad? From this time forward, take counsel so as to put a stop to the following of the dead.' "[6]

Another instance of human sacrifice in Japan is noted in the *Wei Chih* (History of the Kingdom of Wei), a Chinese record compiled in about A.D. 297: "Queen Himiko was the ruler of the kingdom of Wa. She was a shamaness and never married. She was assisted in ruling the country by a younger brother, who was the only man allowed to communicate with her directly. She was waited on by a thousand female servants. When Queen Himiko died the people put up a huge mound more than a hundred paces in diameter. There followed her in burial more than a hundred female slaves. Then they changed to a male ruler. But the people were not obedient. They fell to killing each other. At that time more than a thousand people were killed."[7]

Grave Goods After the third century A.D. clay effigies were substituted for living beings, both animal and human, and for precious articles, because such materials as iron, bronze, cloth, and wood would rust or rot in time and thus be useless to the dead. Moreover, many of the precious things which, according to older rules, should accompany the dead belonged to cult groups or shrines, or were symbols of religious office and therefore not the property of the individuals being buried.

The haniwa figures portray habits of dress which indicate the social, political, and religious structure of the times. They supplement in a very rich way the much smaller number of precious objects, both of a personal and of a religious character, which have been found in burial mounds. Many of the haniwa figures portray religious attendants, dancers, mediums, and leaders of ceremonial rituals—in other words, shamans. This is apparent from their posture and dress and from the accouterments of their office which they carry or relate to, such as thrones, fans, and headdresses. Among the grave goods found in third- and fourth-century tombs are swords, spears, bronze mirrors, bronze bells, gold crowns, armor, horse accouterments, and decorative articles of clothing.[8]

Japanese Shamanistic Practices The origin and character of Japanese shamanism are still unclear today, although it is apparent that two basically different kinds of shamanism were practiced. One seems to have come from northeast Asia and featured the horse-sacrifice ritual, while the other related to agriculture and employed the female shaman, or *miko,* the "dancing girl" of modern Shinto shrines.

In J. Edward Kidder's opinion, the Japanese form of shamanism originated among the nomadic cultures of Inner Asia and was preserved and transmitted to Japan through Korea. This form shared a number of features in common with Mongolian shamanism, such as tree symbolism, the sacrifice of the horse, the concept of the world on three planes, and the "calling of the gods."[9] A gold crown found in Fukui Prefecture, and apparently of Korean origin, has three prongs sticking out like antlers from a simple hat shape. According to Kidder, "the simple antlers were the shaman's way of indicating his capacity for flight."[10] A legend tells of the son of a king in southern Korea who came to Japan wearing such a hat, startling the Japanese with his horned forehead. "Other stories associated with the prince suggest he had unusual powers, and it is tempting to suggest that he represents a formal introduction of well developed Korean shamanism. Japan must have had its share of shamans before this time, but perhaps without the Siberian antler symbols. This Mimana prince was probably following in the footsteps of his father, a priest-king."[11]

Mircea Eliade offers a somewhat different but complementary opinion: "As documented today, Japanese shamanism is rather far from shamanism proper of North Asia or Siberian types. It is primarily a technique of possession by ghosts and is practiced almost exclusively by women."[12]

However, he notes that there is some evidence that connects ancient Japanese shamanism with both Korea and northeast Asia: "What we know, for example, concerning the behavior and role of the sorceress in ancient Japan—despite the effort made by the compilers of the Imperial Annals to pass her over in silence and mention only her rival, the priestess-vestal, the *miko,* who had attained a place among the ritualists at the court of the Yamato— permits her identification both with her Korean colleague . . . and with the Altaic shamanesses."[13]

The symbols and emblems employed by the shaman indicate the character of the ritual that he performed. Some of the instruments used by shamans, such as drums, rattles, mirrors, and sabers, have been found among Japanese grave goods. Referring to such instruments, Eliade observes: "Neither the saber nor the drum are instruments originally belonging to feminine magic. The fact that they are used by shamanesses indicates that they were already part of the paraphernalia of sorcerers and shamans."[14]

Moreover, the horse, a prominent element in Siberian shamanism, appears in Japanese mythology and in the history of the conquest of Japan. Haniwa representing the horse are found in tomb mounds. Legends tell of horses being sacrificed, sometimes in large numbers, and, in fact, unbroken skeletons of horses have been found in some tombs. Quite probably the horse played an important part in ancient Japanese shamanism, although little, if anything, has been written upon this subject.

The Horse in Siberian Shamanism   The ritual sacrifice of the horse by different Siberian tribal peoples as late as the end of the nineteenth century is well known. For example, the Buryats near the town of Usturdi in southern Siberia practiced the Tailgan, or horse sacrifice, in which horses were killed at each of fifteen altars, all at the same time. When all preparations had been made, "a man, his right arm bare to the shoulder, now came with a long sharp knife and with one blow made a deep incision just behind the breastbone. He thrust his hand into the opening, seized the heart of the horse, and wrenched it free from its connections."[15]

The Altaic shamans of northeast Asia, on the other hand, killed horses for ceremonial use by breaking their necks. The congregation participated in the killing, and great care was taken that not a drop of blood should be spilled, inasmuch as contact with blood was considered to be polluting. The horse was skinned bloodlessly and its hide removed as completely intact as possible so that the form of the horse could be reconstructed by draping the hide over a bench or trestle provided for it at the site of the ceremony. This signified the presence of the animal as if it were alive, and at one stage of the ceremony the shaman mounted this effigy and pretended to ride it skyward.[16]

In these rituals the color of the sacrificed horses was always white, or nearly so. The belief that white is an auspicious color and pleasing to the gods is old and is widespread through much of the Asian continent. In Japan this belief is reaffirmed in the ritual started by Mitoshi-no-Kami, who was worshiped until recently in the Shinto Bureau with offerings of a white wild boar, a white horse, and white domestic fowl.[17]

Horse-viewing Festival   The *Kuji Kongen,* an account of ancient customs in Japan, describes an event called Hakuba-no-Sechi-e, White Horse Festival, or Aouma-no-Sechi-e, Blue Horse Festival.[18] The Japanese characters for the adjectives describing such horses can be read as meaning either "white" (*haku*) or "blue" (*ao*). The apparent confusion in colors may be explained in part by the fact that white horses (which are called "grays" by Occidental horsemen) are born black, become dappled (bluish-gray) at three or four years of age, and white at five to eight years. The famous Lippizan horses of Vienna change color in this manner. Usually, white horses (or "grays") are born with brown eyes, but on rare occasions one will be born with blue eyes. According to geneticists, the true albino horse, with white skin and pink eyes, never seems to survive.[19]

The significance of Hakuba-no-Sechi-e lies in the associations of word-magic with symbols and of vital forces with spirit powers.* Inasmuch as horses are animals of good omen; and inasmuch as white or dappled horses sometimes have blue eyes; and since blue (and green, also *ao* in Japanese) suggest spring, which is the beginning of a new life cycle, the chance to attend a Hakuba-no-Sechi-e would preserve one from ill fortune throughout the following year. Other ceremonies in Japan also relied on the horse, and some of these have been revived in modern times. Whether the horse was sacrificed in shamanistic rituals in ancient times has not been established, although there is some slight indication that this ritual practice may have been followed, since "Late Jomon people knew about the horse and the bones from sites are unmutilated, . . . and those from the Yayoi period show that both small and medium horses existed in Japan."[20]

Shamanistic Cults The study of shamanism is becoming popular in Japan today, and all sorts of religious practices are being identified as shamanism or shamanistic. Actually, nearly all of the religious folk cults in current practice reflect influences or tendencies which derive from authentic shamanism, but they cannot be called shamanism in the true sense.

Ichiro Hori has referred to three kinds of shamans in Japan today. *Kannagi*: this category includes *miko* who are attached to Shinto shrines. In Japanese, the general term for a shamanic figure is *miko*, which means explicitly a shamaness. There is no special term for a male shaman. *Kuchiyose*: this category includes female shamans, itinerant or resident, who engage in telepathy, mediumship, fortune-telling, and divination. Moreover, the ritual performed most often by the *kuchiyose* is the seance, in which she contacts the spirit of the dead while in a trance. The Siberian shaman never practiced this form of occultism and the Ainu shaman of Hokkaido is still extremely reluctant to perform in this manner. *Jussha* (magician)

Hakuba seems to be of Chinese origin, where heaven is symbolized by the white dragon, the earth by the horse, and man by the turtle. Hakuba-no-Sechi-e takes place on January 7; twenty-one horses are presented in the promenade because the date (the number 7) is multiplied by 3 (for the three symbols of heaven, earth, and man).

or *gyoja* (practitioner): these individuals experience a vision at which time they are chosen by a guardian deity to serve as "priests" to carry out a mission. These ascetics are found among the yamabushi and itinerant medicine men and magicians.[21]

The most recent reports of Japanese shamans concern those of the kuchiyose type, who are still active in Akita and Aomori prefectures in northeastern Honshu and among the Ainu of Hokkaido. The kuchiyose type of shaman usually serves a long apprenticeship to a master-teacher. This period includes three to five years of training, during which time the novice learns the techniques of achieving a trance and of communicating with spirits, chanting, prayers, ballads, magic, and other formulas of the art. She attains full professional status after a long and complicated ritual of "first communion," so to speak, with her ancestral patron spirit. "The [itinerant] shaman-ess usually carries a black case on her back in which talismans, fetishes, written formulas, and Buddhist sutras may be found; she also has a rosary which is made of 180 wooden or stone beads strung together with several polished skulls and fangs of badger, fox, sable, bear, or antelope, as well as several old coins."[22]

In the Tohoku region of Honshu, during the festival of Jizo, held from the thirteenth to the fifteenth day of the sixth month (or the seventh month, in rural areas), shamans from the region meet at a kind of annual convention.[23]

Shamanistic Symbols   The paraphernalia of the shaman's trade usually were owned by his family or by the community he served. In northeast Asia, the main shamanistic instrument of power was a leather coat decorated with hundreds of miniature dangling talismans. Such a coat could weigh more than a hundred pounds. Very old talismans were imbued with greater magic than new ones could possibly possess, and so were highly treasured.

One of the important symbols for the Japanese shaman was a metal mirror. It was different from all other mirrors: to its edge small metal discs were attached, which jingled when the shaman danced.[24] The tinkling disks were meant to attract the attention of the deity or spirit being invoked.

The symbol of status carried by the shaman was a small stone baton of phallic shape. Often this was made of greenish steatite, and the upper part was stained with ochre. Stone was used simply because it was permanent, not for any innate power.

Objects worn for personal adornment by the Japanese shaman, as evidenced by grave goods, included gilt bronze shoes, gold or silver ear pendants, belt buckles, gold or gilt-bronze crowns, and various kinds of peaked and unusual hats. Of these, the metal crowns are the most important because of their rarity, delicacy of workmanship, and symbolic character. The crowns were never ornate or unusually tall, else they would have toppled while being worn. One gold crown found in Ibaraki Prefecture features three wavy bands of stylized tree branches, from which hang numerous tiny circular pendants or mirrors. Atop the wavy crest of the crown, series of horses and small upright trees are arranged alternately. Another crown found in Gumma Prefecture is made of gilt bronze. About eleven inches in height, it terminates in five stylized trees, the nine branches of which end in the shape of the tama, or jewel, like an inverted heart. Numerous mirror-disks are hung from every part of the crown.[25]

Drums were a very important part of the shaman's equipment and were thought to possess great magic. They were used as musical instruments in calling the spirits of the deities, not as noisemakers to chase away evil spirits. The shell of the drum was made of wood, and the particular tree that was to provide this wood was chosen in a special ceremony conducted deep within the forest. The shaman, while in a trance, was directed by his patron deity to strike with his ax the one and only tree in the forest from which the drum could be made. This having been done, the tree was felled and its trunk was cut into thin boards from which the drum's shell was shaped.[26]

The Japanese shaman made use of masks carved from wood and hollowed in back to fit the face. These masks were human in aspect, painted, but never grotesque or taking the shape of animal or bird heads. Neither were they decorated with feathers or hair.

The spear, as has been mentioned, was a sophisticated fertility symbol, which took the place of earlier phallic stones. The gohei, a wand from which hang folded paper pendants, is a key ceremonial symbol even today, apparently as a representation of the phallus. The first gohei seems to have been a wand to which a cluster of pebbles or jewels was fastened. The wand represented the phallus, while the jewels represented the kteis. Another hypothesis to explain the derivation of the gohei supposes that it represents the sakaki as the tree of life; when used ceremonially, this was decorated with a mirror, jewels, and cloth streamers. In time, a more abstract version of this ceremonial tree, and a less rich one, became the gohei.

Techniques of Ecstasy Before conducting rituals in which he communicated with spirits, it was necessary that the shaman purify himself absolutely. In addition, he had to increase his sensibility to a superconscious level, for only then could he gain the power to "talk" with spirits. These preparatory techniques, practiced by shamans around the world, included taking a variety of natural drugs, such as those found in peyote, Jimson weed, cannabis, and certain mushrooms. An alcoholic beverage of one sort or another—

such as grape wine, or a beer brewed from wheat, rice, barley, honey, or other fermentable substances—was commonly used by the shaman, as well as by the congregation, and was presented as an offering to the spirits. Drugs and alcohol have the effect of changing the body's chemistry and affecting the nervous system, thus launching the subject on a "trip" or "flight." But in addition, and unlike the usual drug taker, the shaman practiced such ritual techniques as lustration, fasting, dancing, chanting, listening to music, and self-hypnosis, usually several at a time in some favored combination. Thus purified and "sensitized," the shaman approached the spirit world with the aid of helper-spirits known only to himself.

Lustration and Fasting The devotee of lustration, or washing, the *gyoja,* was usually a hermit who lived in some remote mountain place close to a waterfall. He subsisted on a meager diet of berries, nuts, greens, and roots garnered from the habitat about him. Emaciated in body, the gyoja sought to purify himself physically and spiritually by entering the waterfall as often as possible, and not less than once every four hours, day and night. In time, under this regimen, his mind lapsed easily into a trance, and he lived on the very edge of ecstasy. The gyoja, while not a true shaman, was a go-between or spirit-medium whose powers were not developed enough to deal with other than lesser matters.

In principle, everyone in Japan, from the emperor on down, practices some form of purification on the many occasions of personal and national ceremonies. The rituals are based upon bathing, abstinence, and meditation. While less severe than those of the cultists, their purpose is the same—to regain a spiritual purity.

Spirit possession The procedure for attaining divine possession, still performed in Japan, requires a chief ritualist who has the ability to induce a trance in himself or to achieve the state of ecstasy. Percival Lowell has described a complex ritual performed indoors by a team of eight men. After purification by bathing, they assembled in a prescribed pattern around a sanctified space. A complicated sequence of prayers, exhortations, chanting, bell ringing, and finger twisting came to a climax, at which point the chief ritualist was seated in the center, utterly still and with eyes closed, holding a gohei in both hands before his chest. Suddenly the gohei began to quiver, and the motion gained in strength, forcing the man's body into convulsive throes. The deity spirit of the occasion was said to have entered the ritualist's body by way of the gohei. When addressed by an assistant, the spirit answered through the voice of the possessed ritualist.

This rite was practiced extensively forty or fifty years ago by cults affiliated with Ryobu Shinto, a Buddhist-influenced form of Shinto, and still survives in some form. There is no question about its origins, for the gods invoked are Shinto, and the gohei, the symbol of the deity-receiving tree, is also Shinto.[27]

Divination Japanese mythology mentions the performance of divinations in several instances, but not much else is said about this occult art except that it was done by burning a tortoise shell or the shoulder blade of a stag in a cherry-bark fire. Divination was practiced at many levels in society, especially by religious leaders and chiefs of the government, as a way of arriving at important decisions. It was necessary that these decisions be in accord with the Way of the Kami and the forces of nature. Divination was practiced as part of shamanistic rituals to determine the exact form a ceremony should take, because all of its details had to conform with the divine will. Selecting the fields for the planting of rice that would be harvested for ceremonial purposes, deciding on the strategy for a battle, choosing the dates for marriages and journeyings: all these and more were determined by divination.

In the mythological era, divination was the responsibility of the deities Ame-no-Koyane and Ame-no-Futodama. These were the ancestors of the Nakatomi and Imbe hereditary corporations respectively, whose members for many generations performed the divinations at the emperor's court. The knowledge upon which their divinations were based was highly secret and was passed on within the corporations only. R. J. Kirby has suggested that these occult practices derive from Chinese numerology and divination.[28] Today their mystery has been somewhat dispelled, at least for Occidentals, and the practice has been popularized among Westerners since publication of translations of the *I Ching,* the Book of Changes.

The Elements of Divination Kirby related the principles of the Chinese Way of Divination, also used in Japan, to three components: time, numbers, and light and shade.

First, there is time. Time is called the eye of divination. The affairs of man on earth undergo numerous changes. Changes are occurring all the time. Life moves to the rhythm of a pendulum, to and fro. There is an appropriate time for "doing" and for "not doing." Safety and danger, peace and rebellion, good and bad: there are many such dichotomies. One must know how to discern what kind of time the present is, and then make his decisions accordingly. The knowledge of how to do this is contained in the sixty-four hexagrams and three hundred and eighty-four *ko* (pieces or parts) of divination. Each hexagram contains six ko, and a diagram shows the lines of divination.

Second, there are numbers. Divination has always been intimately connected with numbers. There is a natural number ruling over every kind of thing in heaven and on earth. When the numbers run out, death must occur. Thus is all life governed. The numbers of earth are the even numbers: 2, 4, 6, 8, and 10. Those of heaven are the odd numbers: 1, 3, 5, 7, and 9. The earth numbers add up to 30, the heaven numbers add up to 25, and the sum of the two is 55. From these numbers are made eight signs which total 64, and these eight signs give the reason for everything in heaven and on earth.

The third principle, that of light and shade, establishes "the center," which divides a space in two, producing two laws—light and shade. This center line divided gives four shapes, which are called Great Light, Small Shade, Small Light, and Great Shade. These correspond to the four seasons, summer, spring, autumn, and winter. The four shapes of the seasons divided in two give eight signs, and these divided in both directions give sixty-four signs, which become the way of divination. Each sign has six ko, which gives a total of three hundred and eight-four ko, or pieces.

In divination, the shoulder blade of the stag is divided into this pattern of ko, and variations in the light and dark areas produced by burning the bone in a cherry-bark fire, or by soot from the fire, are then interpreted.

Heaven is light, and earth is shade. All things come from these two. Everything is arranged and explained according to the interrelationships of the Two Laws, Four Shapes, and Eight Signs. Life waxes and wanes, just as when light grows shade must wane and when shade grows light must wane. Time, number, and light are the three great "ropes of divination." These cannot be comprehended without profound scholarship and discipline. The wisdom of ancient rulers and scholars is preserved in the Six Books, which are Poetry, Writings, Etiquette, Music, Divination, and the Spring and Autumn Annals. The first is an expression of human feelings, the second an account of the way of governing and the history of the Two Emperors and Three Kings. The third book contains the laws of the state and the rules that govern the affairs of men. Music is the fourth book, and it is used to soften etiquette when that becomes too severe. The fifth is the book of divination, now called the *I Ching,* or the Book of Changes, and this deals with the causes of light and shade, of waxing and waning; with long and hard study, this book leads to the Way of Divination. The Spring and Autumn Annals are the sixth book, and this is the way of reward and punishment, that is, the book of laws, the civil code that regulates and governs daily life.

Through the use of the fifth book one learns how to make use of the other five. A head of government, a spiritual leader or teacher of men, or a man of ideas needs to be versed in these many things—history, the arts, law, human behavior. In addition, he needs good fortune and the help of the gods if he is to perform successfully on behalf of his people and the times.

Many lesser rituals have been devised for divinations, and some of these may be observed as part of cultural festivals. The four that are described below use horses and thus invoke the deity of the horse.

In the Oide, or Greeting Festival, held in Nanao, Ishikawa Prefecture, the procession is led by a priest riding a horse. As he approaches the shrine, the parishioners shout in order to alarm the horse. If the priest falls from the rearing horse, the people believe that the prices of crops will drop.

Yabusame is shooting with bow and arrow at a wooden target while the rider's horse is at full gallop. A shot that breaks the target predicts good fortune, and a miss foretells bad luck.

In *horohiki* the rider slowly unfurls a silken banner (*horo*) while increasing the speed of his horse until the thirty-three-foot banner is fully extended and floating behind him. If no part of the banner touches the ground before his course is run, the omen is good.

A more common method of divination, perhaps because it was simpler, allowed horses confined in a corral to mill around at random. The patterns their moving bodies made were interpreted in somewhat the same way as tea leaves in a cup are read.

Some scholars believe that these events were offered to kami as entertainment only.

Older popular forms of divination include *tsuji-ura,* or crossroads divination. This was much practiced in ancient Japan, especially by women and lovers. It required going out to the road at dusk, thrusting a stick into the ground to represent Kunado, the phallic deity of roads, and interpreting the fragmentary talk of passers-by as an answer to the question posed. Another method was to go to a crossroads, carrying a boxwood comb, and there make the comb sound three times by drawing a finger along it (because *tsuge,* or "boxwood," also means "inform me"). Then, with devotion, this verse was repeated three times to Sae-no-Kami: "Oh, thou deity of the crossroads divination, grant me a true response." Good luck or bad was to be inferred from the words of the next person to appear—or of the third, in other versions.[29]

Hashi-ura, or bridge divination, is a variation of tsuji-ura, and here too the deity concerned was probably Sae-no-Kami. The end post of a bridge, the *o-bashira,* is most obviously a symbol for the phallus. The words uttered by the first person crossing the bridge after the questioner's arrival would be the omen.[30]

In stone divination, *ishi-ura,* a wish was granted if one succeeded in carrying a stone (representing a deity) around a mound of dirt or rocks and back again to its resting place.[31] Such stones were called *ishi-gami,* stone gods, and no doubt were phallic. In other words, they represented Kunado or Sae-no-Kami.

Aston described a gruesome method by which a diviner could be assured of aid from knowledgeable spirits: "Amongst the ordinary diviners is one called Kitsune-tsuki, i.e., a fox-possessor. The divination is carried on by means of a small image of a fox, made in a very odd way. A fox is buried alive in a hole with its head left free. Food of the sort of which foxes are known to be fond is placed just beyond the animal's reach. As days pass by the poor beast in its dying agony of hunger makes frantic efforts to reach the food; but in vain. At the moment of death, the spirit of the fox is supposed to pass into the food, which is then mixed with a quantity of clay and shaped into the form of the animal. Armed with this extraordinary object, the *miko* is supposed to become an infallible guide to foretelling future events of every kind."[32]

Percival Lowell mentioned two popular kinds of divination used formerly for determining the guilt or innocence of an accused person. These are ordeals of the usual type, the one by boiling water and the other by the crossing of fire. When performed by a skilled diviner (who serves as surrogate for the accused person), these rituals begin with purification by bathing, followed by a long and involved ritual of chanting, bell ringing, finger twisting, marching in procession, and other exercises, which lead finally to the collapse of the chief participant in a trance. The fact that, when he is in this state, the ritualist can endure scalding water or walking upon hot coals is explained as the consequence of his being possessed by a deity.

Still other forms of divination are known, but they are too numerous to discuss here. Others have been described in Chapter III in connection with the so-called naked festivals.

PART FOUR

THE MYTHIC ROOTS
OF FOLK WORSHIP

VII

JAPANESE MYTHOLOGY

The sacred stone carvings found by the wayside in Japan, together with the customs and rituals that relate to them, connote religious ideas and beliefs of ancient origin. The oldest expressions of these ancient beliefs are preserved in the myths and folk tales of the people who lived in prehistoric times. Japan's mythology and other facets of its prehistory are recorded in two valuable compilations, the *Kojiki* (Record of Ancient Matters), said to have been written in A.D. 712, and the *Nihongi* (Chronicles of Japan), completed eight years later. These records might never have been written but for the introduction of Buddhism into Japan in about the year 552. The new religion and its priests had dramatic effects on people of all classes. During the seventh century, strong attempts were made to establish Buddhism as the national religion. One of the reactions to this effort was a countermovement to establish indigenous concepts, deities, and rituals in a religious system that would be acceptable within the traditions of the indigenous populace.

Emperor Temmu (673–86) was the first to suggest that a record of ancient matters be written, but he died before anything was done. Twenty-five years later, Empress Gemmei (707–15) ordered Hideya-no-Are, who had committed to memory all of Japan's early history, to dictate a complete account of it for the benefit of posterity. This compilation was finished in 712. (Some modern authorities believe that an earlier account was destroyed in a fire about fifty years earlier.) Known as the *Kojiki,* it recounted the mythology, manners, language, religious and political ideas, and traditional history of the country.[1] The accounts of manners and customs included sections on courtship, marriage, the confinement of expectant mothers in parturition houses, blood and death as sources of pollution, and many other matters. Dwelling places were described, and the use of utensils, the making and wearing of clothing, jewelry, and hair styles. Animals and their domestic uses were mentioned, including the horse, cormorant, barnyard fowl, and dog. References of this kind are so plentiful that a deep sense of reality is gained from what many people have chosen to regard as a fabrication.

Religious and political ideas and systems, while difficult to interpret and evaluate, are presented with the same strong sense of factualism. We are made aware of the existence of three regional centers of political power, in Izumo, Kyushu, and Yamato; of how they interacted; and of what happened in their contest for supremacy. There are references to nature gods, deified heroes, and ancestor deities, and to the rituals with which they were worshiped. This account established the lineage of the imperial house, and through that the continuity of the long succession of emperors from prehistoric times to the present. And, as Chamberlain has remarked, "even in what is not to be accepted as historic fact there is often much that is valuable from other points of view."[2]

The *Nihongi,* which followed in 720, covered much the same subjects as did the *Kojiki* but attempted to correct certain "injustices" in the first compilation that had been unacceptable to some important families and chieftains. In the *Nihongi,* "Chinese philosophical speculations and moral precepts are intermingled with the cruder traditions that had descended from Japanese antiquity."[3]

Many other books followed those two great works. They dealt with such matters as the local geography, the fauna and flora of the country, codes of law, liturgical prayers, government administration, and the histories of different clans and families. In 867 the *Kogoshui,* or "Gleanings from Ancient Stories," appeared. The *Engishiki,* completed in 927, was a record of norito, or liturgical prayers, which dealt with many of the same matters as the *Kojiki* and the *Nihongi.* A number of chronicles, such as the *fudoki* (regional gazetteers compiled in the eighth century) and the *Shojiroku* (815), attempted to describe at length the characteristics of the several provinces and the genealogies of the nobility, respectively.

These accounts, and others of a similar kind, taken together provide the foundation for much of what is known about Japan's early society. The core of this body of knowledge is the *Kojiki,* and the summary of Chamberlain's translation of the first book of that work, which is presented below, relates the mythical beginning of the Japanese nation.

As has been shown in Part Three, the very first stories in Japan's mythology establish a cosmos of three neighboring planes: the realm of the sky, the realm of the earth, and the land of darkness, Yomi, where evil spirits and those of the dead dwell deep in the bowels of the earth. There were deities who lived in each of these realms, and sky deities could move from one plane to another. Not much is said about the deities of Yomi, since the Japanese seem to have been concerned more with the living than with the dead. The Japanese concepts of creation and of the cosmic structure of their universe and how it worked are not much different from those of many other peoples, but some of the elements and subtler touches in their imagery are distinctively their own.

THE NARRATIVE

At the time that the sky and the earth first began, three wondrous deities appeared, and one of these was Deity Master of the August Center of Heaven. These three disappeared or died. Later, when the earth was still forming, swimming around like a huge jellyfish in an oily sea, three more deities came into being. These three also died. After that seven more generations of deities were born, and the last of these were Izanagi-no-Mikoto, Deity the Male Who Invites, and Izanami-no-Mikoto, Deity the Female Who Invites. The deities of heaven ordered these two to consolidate the earth, and they stood on the Bridge of Heaven (which is the Milky Way) and stirred the waters below with a spear, causing them to curdle. An island was formed from the drops that fell from the point of the spear, and Izanagi and Izanami descended upon it. They set up a pillar in a Hall of Eight Fathoms, and wooed each other by walking around this pillar. In time they gave birth to the Eight Islands of Japan, and also to many nature spirits, including the gods of the wind, trees, and mountains. The last of their offspring was the deity of fire. In being born he burned Izanami, causing her death. Whereupon Izanagi slew the deity of fire, from whose body many new gods were born.

Perforce, Izanami went down to the Land of Yomi, and Izanagi lamented bitterly and could not console himself. At last he followed Izanami and implored her to return. Izanami asked him to wait while she went to discuss the question with the god of Yomi, and told Izanagi not to look into her chamber. However, Izanagi was impatient and lit a torch so that he might look about. He saw Izanami's rotting body, crawling with maggots and infested by the Eight Thunders. Izanagi fled in horror, and Izanami, greatly humiliated, sent the Ugly Women of Yomi and the Eight Thunders to pursue him. Izanagi foiled them by throwing magical things in their path. When he reached the top of the Even Pass of Yomi he blocked the way with a large boulder, and thus the two deities who so recently had been husband and wife found themselves on opposite sides of the rock, each threatening the other with great harm. The rock which blocked the path later was deified as the god of blocking the road.

Izanagi, feeling sullied by his contact with the land of the dead, went to bathe in the Tachibana River. He threw down his walking stick, and from this was born the god Kunado, Deity Thrust-erect Come-not Place.[4] Other gods were born from the clothing Izanagi cast off. The three who were born from the washing of his left eye, his right eye, and his nose were Amaterasu, goddess of the sun; Tsukiyomi, god of the moon; and Susano-o, the rainstorm god, respectively.[5]

The sun goddess and the moon god took possession of their dominions, but Susano-o moaned and wailed. When Izanagi asked him the reason for his lamenting, he said that he wanted to visit his mother Izanami in Yomi. Izanagi was furious and drove Susano-o away. Susano-o then said he wanted to visit his sister in heaven before going to Yomi. He went to heaven to see Amaterasu, making a great noise and a disturbance which shook the mountains, flooded the rivers, and made the earth shake. The sun goddess took several precautions before meeting her brother: she slung a quiver on her back, and stuck a bow upright into the ground and plucked the strings, stamping her feet in warning. Susano-o assured his sister that his intention was merely to say goodbye before going to visit Izanami. The sun goddess asked for proof of his good will, and he proposed that each of them should create children and wagered that his would be boys. Amaterasu took her brother's sword, broke it into three pieces, chewed them thoroughly, and blew out a mist from which three divine daughters were born. Susano-o borrowed her string of jewels and likewise chewed them up, and blew out a mist from which five sons were born. Amaterasu declared that the male deities belonged to her, because they came from her jewels, and that the daughters were his.

But Susano-o was so elated with his success that he lost control of himself and rampaged about, destroying the rice fields, filling in the irrigation ditches, tearing out the dikes, and strewing excrement in the temples where the Festival of the First Fruits was being held. The sun goddess made excuses for her brother, but he would not stop. Amaterasu retired to a sacred hall with her attendants, where they occupied themselves in weaving cloth. Susano-o tore a hole in the roof and threw down a piebald horse that he had flayed backward. This horrible deed caused such a shocked disturbance that some of the weaving maidens were frightened into committing suicide by stabbing themselves with their shuttles. The sun goddess was terrified and hid herself in a cave, blocking the entrance with a great boulder. The world was plunged into darkness, and the evil deities of pestilence came out in great numbers to wreak havoc upon the world.

The eight hundred myriad deities of heaven met in the dry bed of a river to prepare a plan to lure Amaterasu forth from her cave and thereby restore light to the darkened world. They scorched the shoulder blade of a stag in a cherry-bark fire, and with the help of this divination they decided what must be done. They made an eight-hand-span mirror, strings of jewels, and streamers of cloth, and hung all of these upon a sakaki tree. They gathered cocks whose crow comes at dawn, and they made musical instruments. They recited many prayers.

The beautiful Ame-no-Uzume-no-Mikoto, or Uzume as she was known to her fellow deities, dressed herself in an elaborate costume and performed a dance before the assembled divinities. Faster and faster she danced until, possessed by ecstasy, she threw off her clothes. The deities roared with laughter. The crowing of the cocks, the music, the stamping of Uzume's dancing feet, and the loud laughter of the myriad gods at last made the sun goddess exceedingly curious, and she peeked out of her cave to inquire the reason for all the merrymaking. The mirror hung on the sakaki tree set up before the cave cast her reflection back into her eyes and dazzled her. She ventured a little way out of the cave, and one of the gods stationed there seized her by the arm and drew her out of her refuge. Other gods stretched a straw rope across its entrance so that she could not return. Then all the gods escorted Amaterasu to a new palace that they had built for her. And so light was restored to the world with the rays of the sun goddess, and everything was as before.

Now the deities of heaven decided to punish Susano-o for having affronted Amaterasu, and they forced him to pay a heavy penalty. They cut off his mustache and beard, and pulled out his fingernails and toenails. Then they expelled him from heaven. Susano-o resumed his journey to Yomi, but before he had gone any distance he came upon the goddess of food and begged her for something to eat. She offered him all sorts of dainty morsels, which she took from her mouth, nose, and other parts of her body. He was outraged because he thought that she was offering him filthy things. And so he killed her. Whereupon rice, beans, millet, barley, and other grasses, as well as farm animals, grew from her body. These things were brought to the sun goddess, and she took the seeds and planted them in her garden.

After killing the goddess of food, Susano-o descended from heaven and settled at a place on the headwaters of the River Kii in the land of Izumo. Here he met an old couple whose eighth and last daughter was soon to be claimed by an eight-headed dragon. He thought of a clever scheme to kill the dragon by setting out eight tubs of sakè so that each of the eight heads could drink its fill. He easily killed the drunken dragon, cut off the heads, and hacked its body in two. At the last stroke, his sword glanced off with a metallic sound. Upon investigating, he found a magic sword hidden inside the dragon's tail. He sent this wondrous object up to Amaterasu as a final gesture of his good will.

(At this point in the myth-narrative, it should be explained, the main story line is interrupted by a secondary plot, so to speak, which follows Susano-o and his relatives through a series of adventures that account for the "consolidation and pacification of the land." When finally it had been made ready, this land was given over to the rule of the sun goddess's grandson, Prince Ninigi. The following account omits those tales because they tend to confuse the story of how a divine emperor came to rule the land that had been created by Izanagi and Izanami.)

Amaterasu sent several envoys down to earth to take command of it in her name, but all of them failed, and finally the task was given to Prince Ninigi. Before he descended to earth, he sent out scouts to learn whether the way was clear. They came back and reported that the Heavenly Eight Crossroads were blocked by a god, Saruta-hiko, who was seven fathoms tall, and that such a brilliance radiated from him that they were blinded. Ninigi commanded the beautiful female deity Uzume to go and find out why the roads were being blocked. She confronted Saruta-hiko and so disturbed him by exposing her body that he admitted that he was there to serve as a guide on Ninigi's journey. Saruta-hiko escorted Prince Ninigi by means of the Floating Bridge of Heaven to Mount Takachiho in Hyuga Province. Thus did Prince Ninigi become the first of the sun goddess's line to rule in Japan. Many years later, one of his great-grandsons became the first emperor of Japan, Jimmu.

This brief summary of the first book of the *Kojiki,* although it omits some sprightly tales and exciting events, identifies certain main characters and the important elements that form the core of Japanese mythology as it considers the creation of the earth, the forming of the Japanese state, and the origin of its deities and rulers. In the following chapters, some of these events will be reviewed in greater detail, and the meanings of certain myths will be explored in their possible relationship to concepts of creativity. The presence of the two deities Uzume and Saruta-hiko, who are clearly identified with sex in these myths, suggests that the ancient beliefs rooted in phallicism became vested in those two deities in human form, and that, furthermore, those two seem to be the phallic deities who are portrayed in sculptured form as Dosojin.

VIIII

THE CREATION MYTHS

Japanese mythology is surprisingly rich in the number of its references to acts of creation, courtship, sexual intercourse, defloration, and feats of magic. The first of these is Izanagi's and Izanami's creation of the island of Onogoro by means of the Heavenly Jeweled Spear, a phallic symbol of the first importance. But Japanese mythology is by no means orderly in its structure and presentation; and adding to this confusion is the failure of many scholars in other disciplines to recognize in specific incidents or components of those incidents the archetypes that appear in all mythologies. Typical of such an archetype is the creation myth telling of the "separation of the World Parents, the splitting off of opposites from unity, the creation of heaven and earth, above and below, day and night, light and darkness. . . ."[1]

In the series of myths presented below we recognize Izanagi and Izanami as the World Parents, the Sky Father and Earth Mother. Their function is to create order out of chaos, to establish the form of the cosmos and bring it under control, to make it productive and fruitful. They are part of the endless cycle of birth, death, and rebirth. When their task is done they disappear and are replaced by new deities who perform similar functions on another plane of responsibility. Discussion of this aspect of the creation myths will be resumed after we consider the more apparent manifestations suggested by a variety of symbols, and by Izanami's and Izanagi's ritualistic behavior as that is described in the myths.

The Island of Onogoro   The first deities of the cosmos appeared mysteriously in the Plain of High Heaven before the earth was created. Those heavenly deities commanded the last two of their group, Izanagi and Izanami, to create the earth.

"Granting to them an heavenly jewelled spear, they [thus] deigned to charge them. So the two Deities, standing upon the Floating Bridge of Heaven, pushed down the jewelled spear and stirred with it, whereupon, when they stirred the brine till it went curdle, curdle, and drew [the spear] up, the brine that dripped down from the end of the spear was piled up and became an island. This was the Island of Onogoro."[2]

The symbolism of the jeweled spear, in this act of creation, is inescapable: the magic power of the phallus in the procreative act is assumed here by the spear. As Jean Herbert has recognized, the fact that the spear should be given this kind of significance has bothered some writers up to the present time: "The jewelled spear has given rise to a considerable literature, and sex-obsessed western scholars have eagerly seized the opportunity for dilating upon this 'proof' of the existence in Japan of a phallic cult—of which it is no more difficult to find traces there than in any other country in the world."[3]

Phallic symbols are found in Japan even today in profusion, not only in fields and at roadsides in the country, but also concealed behind altars in shrines and temples. During certain festivals in the time of rice planting, such fertility symbols are prominently displayed, as at Tagata Shrine near Nagoya, which also holds regular celebrations on the first and fifteenth days of every month. Miniature phallic symbols are sold as souvenirs at such shrines, and toys based upon phallic deities and symbols are available in large variety along the beaten path followed by tourists.

In Jomon times, apparently, stone clubs resembling phalli stood along paths and frontiers to safeguard the countryside. The metal spear, introduced from China in early Yayoi times, was used first in hunting and in battle. The Yayoi period saw the introduction and development of rice cultivation, when man the hunter became tied to the soil and the seasons of the year. The patterns of life, economic, social, religious, and political, became more complex, and a need for specialization among both gods and men was recognized. In religious matters, these changes called for new deities, rituals, and symbols, which slowly replaced the older ones. In this new developing agricultural society, political power was secondary to religious authority, which was vested primarily in men and women who served their people as shamans. The spear as a weapon was set aside in favor of its use as a religious symbol having divine power and at times signifying the presence of a particular deity.[4]

The spear as a symbol functioned in several ways and could fulfill these functions either singly or all at the same time. It assumed divine power in protecting boundaries, or representing the authority of high office, or signifying the procreative power of different deities. The spear as a symbol appears in a number of myths, notably in the hands of Uzume, the deity of sexual attraction, during her dance before the cave in which the sun goddess had hidden herself; and in the hands of Onamochi-no-Kami, Great Name-possessor Deity, when in abdication he gave up the Land-subduing Broad Spear; and when Empress Jingu, having conquered the kingdom of Silla in Korea, set up her spear at the palace gate as a sign of her authority. The Goryo festival in its original form featured sixty-six halberds that were placed around the ceremonial site to purify it and to designate it as a sacred place. The Goryo festival was dedicated to the phallic gods known collectively as Sae-no-Kami, the preventive deities against pestilence, evils, and sickness. And, of course, the jeweled spear used by Izanagi and Izanami in the creation of the island of Onogoro—that is to say, the earth—can hardly be misunderstood as a symbol of a divine force, used in the same way as was the phallic stone which preceded it in more primitive times.

The Courtship of Izanagi and Izanami When Izanagi and Izanami descended from Heaven to the island of Onogoro, a great loneliness surrounded them. Then Izanagi plunged the Heavenly Jeweled Spear into the ground and from it grew a heavenly pillar, and then a great palace, the Hall of Eight Fathoms, rose around them. They regarded each other with open hearts, and talked of their desire to become man and wife.

"Then Izanagi addressed Izanami, saying: 'How is thy body formed?' Izanami replied, 'My body is completely formed except one part which is incomplete.' Then Izanagi said, 'My body is completely formed and there is one part which is superfluous. Suppose that we supplement that which is incomplete in thee with that which is superfluous in me, and thereby procreate lands.' Izanami replied, 'It is well.' Then Izanagi said, 'Let me and thee go around the Heavenly August Pillar, and, meeting on the other side, let us become united in wedlock.' This being agreed to, he said, 'Do thou go round from the left, and I will go round from the right.' When they had gone round, Izanami spoke first and exclaimed, 'How delightful! I have met a lovely youth.' Izanagi then said, 'How delightful! I have met a lovely maiden.' "[5]

The child of this union was born without legs and could not stand (it was a so-called leech-child). They refused to accept it as their own, and cast it adrift in a reed boat. On their second effort, the island of Awa was born to them, and they refused to own that, too. Thereupon, the two deities ascended to heaven to seek the counsel of the heavenly deities in their misfortune. The gods performed a grand divination, and advised Izanagi and Izanami, saying, "The bearing of children had not been good because the woman had spoken first. Descend again and amend your words."[6] Descending, they again went round the Heavenly August Pillar as before, except this time Izanagi went round from the left and Izanami from the right. And this time Izanagi spoke first, saying: "Ah! What a fair and lovely maiden." Izanami replied: "Ah! What a fair and lovely youth."[7] Thereafter the gods were appeased, and the pair lived in great contentment and so gave birth to the Eight Islands which became Japan.

This courtship myth immediately indicates that the shamanistic concept of the cosmos as existing on closely interrelated planes was understood by the ancient Japanese. The pillar is one form of the central axis which connects the three planes of the cosmos and which makes communication among all three possible. This axis takes many forms, as we have seen—a pillar, a tree, a mountain, a tent pole, the hole at the top of a roof or a tent, and so forth—and thus the central axis, the cosmic tree, and the heavenly pillar represent the universe in a process of continual regeneration. These are symbols of fertility, creation, and recurrent life and immortality.[8] Therefore, the protective power of the phallus is synonymous with the Heavenly August Pillar; and the center post on which the home, the Hall of Eight Fathoms, stands is also the procreative power of the phallus.

The Hall of Eight Fathoms has been identified as a house of coition and as a house of parturition. It seems fitting that heavenly deities should consummate their courtship in such a suitable setting. But more than this, the story reflects the old customs of ceremonially avoiding the contaminating of a regular dwelling house by consummating a marriage within it. Shinto regards the worst defilements, kegare, to be those connected with death, the blood of childbirth, and the blood of menstruation. The parturition house was considered to be a sacred place, where life was born, even though the treatment of the mother while she stayed there was anything but considerate. The expectant mother was isolated, often for weeks and even months, both before and after childbirth. Because of the fact of kegare, she was ignored and abandoned to loneliness and want. The mother and child were not allowed to return to the family circle until both were out of danger and their "illness" would not contaminate the family.[9]

The ritual of Izanagi and Izanami's courtship around the Heavenly August Pillar and the culminating act of coition are unusual in mythology because the event is described in realistic terms: here gods behave like people rather than appear in abstract or symbolic terms. From this and other such details, we can conclude that the

　　　　　　　　　　　　　　　　THE MYTHIC ROOTS

early Japanese understood the mysteries of conception and considered it to be a divine gift. This advanced degree of knowledge contrasts most favorably with the beliefs of more primitive peoples, such as the Trobriand Islanders in the Pacific, who until very recent times believed that women were impregnated when they bathed in the sea or exposed their buttocks to the wind.

Another interesting aspect of this myth about the parent gods is the incompatibility that Izanami caused when she presumed to speak first and walked around the pillar in the wrong direction, from the left. (In Shinto belief, the place of honor in the arrangement of individuals is the first position to the left of center. Thus, the position farthest to the right is for the individual lowest in rank.) This myth does not teach that the male is superior to the female but merely that a proper procedure must be followed to insure compatibility between husband and wife if the sexual act is to have good results.

In the marriage ceremony, the masculine and the feminine parts, the left and the right, are to be united; and the gods advised that, in order to have a harmonious and fruitful union, Izanagi and Izanami should follow their own essential masculine and feminine natures, with Izanagi going left around the pillar and Izanami going right.

The Death of Izanami The courtship of Izanagi and Izanami and their creating of islands were followed by the creating of many deities —those of the rivers, oceans, mountains, valleys, winds, passes, and others, some thirty in number. The last of these was the deity of fire, the consequences of whose birth were tragic. Through giving birth to this child Izanami's private parts were burned and she sickened and died. Izanagi was stricken with grief and so great was his sorrow that he crawled around her head and feet weeping, and from his falling tears was born the deity of weeping. Izanagi buried his wife and then his tremendous grief burst in great fury. He slew his child, the deity of fire, with his ten-grasp sword, and from the spattering blood that dripped from the sword there were born eight deities and from various parts of the dismembered body of the child there were born still eight more.[10]

Izanagi loved his wife so much that her death haunted him incessantly and he could not find peace of mind. He determined to seek her in the underworld kingdom of Yomi. After a long journey he arrived at the gate of Yomi, and, striking it, he cried aloud, "Oh, my beloved sister, come back to me!" And she answered, "Oh, my beloved elder brother, gladly would I come, but alas, I have eaten of the cooking-furnace of Yomi and am beholden to the deities of this place. Look not upon me and I will go to speak with them."

Izanagi waited a long time, and becoming impatient, he broke off the "male" end of the wooden comb stuck in the bunch of his hair, lighted it, and went looking for Izanami. He came upon her body and it was rotting, full of worms, and the Eight Thunders infested her head, body, hands, and feet. Izanagi, greatly shocked, exclaimed, "What a hideous and polluted land I have come to unaware." He fled in horror. Izanami called after him, "You have shamed me," and she set the Eight Ugly Women of Yomi to catch him.[11]

But each time they were about to seize him Izanagi prevented his capture by magical means. First he threw down his black head-wreath, and it became a bunch of grapes. The pursuers stopped to eat them. Next he threw down his wooden comb of many teeth, and they became young bamboo sprouts. Again the pursuers stopped to eat them. Then Izanami sent the eight thunder deities and the five hundred soldiers of Yomi after him. Izanagi drew his great sword and brandished it behind him, but still they pursued him. Finally he reached the end of the slope leading from Yomi to the land of the living. At the entrance he stopped to rest and at the base he saw three peaches growing. He picked the peaches and smote his pursuers with them and they fled back down the path of Yomi.[12]

Then Izanagi took a great rock (which in time was deified as Chigaeshi-no-Okami, or Great Deity of the Road Turning-back),[13] and he blocked the pass with it, pronouncing at the same time the formula of divorce, namely: "Our relationship is severed." Izanami threatened him, saying, "If you divorce me I will in one day strangle to death one thousand of the people of your land." He replied, "If you do so, I will, in one day, build one thousand and five hundred parturition houses."[14]

Izanagi then said, "Come no farther," and threw down his staff, from which was born the deity called Funado-no-Kami, Deity Pass-not Place, or Kunado-no-Kami, Deity Thrust-erect Come-not Place.[15]

In the *Kojiki* version of this myth, Izanagi does not throw down the staff until he reaches the bank of the river where he intends to bathe. In the *Nihongi* version, however, the staff is thrown down at the time of the road-blocking and the pronouncement of divorce. In any event, the details of the sequence are not important. Rather, it is the function of the rock and the staff as magic symbols that is significant: they represent the blocking of evil through phallic power.

Chamberlain recognized the phallic character of Kunado, as he made evident by his translation of the deity's name, Deity Thrust-erect Come-not Place. Usually the name is shortened to Deity Come-not Place, and thereby its phallic meaning is lost.

Another source suggests a much more involved derivation of the name Kunado. *Kunagu* is an archaic word meaning sexual intercourse. *Kunado* means "a thing of Kunado," in other words, the phallus. *Kuna* of Kunado means "to mate." *Hoto* is a name for the female genitalia. *Mito* is a name for the genital organs of both sexes.[16] A literal translation of Kunado-no-Kami, then, would be "Deity of the Male Organ."

The Ritual of Purification   Secure in his escape, Izanagi observed himself in disgust, for he had become hideously polluted during his journey to the world of the dead. He chose a small stream on the island of Tsukushi (an ancient name for a part of Kyushu) in which to cleanse and purify himself. From the soiled clothes that he took off and threw down, twelve deities were born: from his girdle, the Deity Road Long Space; from his skirt, the Deity Loosen Put; from his upper garment, the Deity Master of Trouble; from his hat, the Deity Master of the Open Mouth; and from his trousers, the Road-fork Deity. Then he plunged into the quiet waters of the stream, and as he washed fourteen deities were born from his bathing. From the washings of his left eye was born the sun goddess, Amaterasu Omikami, the Heaven-shining Great August Deity. From the washings of his right eye was born the moon god, Tsukiyomi-no-Kami, Deity Moon Night Possessor; and from those of his nose the deity of the sea, or the rainstorm god, Susano-o-no-Mikoto, Brave Swift Impetuous Male Augustness.[17]

Izanagi rejoiced that at his final begetting he had brought forth three such illustrious children. He ordered Amaterasu to rule the Plain of High Heaven and gave her his sacred necklace of jewels. To the moon god he entrusted the Kingdom of the Night, and to Susano-o the Kingdom of the Waters of the Sea. The first two children obeyed, departed, and took possession of their dominions, but Susano-o wept and groaned and did not leave. Izanagi confronted this third child, saying, "Why do you wail and weep instead of assuming the command I have given to you?" Susano-o replied, "I wish to visit the Land of Yomi to see my dead mother."[18] Angered, Izanagi banished Susano-o to the nether land of Yomi, and then he retired to live in a cave until the end of his time.

Significance of the Myth   Izanagi's flight from the depths of the underworld is significant in that it reveals the nature of the evil spirits of Yomi and of the magic symbols that could be used to control them. It describes the ritual of divorce as a realistic event that separates the Earth Mother from the Sky Father. And it also reveals the manner of creating the phallic deities of the sun, moon, and rainstorm, which he does almost incidentally while cleansing himself of the pollution acquired during his unsuccessful journey to Yomi. Let us examine these magic symbols and phallic elements before we consider the meaning of Japan's creation myths on another level.

The Comb First, there was the end tooth of the wooden comb that Izanagi wore in his hair. The end tooth is known as the "male pillar," or o-bashira. This term is applied also to the end post of the railing on a bridge or of the balustrade for a staircase. Such a post is crowned with a wooden or metal head in the form of a *tama,* or jewel, a bulb shape pointed at the top. The o-bashira is seen everywhere in Japan. Originally it was placed in positions that commanded throughfares to prevent the passage of evil spirits or pestilences. Many other forms of the "male pillar" are made, such as the spoon, the ladle, and especially the pestle that is used in pounding rice into flour or paste. A special ceremonial form is the kezuri-kake, which has been described more fully in Chapter III. The regular or small teeth of the comb which Izanagi threw down before the Ugly Women of Yomi sprang up as bamboo shoots—phallic symbols of the most obvious kind. There are many other vegetable phalli as well, among them the *daikon* (long white radish), carrot, and asparagus. Vegetables of this kind are presented as offerings to images of phallic deities. The sword that Izanagi brandished behind him in his flight from Yomi is a sophisticated phallic symbol, whose development as a magic talisman parallels that of the spear.

Swords were buried in boxes at strategic locations in order to repel evil forces from crossing borders. Some swords have been deified, and it is probable that one of these most sacred objects is enshrined at Ise.[19] A special ceremonial sword, with seven flamelike points and three spurs on each side, resembling the Tree of Life, is preserved in Isonokami Shrine near Nara.[20]

The Headdress and the Peaches Izanagi also threw down a headdress made of leaves, and these turned into bunches of grapes. The peaches that he found at the base of the Even Pass of Yomi turned back the five hundred warriors who were pursuing him. Izanagi later deified those peaches. Soft, round fruits, such as grapes, peaches, plums, persimmons, and pomegranates, are regarded as symbols of the female sex organs, and have the same magic power as does the phallus. Several kinds of Dosojin sculptures are made in the form of a pillar and a sphere, denoting male and female genitalia, respectively. Offerings of such fruits and vegetables are made to Dosojin, especially in conjunction with prayers from women who wish to bear children.

The Rock and the Staff The most significant part of the myth is the blocking of the entrance to Yomi with a huge boulder. Thereupon Izanagi and Izanami are separated forever: death is on one side of the rock, and life is on the other. The final curtain has been drawn upon the drama: the dead may not return to this world. As if the physical barrier of the rock were not enough, Izanagi takes advantage of the situation to part from Izanami simply by repeating the ritual formula for divorce. And indeed, in old Japan, if a wife proved to be unsatisfactory, unable to produce children (whether or not it was her fault), unable to contribute to the productivity of the home and fields, or was a nag and an unfit companion, she could be sent back to her parents, and the marriage would be dissolved by such a simple pronouncement.

If we consider from the animistic point of view of magic the great rock which blocked the entrance to Yomi, we observe that it prevented the five hundred warriors, the Ugly Women, and the Eight Thunders from escaping from the underworld. These evil spirits are equated with sicknesses and pestilences that spread terror and death among the people of early Japan. The rock that Izanagi used to block the way, Chigaeshi-no-Okami, and the staff that he threw down, Kunado, were divine objects and deities in their own right. Scholars of the seventeenth and eighteenth centuries explained the creation of these two phallic deities in this way: while Izanagi was engaged in his great struggle to return from Yomi, in placing the rock in position a portion of his mitama, or august spirit, was jarred loose from his body and adhered to the great rock and to his staff. From this mitama were born the two deities. Having been born in this manner, they are considered to be one and the same, that is, one deity produced in one birth. Moreover, the peaches growing at the base of the great rock suggest that it was female, while the staff, as its title indicates, was unquestionably male.

In ancient times, the crossroad deities were regarded as mitama, and they appeared in the form of carved wooden male and female statues placed across from each other on opposite sides of the road. As august spirits, they were called Chimata-hiko, Road-fork Prince, and Chimata-hime, Road-fork Princess.[21] In other words, the phallic deities of the rock and the staff were personified in the form of wooden statues, female and male. Undoubtedly these wooden statues were the predecessors of the Dosojin couple sculptures carved in stone. Since those earlier forms were made of wood, they may have been burned in the annual festival fires or have rotted away because there is no evidence of them today.

Izanagi's concern with creating deities continued as he disrobed to purify himself in the stream. Of those that were born from the pieces of his clothing, naturally the road-fork deity, Chimata-no-Kami, was born from his trousers. It seems that the abundance of phallic symbols, the male staff, the female rock, and the obliging connecting crotch, lent themselves to the creation of deities endowed with magic powers.

It is apparent, from this brief analysis, that originally the phallic gods of roads, of road-blocking, of road-forks, passes, tunnels, and other routes of access were preventive deities, called Sae-no-Kami; and that in later times the male and female principles were conjoined into a single image and ultimately into a single deity. Under whatever name he may have been called, and he had many names, his function was always the same: to be the guardian of the way.

Archetypes in Creation Myths: The World Parents Creation myths, or myths about the emergence of order from chaos, follow a pattern that is much the same in all the major cultures of mankind. The phases in a society's cultural evolution stand in the same relationship to one another as do the successive stages in the conception, birth, and development of an individual human being. The elements of any mythological record may be more easily read and understood if we recognize and understand that "a series of archetypes is a main constituent of mythology . . . they stand in an organic relation to one another, . . . and their stadial succession determines the growth of consciousness. In the course of its ontogenetic development, the individual ego consciousness has to pass through the same archetypal stages which determined the evolution of consciousness in the life of humanity."[22]

The successive stages of development observed in the cosmic myths of Japan, according to Eliade, are:

1. The primordial situation, the androgynous whole in which nothing is separated and sex is undifferentiated; identified as Chaos, World Womb, and so on.
2. The presence of a germ, seed, or shoot, regarded as the progeny of the divine androgyny. Deities are born from the shoot grown into a stalk.
3. The first deities create brother and sister deities of heaven (Izanagi) and earth (Izanami) and they marry.
4. The deity of heaven and the deity of earth create, that is, they separate heaven from earth.
5. After the separation the marriage is consummated; a hierogamy is established through the union of two cosmic principles creating the world.
6. The Earth Mother dies—is sacrificed—in giving birth to the deity of fire.
7. The fire deity is dismembered; earth and vegetative deities are born from this second gory sacrifice.
8. The Sky Father creates the sun, moon, and rainstorm deities and retires.[23]

The cycle of these successive stages begins with the origin of the universe. This is separated into parts by deities specifically created for the purpose, and when their task is done they sacrifice themselves to generate a new cycle of responsibilities at a different level of existence, while they themselves return to the primordial situation. This is the cycle of birth, emergence of being, fulfillment, and death.

In the Japanese cosmogonic myths, the appearance of Izanagi and Izanami as brother and sister (implying sexual noninvolvement) is analogous to the creation of heaven and earth in an undifferentiated state of wholeness. These two deities themselves were created by other deities, who sprang from a germ or root present in the primordial unity, or World Womb.

Izanagi and Izanami were assigned the task of creating the world, that is, of separating the sky from the earth. They accomplished this by creating an island to which they descended; and, by taking each other as husband and wife, they established the two principles of maleness and femaleness. Symbolically, the separation of sky and earth is accounted for in the new identities of the Sky Father and the Earth Mother. The creative aspects of these myths thus far delineate the emerging psyche of humanity.

"When the ego begins to emerge from its identity with the uroboros, and the embryonic connection with the womb ceases, the ego takes up a new attitude to the world. . . . Detachment from the uroboros means being born and descending into the lower world of reality, full of dangers and discomforts. The nascent ego becomes aware of pleasure-pain qualities. . . . Consequently the world becomes ambivalent. . . . The world experienced by the waking ego of humanity is the world of J. J. Bachofen's matriarchate with its goddesses of motherhood and destiny. The wicked, devouring mother and the good mother lavishing affection are two sides of the great uroboric Mother Goddess who reigns over this psychic state."[24]

Having created the world and separated it into the sacred and profane realms, sky and earth, Izanagi and Izanami created deities to control specific aspects of these cosmic regions in order to ensure productivity and fruitfulness. When Izanami died in giving birth to the deity of fire, from her body were born eight deities of fertility related to the earth and to food. Izanagi slew the deity of fire, and from his dismembered body a second series of similar agricultural deities was born.

At this point, Izanagi and Izanami, the World Parents, are separated symbolically. The separation of the World Parents is symbolically identical with killing, sacrifice, dismemberment, and castration. Mutilation is the condition of all creation. So here we come upon two archetypal motifs that belong absolutely together and appear in all creation myths. Without the slaying of the old parents, their dismemberment and neutralization, there can be no beginning.[25]

The death of Izanami and the killing of the fire deity are two acts of creation based upon the principle of sacrifice. If these two events are not readily recognizable as such, there is still a third instance—when hasty Susano-o kills the goddess of food, Ugadama or Uke-mochi. Susano-o takes offense at the foods he is offered from diverse parts of the goddess's body, and so he kills her.[26]

Whereupon "from Uga-dama's body, *aha* (millet) grew on her forehead, a silkworm and mulberry tree grew on the eyebrows, *hiye* (barnyard grass) grew on the eyes, a rice-seed on the belly, barley, a large bean and a small bean on the private parts, and the head changed into a horse and a cow. . . . [Amaterasu] appointed lords of the villages of Heaven and for the first time made them plant these rice-seeds in the narrow fields of Heaven . . . also . . . mulberry trees . . . and silkworms. . . . The arts of silkworm rearing and weaving commence from this time."[27]

The killing of Ugadama is a symbolic returning to the earth of that which grew from it: "The womb of the earth clamors for fertilization, and blood sacrifices and corpses are the food she likes best. This is the terrible aspect, the deadly side of the earth's character. In the earliest fertility cults, the gory fragments of the sacrificial victim were handed round as precious gifts and offered up to the earth, in order to make her fruitful. These human sacrifices for fertility occur all the world over quite independently of one another, in the rites of America and in the Eastern Mediterranean, in Asia and in northern Europe. Everywhere blood plays a leading part in fertility ritual and human sacrifice. The great terrestrial law that there can be no life without death was early understood, and still earlier represented in ritual, to mean that a strengthening of life can only be bought at the cost of sacrificial death. . . . Slaughter and sacrifice, dismemberment and offerings of blood, are magical guarantees of earthly fertility."[28]

Myths about the killing of the food goddess, whether she is the Corn Mother of Europe or the Rice Mother of Southeast Asia and its islands, are based upon actual rituals of human sacrifice, in which the blood and the flesh or the ashes of the victim who represented the grain deity were sprinkled over the seed as it was placed in the ground at the time of planting. The Pawnees and the Sioux in North America, the Bagados of Mindanao in the Philippine Islands, the Gonds of Dravidian India, and the Incas of Peru, among others, all practiced human sacrifice to ensure the fertility of crops.[29]

Violent sacrifice, including dismemberment, adds another dimension to the concept of fertility. "The violent death is creative . . . the life which is sacrificed manifests itself in a more brilliant form upon another plane of existence. . . . A living 'whole' bursts into fragments and disperses itself in myriads of animated forms . . . by the act of Creation."[30]

And so it was with Izanami, and with the deity of fire, and with Ugadama: from their several bodies many divinities of land, mountains, rocks, roots, and water were born, so that life could be renewed among men and all the creatures of the earth on a higher level of existence.

These references in mythology to the establishment of agricultural husbandry on a systematic scale prove that the culture of the Japanese people had risen to a new level. Apparently this marked the change from a hunting society to an agricultural society. In consequence, the people found it necessary to create or accept new deities to relate to the new procedures that were required by their evolving system.

Izanami descended to Yomi after her death, and Izanagi followed, hoping to bring her back. But just as Orpheus failed in his quest for Eurydice, so did Izanagi fail in his for Izanami. It could not have been otherwise, because what we see here is "the funerary aspect of the Earth-Mother as the Goddess of Death . . . simply because she is felt to be the universal womb, the inexhaustible source of all creation. Death is not, in itself, a definitive end, not an absolute annihilation, as it is sometimes thought to be in the modern world. Death is likened to the seed which is sown in the bosom of the Earth-Mother to give birth to a new plant. Thus, one might speak of an optimistic view of death, since death is regarded as a return to the Mother, a temporary re-entry into the maternal bosom. That is why bodies buried in neolithic times are found lying in the embryonic position; the dead were laid in the earth in the attitude of the embryo in the womb, as though they were expected to come back to life again and again. The Earth-Mother, as the Japanese myth told us, was the first to die; but this death of Izanami was at the same time a sacrifice made in order to augment and extend the Creation."[31]

The creation myths of Japan conclude with Izanagi's creating of the sun goddess, the moon god, and the rainstorm god. These acts complete the cosmic structure and its hierarchy, and now the world is able to function. "The world begins only with the coming of light which constellates the opposition between heaven and earth as the basic symbol of all other opposites."[32]

The sun goddess, Amaterasu, ascends to heaven to govern the realm of day; the moon god ascends to rule over the night. The rainstorm god was meant to rule over the sea, but he was inconsolable at the loss of his mother and defied his impatient father. The consequences of Susano-o's rebellion, the subject of succeeding myths, will be considered in the next chapter.

RAVAGES AGAINST HEAVEN
AND EARTH

The tempestuous events that occurred during Susano-o's visit to heaven to bid goodbye to his sister Amaterasu are known as the August Ravages of Susano-o. As the very appellation suggests, they were both bizarre and dramatic. The August Ravages were preceded by the magical act in which vaunting Susano-o and competitive Amaterasu created princes and princesses from each other's possessions. When they bickered over the results of this contest, matters went from bad to worse:

"Then His-Swift-Impetuous-Male-Augustness said to the Heaven-Shining-Great-August-Deity: 'Owing to the sincerity of my intentions I have, in begetting children, gotten delicate females. Judging from this, I have undoubtedly gained the victory.' With these words, and impetuous with victory, he broke down the divisions of the ricefields laid out by the Heaven-Shining-Great-August-Deity, filled up the ditches, and moreover strewed excrements in the palace where she partook of the great food. So, though he did thus, the Heaven-Shining-Great-August Deity upbraided him not, but said: 'What looks like excrements must be something that His Augustness mine elder brother has vomited through drunkenness. Again, as to his breaking down the divisions of the rice-fields and filling up the ditches, it must be because he grudges the land [they occupy] that His Augustness mine elder brother acts thus.' But notwithstanding these apologetic words, he still continued his evil acts and was more and more [violent]. As the Heaven-Shining-Great-August-Deity sat in her awful weaving-hall seeing to the weaving of the august garments of the Deities, he broke a hole in the top of the weaving-hall, and through it let fall a heavenly piebald horse which he had flayed with a backward flaying, at whose sight the women weaving the heavenly garments were so much alarmed that impegerunt privatas partes adversis radiis et obierunt."[1]

As might be expected, the sun goddess was terrified by her brother's horrible deeds. She fled and hid herself in a cave, blocking the opening with a huge rock. In his tantrum, Susano-o destroyed the ricefields and crops, desecrated Amaterasu's sacred chamber, caused the death of her handmaidens, desecrated a living animal, and caused the world to be plunged once again into darkness. The interpretation of the symbolism in these events holds more than is immediately apparent, although in this myth some of Susano-o's misdeeds seem to be included simply to record the rules of conduct governing agrarian life. In the agricultural society of that time, the staff of life was rice, and religious ideas were shaped to protect and fortify this relationship.

Rules governing the agricultural way of life appear in the *Engi-shiki,* the ancient records regulating the conduct of rituals; and a reading of the Tenth Norito shows that Susano-o's offenses were considered to be extremely serious: "Now of the various faults and transgressions to be committed by the celestial race destined more and more to people this land of his peaceful rule, some are of Heaven, to wit, the breaking down of divisions between rice fields, filling up of irrigation channels, removing water-pipes, sowing seed over again, planting skewers, flaying alive, flaying backwards. These are distinguished as Heavenly Offenses."[2]

Those tribal taboos, or heavenly offenses, are curious in one respect: all of them apply to rice cultivation except those concerned with flaying. If rice was considered to be sacred, then, by association, we can assume that certain animals, specifically the horse, to which those phrases about flaying apply, were also considered to be sacred. However, the horse was not part of the religious system based upon rice cultivation, because the horse was not employed as a farm animal in early Yayoi times. Rather, it was regarded as a noble creature, whose use as food was prohibited, just as was the use of the ox and the stag. In later times, white horses were kept at Shinto shrines, to be employed ceremonially in performing divinations or for carrying a mikoshi or sometimes a miko or a high priest. On special occasions, the emperor, a living kami, rode a white horse.

In this myth, the violence of Susano-o's acts suggests that there was a conflict not only on the politicoeconomic level but also between two systems of ritual, one characterized by cultivation of rice and the other by the use of the horse for ritual purposes. The key to interpreting the symbolic meaning of this myth, especially the

THE MYTHIC ROOTS

significance of the flaying of the piebald colt, lies in the two disparate cultural heritages and the two religious systems represented by Amaterasu and Susano-o. Mythic accounts do not tell us clearly that these deities belonged to different cultures in different ages, but recent theories regarding the conquest and consolidation of the "rice cultivators" by a race of "horse riders" are being substantiated by archaeological and anthropological evidence.

The development of Japanese culture extended over a long period of time, the earliest dates of which are being pushed back further and further as more research is done. The present opinion is that the Jomon period extended from about 7500 B.C. to about 200 B.C., and that it can be subdivided into five phases. The preceramic age in Japan is thought to go back to 15,000 B.C. or earlier. The first inhabitants of Japan—the first "Japanese" as well as the Ainu—were followed by waves of immigrants from the area of New Guinea and the Indonesian islands, the Korean peninsula, Manchuria, and central and southern China.

The first immigrants from the Asian continent to settle in the Izumo region on the Japan Sea coast were members of an ethnic group who had farmed the harsh, dry, semiarid lands of the Korean Peninsula and southern Manchuria. These were Tungus farmers, who cultivated millet, were organized in a patrilineal society, and introduced a cultural heritage originating in the Siberian bronze culture. The bronze grave goods attributed to the early Yayoi culture, such as the spear, crescent-shaped knife, bell, mirror, and jewels of jade, must have been introduced into Japan at that time.

These people from northern Asia brought religious concepts that found expression in rituals performed by shamans. The shaman had tutelary deities who helped him in the ritual of ascending to heaven along a "rope road" which connected the earth with the sky.[3] Shamans performed seances for the usual reasons—to ward off disease and death, to appease the spirits, and for special reasons concerned with the souls of the dead and the nether world.[4]

There is also, undeniably, an Oceanic tradition among the people of the west coast of the Izumo region.

The Rice-Culture People   The introduction of rice cultivation at the end of the Jomon period by members of an ethnic group who seem to have come from south of the Yangtze River in China marked the end of a hunting society in Japan and the beginning of one based upon agriculture. The newcomers brought not only the knowledge and skills needed to manage the growing of rice in irrigated fields but also the tools, implements, religious beliefs, rituals, and deities for a complete system of life. It was this group that brought to Japan the myths and religious cult of Amaterasu, the sun goddess,[5] as well as a multitude of nature deities, animal deities, and a belief in the magic of symbols, such as the stone phallus.

The Horse-Riding People Sometime during the third and fourth centuries A.D., a very aggressive people, whose mounted horsemen were equipped with the bow and arrow and the long sword, migrated to Japan, probably from Korea. This was a patriarchal society, highly organized in clans and classes, and distinguished by a marked specialization of labor, a slave system, a military elite, and knowledge of the techniques involved in working iron.[6] Its clans seem to have been grouped into units of five, based on a tradition followed by Siberian "military democracies" of that age. The Western Turks, also a horse-riding people, for example, were divided into five eastern and five western "generations." This organizational grouping of five families is found in both the early stages of the Japanese state and in its mythology.

The religious system of the horse-riders was characterized by the worship of celestial divinities, the deification of heroes, the belief that deities could descend from the sky to mountain peaks and the tops of trees, and the use of shamans.[7] The shamanism of the Ural Altaic tribes is characterized by the ritual of horse sacrifice and by the belief that the spirit of the sacrificed horse could fly to the sky, guiding the shaman's spirit to an audience with celestial deities.

During the Yayoi period in Japan, the society was dependent upon the cultivation of rice, gentle in manner, immersed in religious affairs, and nature-oriented. Evidence from the early Tumulus period (c. 250–c. 375) reveals the gentleness of those rice-cultivating farmers. The tombs were small shaft-chambers, higher than they were broad; and the grave goods usually consisted of bronze mirrors, jewelry, swords, hoe-shaped stones, stone whorls, and other precious symbol-objects of religious character.

In contrast, the burial mounds of the late Tumulus period (c. 375–552), after the horse-riders came, were gigantic in size and keyhole-shaped, and usually the inner chamber was broader than it was high in order to accommodate the larger trunk-shaped outer coffin made of stone. The grave goods included weapons, horse accouterments, body armor, clothing, and models of men, women, and things known in daily life, such as birds, beasts, houses, and other ordinary articles. The greater number of these objects, especially the weapons, horse accouterments, and decorative articles of apparel, were practically the same as those of the horse-riding people of the so-called Hu Barbarians in northeast Asia, who were active in northern Korea in the third to fifth century.[8] This kind of evidence supports the theory that the horse-riding invaders from the continent subjugated the agricultural population in Japan during the late Yayoi period. In time, the horse-riders dominated the country administratively and politically, while allowing the religious structure of the preceding culture to continue—of necessity, because they could not change the beliefs and attitudes of the people whom they had subjugated. In this respect, at least, the new culture was absorbed by the old.

The effects of these successive immigrations are condensed in such myths as that of Susano-o's descent from heaven to a place somewhere in Korea, after which he made his way to Japan. Other accounts place his arrival directly in Izumo, on Mount Torikami. Susano-o must be recognized as being a composite of ancestors, a figure who was invented to explain some of the complicated and compromising prehistorical events in the founding of the Japanese nation. It is scarcely surprising, then, to find that Susano-o is not one of the six deities housed at the Great Shrine of Izumo. Instead, he is relegated to a small minor shrine at the rear of that sacred compound.[9] The highest-ranking deity of the six who are enshrined at Izumo Taisha (Great Shrine) is Okuni-nushi-no-Mikoto, Great Land-possessor Deity, who is sometimes called Susano-o's son and sometimes his descendant in the sixth generation.[10]

Mythology also tells us that when Okuni-nushi was forced to abdicate the Izumo lands, he handed over his authority to Ame-no-Hohi-no-Mikoto, Deity Heavenly Fire-shine, who, as a heavenly messenger, brought with him a divine fire drill by virtue of which he became the "master of worship," or the first high priest of Izumo Shrine.[11] Ame-no-Hohi's children and their descendants continued to hold this position for many generations.[12] "All of the [Izumo] priests are said to have discharged their office solely in virtue of being possessed of the 'Marvelous Drill' bestowed upon Ame-no-Hohi-no-Mikoto by his 'parents' Susano-o and Amaterasu."[13]

The indication here is that the "house" or family line of the Izumo high priests descended from those mythological ancestors, or others like them. These men were deified because they were heroes who had distinguished themselves in settling and conquering the country during conflicts with defending aborigines, and still later as the horse-riding warriors who had established a unified state. In time, those hero-ancestors were elevated to the rank of kami. And as, eventually, the stories told about them were transmuted into myths, their experiences in the dim past were preserved for their descendants to remember and to look upon with reverence.

In the context of this background, we can see that Susano-o's association with the horse in this myth is not casual or accidental but rather is based upon the character of prehistorical events that included the settling of the western shores of Japan by several waves of tribesmen from the Asian continent. These included the horse-riding people who invaded Japan from Korea, and who in time became known as the Children of Heaven and the founders of the imperial clan. Moreover, their religious heritage seems to have been derived from shamanistic practices. Foremost among those was the sacrifice of white horses, which were regarded as beasts of good omen, if not actually sacred.

The Symbolism of Susano-o's Deeds The myth of Susano-o's Ravages mentions three events whose symbolic meaning is significant: the disappearance of the sun goddess, the death of the weaving maidens, and Susano-o's throwing of the flayed horse through the hole in the roof.

The first two of these events are undoubtedly connected with agricultural fertility. The waning of the sun with the end of the harvest season and the coming of winter is a theme common to all mythologies based upon agriculture. The symbolic meaning of a sacrificial act involving human or animal life lies in the belief that the sun's generative power, declining with the coming of winter, will be restored when it takes to itself the life offered to it in that sacrifice. The death of the handmaidens is also a reference to agricultural fertility, in this case the offering of human life to the sun goddess in her role as a primary deity of agricultural production. The maidens represent the fruits of the bountiful land, which must be harvested and put back again into the earth to render it fertile. However, the grotesque manner in which those maidens took their lives implies another and more sinister meaning: in thrusting the weaving shuttles (which are symbolic phalli) into their wombs, the maidens destroyed their ability to reproduce. This is a gross and violent imitation of the sexual act—it is, in essence, a symbolic rape. The victim of this rape, which the handmaidens represent, is the rice-growing culture, ravished by the inferior but more aggressive horse-riding people. This interpretation will be reinforced by the analysis of the myth about the backward flaying of the piebald colt.

The Flaying of the Piebald Colt Among the heavenly offenses listed in the Tenth Norito is the prohibition against "flaying alive" and "flaying backward." Although these appear to be two separate offenses, a commentary explains that the two phrases, *ike-hagi* and *saka-hagi,* are customarily used together, so that they relate to one act, that is, to "flaying alive backward."[14] Thus, the colt that Susano-o flung through a hole in the roof had been flayed alive backward. The symbolism of this act is perplexing, but its meaning is satisfactorily explained when viewed against the context of shamanistic rituals, which featured the sacrifice of horses.

The most frequent explanation of "flaying alive backward" is that the skinning was done from tail to head. But this is a naive explanation, inasmuch as the standard method of flaying animals is exactly that way. However, the significance of the phrase lies in its symbolism rather than in the technique of flaying.

What, then, is the symbolism of Susano-o's act? The sacrilegious aspects of his terrible deed seem to be obvious. He removed the horse's hide backward, that is, contrary to ritual requirement. Then, having polluted the hide and the carcass of the horse, thereby rendering them unfit for ceremonial use, he proceeded to violate the sacred Pathway to Heaven by casting the defiled carcass through the hole in Amaterasu's roof.

Susano-o's outrageous behavior in this offensive act was preceded by other acts of violence, protest, and trickery, as we have seen. In her translation of the *Izumo Fudoki* (Topography of the Izumo Area), Michiko Aoki interpreted Susano-o's effort to wrest Amaterasu's dominion from her, and his subsequent banishment to the Land of Yomi, on the level of political and military conquest.

But the ravages of Susano-o, beginning with his ascent to the sky to challenge his sister's dominion and including the backward flaying of the colt, can also be interpreted in a religious context. Amaterasu and Susano-o were sister and brother, in effect creator deities in the same sense that Izanagi and Izanami were, but on a different level of consciousness. Izanagi and his consort represent the creation of the lands of Japan, while Amaterasu and her brother represent the rise of a nation to maturity, the forming of a state and the line of its rulers. Amaterasu represents the religious beliefs and attitudes of the older rice culture, with its broad base in the masses of the people. Susano-o, on the other hand, represents the invading elements, the successive waves of foreigners that came from the mainland to the west coast of Japan. Susano-o represents "seven generations" of ancestors, not just a certain group of rulers in Izumo at one particular time in history. One of those waves of invaders finally consolidated the provincial governments into a single unit for the first time, and this became the Yamato court during the fourth century A.D.

If that victorious horde was indeed made up of horse riders from Korea, as present theory suggests,[15] their religious beliefs contrasted strongly with those of the rice-culture people. The resulting dilemma had to be resolved. The state having been formed by force, the rulers had to perpetuate their control and saw that there was no better way to do so than to establish that right by claiming divine origin and divine right. Since Amaterasu represented the beliefs of the masses of inhabitants, and they could not be changed, the political hierarchy had to be built upon that base. Amaterasu was the obvious choice for the rulers to claim as their divine ancestor. The events that are described in Japanese mythology are so arranged that the ruling families ever since have been able to claim descent from that supreme deity.

Susano-o's religious background, however, was so alien to the masses of Japan's people that he had to be sacrificed, in a sense, to the needs of his people, the very conquerors who brought him with them to Japan. Because Susano-o's cult contained shamanistic elements and the worship of heroes whose ancestors came from a foreign land, the rulers of the new nation they had established in Japan quickly saw that this religious orientation was unacceptable to the aborigines of the conquered land. They decided, therefore, not to build their hierarchy upon the basis of those alien religious ideas.

The conflict between the two cultures, with their different religious beliefs, was resolved eventually—according to a process that has become "typically Japanese"—through adaptation and compromise. The protest of the rice-culture people is recorded dramatically in the bizarre myth of the desecration of Amaterasu's weaving hall with the August Ravages of Susano-o. And Susano-o's "punishment and banishment" to Izumo—the Land of Yomi, the world of darkness—is the symbolic expression of a falling from power of the indigenous rulers of Izumo at the time that they were being subjugated by the founders of the Yamato state.

THE CELESTIAL MATSURI

The myth of the sun goddess's withdrawal following the horrendous act perpetrated by the rainstorm god is actually the concluding part in the Japanese version of the universal drama about the cycles of nature's seasons. However, and happily, the Japanese version of this universal archetype differs from many others in that it adds an account of the festival that was designed to induce the sun goddess to come forth again from her cave. This celestial festival can be regarded as the very foundation of the religious system of the Japanese nation.

In a later myth, we are told how the Celestial Matsuri—the Way of the Kami—was brought down to earth by some of the deities, who performed it here as expert ritualists. The descendants of those deities claimed their high positions in life on this earth by virtue of their descent from that divine hierarchy.

The following account of the heavenly festival is a composite drawn from the *Kojiki* and the writings of Ernest Satow.

The Door of the Heavenly Rock Cave At the horrible sight of the flayed and disemboweled piebald horse, the sun goddess, angered and terrified, fled and hid herself in the Cave of Heaven, closing the entrance with a huge boulder. The world was plunged into total darkness, and the deities of evil profited by this to create chaos and malice. Their activities sounded like swarming flies. Facing this sudden crisis, the eight hundred myriad deities of heaven assembled for a grand conference in the dry bed of the Tranquil

227

River of Heaven. After long deliberation, they bade Omoi-kane-no-Kami, Deity Thought-includer, to think of a plan to draw the sun goddess out of the cave and thus restore the world to order. He quickly set about making many preparations. Bonfires were lighted so that all might see to work. He ordered many crowing cocks to be gathered, and a perch to be built, a *torii*, for the cocks to rest on. He ordered a large hard rock to be brought from the riverbed to serve as an anvil, and iron to be mined from the Heavenly Metal Mountain. A bellows was made from the whole skin of a deer.

Her Augustness, Ishikori-dome-no-Kami, Again-forging Old Woman, was charged with making an eight-sided mirror (or a mirror that was eight handspans in width). The first two attempts were not successful, but the third effort produced a perfect mirror, and it was polished to a shining brightness. Next Ame-no-Futo-dama-no-Mikoto, His Augustness Jewel Ancestor, was commanded to make a complete string of five hundred curved jewels in the commalike form called *magatama*. Two deities were sent into the mountains to cut down tall straight trees for posts, and others dug holes in the ground in which the posts were set, and a new palace was built there. Two deities were put to preparing bark and fibers to weave into coarse and fine cloth. Two other deities made *tamagushi* from the branches of the sakaki tree and the *suzu*, a kind of small bamboo. Ame-no-Koyane-no-Mikoto, the Deity Beckoning Ancestor, pulled up a sakaki tree of five hundred branches, roots and all. The string of five hundred jewels was wound throughout the top branches, the mirror was placed in the middle branches, and from the lower branches were hung strips of blue and white cloth, both fine and coarse.

"When these preparations were complete, Taka-mi-musubi-no-kami then called before him Ame-no-koyane-no-Mikoto and Ame-no-futodama-no-Mikoto and instructed them to find out by divination whether the goddess was likely to be induced to reappear."[1]

They caught a heavenly stag, pulled out its shoulder blade, and set it free again. Then they placed the great bone in a cherry-bark fire and scorched it until cracks appeared in the surface. From the interpretation of these cracks, they drew a favorable omen and devised a plan for a ceremony.

Now the cocks that had been gathered were set to crowing in concert. Ame-no-Tajikara-o-no-Mikoto, whose name signifies that he possessed great strength in his arms, was placed in concealment by the door of the cave. Ame-no-Uzume-no-Mikoto, Heaven-alarming Female Augustness, blew on a bamboo with holes pierced in it, a kind of flute, while other deities kept time to the music by striking two blocks of wood together. "Ame-no-kamato-no-

Mikoto made a sort of harp by placing six bows close together,"[2] and his son Nagashiraha played upon it by drawing a bunch of grass and rushes across the bowstrings.

And now Uzume made a headdress of the leaves of the spindletop tree, and a sash of moss, and she bound the sleeves of her robe close under her armpits with a thin vine. She gathered a bunch of bamboo grass to hold in her hand as a nosegay. She held a spear in the other hand, and it was wound around with *chi,* a kind of grass. Small jingling bells were attached to the spear.

"Now a wooden drum was brought forth and set down for Uzume to dance upon. She mounted upon it and began to dance, keeping time with the music by shaking the jingling belled spear. Faster and faster she danced, until as if possessed, in ecstasy, she stripped off her clothes and danced naked and all the deities roared with laughter. Meanwhile Uzume sang a song of which the words were the numbers from 1 to 10; its true meaning was magic, and it had great power.[3]

At last the sun goddess was made exceedingly curious about the merriment before the cave, and she peeped out. She said, "I fancied that because of my retirement, both heaven and earth were in darkness. Why has Uzume danced, and why do all the gods laugh?" Uzume replied, "I dance and they all laugh because there is an honorable deity here who surpasses your glory."[4] As she said this, Ame-no-Futodama held the sakaki tree with the mirror directly before the sun goddess and reflected Amaterasu's image so that she was dazzled and blinded by its brilliance. Ame-no-Tajikara-o-no-Mikoto seized her by the arm and drew her out of the cave. The deities rejoiced, for once again the world was bright with the rays of the sun goddess. Ame-no-Koyane took a rice-straw rope, a shimenawa, and tied it across the entrance to the cave to prevent the sun goddess from going back into her refuge. As they were putting the mirror into the cave, it struck against the rock and received a flaw which remains in it to this day. Then the sun goddess was ceremoniously escorted to her new palace, where she has dwelt in harmony ever since.

The Elements of the Ceremony   The emergence of the sun goddess from the cave and her installation in a new palace built especially for her signify the beginning of a new productive cycle. This ceremony, in which Uzume was a star performer, is regarded as the foundation of Shinto ritual, the formal procedure in following the Way of the Kami. To Shintoists the Celestial Matsuri, although it is called a festival, is less a joyous celebration than it is a sober religious ceremony. It is held for the double purpose of reintegrating the physical with the spiritual self of a person as an individual and of reaffirming the unity of the nation. In general, the following are the successive stages of the matsuri as it is performed in the Shinto ritual:

1. The purification of the site, premises, participants, utensils, and other religious objects.
2. The invocation, or *kami-oroshi,* to bring down the spirit of a particular kami.
3. The presentation of offerings.
4. The exhortation or recitation of norito, magical or potent formulas of prayer.
5. The presentation of the shintai, such as a tamagushi, gohei, or some other object representing the deity.
6. The offering of songs and dances (techniques to attain ecstasy).
7. The delivery of the oracle, or determination by divination.
8. Withdrawal of the offerings made to the kami.
9. The release, or *kami-age,* to send off the deity-spirit of the festival.
10. The feast, the consuming of the food offerings by the participants in the ritual.[5]

Many of the events in the myth describing the Celestial Matsuri will be readily recognized among these ten steps in the present Shinto ritual. A few will be more difficult to identify. The purification, for example, is not clearly mentioned in the myths, but it must have taken place at the meeting of all the deities when they assembled in the bed of the Tranquil River of Heaven, in itself a sacred place and thus capable of purifying those present. The divination, the presentation of offerings of blue and white cloth, the shintai in the form of the mirror, the tamagushi signifying the sacred place, the offering of prayers, and finally the spectacular dance performed by Uzume: all these events related in the myth fit the pattern of the matsuri as eventually it was elaborated for use by the priests of Shinto.

Uzume's Dance For earthbound folk, the high point of the matsuri in heaven is Uzume's dance. It includes certain features, moreover, which link it with a part of the emperor's investiture ceremonies, the Chinkon-sai. Some of these features derive from shamanistic ritual, while others come straight out of farmers' robust realism. The *Kojiki* describes Uzume's performance in some detail. The motifs of ecstasy, nakedness, and divine laughter appear in these few lines: "laying a sounding-board [tub or drum] before the door of the Heavenly Rock-Dwelling, and stamping till she made it resound and doing as if possessed by a Deity, and pulling out the nipples of her breasts, pushing down her skirt-string usque ad privatas partes. Then the Plain of High Heaven shook, and the eight hundred myriad Deities laughed together."[6]

The response of the deities to Uzume's nakedness was not caused by embarrassment but rather because "peasants the world over are notorious for their broad and earthy humour, and . . . the Japanese peasant is no exception."[7] While deities were not peasants, the setting out of which the myth grew was, of course, the life of the rice-growing farmer. Uzume's dance was a display of her sexual charms, revealed in the unembarrassed manner that is common to all such fertility dances. In Japan, dances of a sexual nature are very common among the farm people. There are always plenty of opportunities in farm communities for gathering to eat and drink. When women are present at such parties, and after plenty of *shochu,* the farmers' cheap rice wine, has been drunk, someone will get up to dance. At first, usually, the dancing is a representation of farm work, such as sowing rice or pulling weeds, but before long the dances acquire a sexual character. A buxom housewife will take the floor and perform a dance, thrusting her hips forward to the accompaniment of some very free verses. A stick may be used by a man as a phallus, and a song will be sung in its praise. A cushion folded adroitly, or a *gara,* a pillow stuffed with chaff, covered with a cloth may also be used in such a dance. These dances invariably bring roars of laughter from the assembled company, and after an especially good performance the dancer is offered many drinks and congratulations.[8] Whether or not the people know this, the character of such dances makes them more than merely entertaining. They are also symbolic, referring as they do to the principles of fertility in agriculture as well as among animals and people. The phallus and the gara, the triangular black pillow, we should remember, are among the symbols hung in the ceremonial tree at the Dosojin festival.

The climax of Uzume's dance, of course, is the point at which she achieves the state of ecstasy. In the *Kojiki,* she is described as "doing as if possessed by a Deity." This is the primary goal of the shaman's performance: the point at which the spirit of the shaman leaves his body on its flight to communicate with a deity upon a different cosmic plane. Dancing is only one of the techniques shamans may use in order to attain ecstasy, or self-induced trance; other techniques are playing or listening to the koto, drumming, lustration, and fasting. If these details are not enough to identify Uzume's role in this ceremony, the parts of her costume certainly do identify her as a shaman. Moreover, the chief insignia of the shaman's office is a phallic wand, or baton. The bunch of bamboo

Uzume held in her hand was just such a symbol. The very presence of the phallic baton establishes a positive ambiance for the shaman's ritual, purifying the scene of all contaminating influences.

Headgear   Uzume's headdress, or crown, was made of spindletop leaves, and she also wore a sash of moss. The crown is significant in that a shaman always wears a crown or hat in the performance of rituals. Shamans consider that a great part of their power is resident in crowns. Altaic shamans never perform true ceremonies unless they are wearing a hat.[9]

The Drum   Uzume danced upon an upturned tub, which re-sounded like a drum beneath her stamping feet. Some versions of this story refer to a dance platform, as if Uzume were performing upon the stage of a Noh or Kabuki theater. Ernest Satow thought it was something other than a tub: "Then the *uke,* a sort of circular box, was laid down for Uzume-no-Mikoto to dance upon. (In a picture illustrating this legend which is given in one edition of the *Nakatomi no harai,* the *uke* is represented as being diverted from its proper use to serve as a drum, which is no doubt an error of the draughtsman)."[10]

Satow himself may have been in error. Mircea Eliade's reference to the shamanic drum is quite different: "The drum has a role of the first importance in shamanic ceremonies. Its symbolism is complex, its magical functions many and various. It is indispensable in con-ducting the shamanic seance, whether it carries the shaman to the 'center of the world' or enables him to fly through the air, or sum-mons and 'imprisons' the spirits, or, finally, if the drumming enables the shaman to concentrate and regain contact with the spiritual world through which he is preparing to travel."[11]

Because the shell of his drum is fashioned from the actual wood of the Cosmic Tree, and the drumhead is made from the skin of a stag, deer, or horse, in the ceremony for animating a new drum it "comes to life" through the agency of the shaman and tells of its birth as an animal and about its parents, childhood, and whole life until the instant it was brought down by the hunter's bow. It ends by promising the shaman that it will perform many services for him:[12] "by virtue of his mystical relations with the 're-animated' skin of the drum, the shaman is able to share in the nature of the theriomorphic ancestor; in other words, he can abolish time and re-establish the primordial condition of which the myth tells."[13]

In northeastern Asia, the shaman's drum was decorated with assorted bits of tinkling metal or small bells and with designs of various symbols, such as the sun and moon, the rainbow, horns of deer or stag, concentric circles, horses, and the male and female sex symbols. These icons added to the potency of the magic of the drum.[14] "The drumming at the beginning of the seance, intended to summon the spirits and 'shut them up' in the shaman's drum, constitutes the preliminaries for the ecstatic journey. This is why the drum is called the 'shaman's horse' (Yakut, Buryat). The Altaic drum bears a representation of a horse; when the shaman drums, he is believed to go to the sky on his horse."[15]

The Spear Uzume's spear, decorated with a slender vinelike grass and jingling bells, is a phallic symbol. Izanagi and Izanami created the island of Onogoro using a similar spear.

When the deity Onamochi turned over the lands of Izumo to the envoys of Amaterasu, he also offered them the "land-subduing broad spear" that he had used to pacify and cultivate the land.[16] The people of the land were not subjugated by the spear in battle: rather, the land itself was subdued by being populated through the magic of the procreative power of real phalli, which are symbolized by the spear. It must be remembered that, in mythology, symbols have more than one meaning; and recognizing the fact that spearlike objects can be symbols of authority and office does not rule out their phallic meaning. Indeed, this dual recognition helps to strengthen the political authority by showing that it is based upon the power to bring life into being—or to end it.

Because of its ritual significance, one other part of Uzume's dance must not be passed over. This is her chanting of the numbers one through ten. One very intriguing interpretation of this chanting of the magic numbers, the result of a study by Satow,[17] proposed that the *sounds* that represent the numbers also mean:

> "People, look at the lid!
> Majesty appears, hurrah!
> Our hearts are quite satisfied.
> Behold my bosom and thighs."

If the derivation of this idea is strained, no matter. The important thing is that Satow recognized that Uzume's nudity was purposeful: in exposing her delectable charms to the sun goddess, a deity of fertility, she was reminding Amaterasu of her responsibility for making the earth fruitful. Uzume's act was a way of giving thanks to Amaterasu for producing life. And it was a reminder, so vividly illustrated by the vigor and the charm of the young female body exhibited before Amaterasu's very eyes. Such rituals, in which the young and most beautiful maidens of a village gather to dance before the god of fertility, are still common among many African and South Sea island societies. The fertility dance is not simply a romantic ritual but usually is sensuous, exciting, frenzied, and even a lewd bacchanal, sometimes lasting for hours until finally the dancers fall exhausted. In such fertility dances, wherever they are held, personal sexuality is glorified to illustrate, praise, and please the universal principle of fecundity, which sustains the earth's productivity.

In Japan, the performance of the fertility dances and of the sexual act in a rice paddy at the time of planting invigorated the fertility of the earth. With the farmers' fertility dances, as with Uzume's dance, the sun goddess is being asked to resume her function: winter has passed, they are saying, and now spring must come.

The Ten Sacred Treasures Another interpretation of the magic numbers in Uzume's chant is suggested by other myths in the *Kojiki,* which refer to the Ten Sacred Auspicious Treasures. These treasures, his heavenly heritage, were given by Amaterasu to her grandson Prince Ninigi, who passed them to his son Uma-shimade-no-Mikoto, who in turn transmitted them to his grandson Jimmu, the first emperor of Japan. Thus, they became the sacred symbols of the imperial family and of Shinto. These treasures are:

1. The Mirror of the Far-off Shore
2. The Mirror of the Near Shore
3. The Eight-hand-span Sword
4. The Life-inspiring Jewel
5. The Jewel of Perfect Health and Strength
6. The Jewel of Resuscitating the Dead
7. The Jewel of Warding Off Evil from Roads
8. The Serpent-preventing Scarf
9. The Bee-preventing Scarf
10. The Scarves of Various Specters and Efficacies

The belief is that these treasures have the power to ward off evil, restore life, control the rise and fall of the tides, and conquer in battle, and have other miraculous attributes as well. The *Kojiki* refers to an ancient ceremony called Mitama Furishiki, that is, Shaking the August Jewels, the ritual for which is described in this way: "In case of illness shake these treasures and repeat to them the words, 'one, two, three, four, five, six, seven, eight, nine, ten.' If thou doest so the dead will certainly return to life."[18]

The magical power of the scarf is illustrated by the story in which Susano-o tests his son-in-law, Okuni-nushi, by putting him into a room filled with snakes, bees, and centipedes.[19]

Many Shintoists believe that the ten treasures actually exist, although it is said that no one has ever seen them. The chief priests of the Grand Shrines at Ise will neither admit nor deny that they do exist.[20] Other people think that they are only epithets applied to concepts of spiritual stages in Shinto exercises, which correspond to the ten numbers used for the stages in the emperor's pacification ceremony (described below). The belief is that the spirit of the devotee comes to life at the fourth stage, becomes constructive at the fifth, and gains the ability to serve others in the succeeding stages. Thus, in the pacification ceremony the tying of the ten knots in the silken cord appears to be an affirmation of the emperor's descent from the sun goddess, and therefore of his divinity.

The Ritualists Among the deities who participated in the Celestial Matsuri were five important ritualists, and these five were included in the entourage that Amaterasu selected to send down to earth with Prince Ninigi. During the fourth and fifth centuries A.D., when the country was being conquered by the horse-riding invaders from Korea, the chiefs of the five companies that dominated the social structure of the Japanese people claimed descent from those five celestial ritualists. At that time the nobility were distinguished according to an elaborate system of ranks, which reflected their power and influence, clan lineage, and occupations. The hereditary chiefs of some clans, corporations, and guilds gained considerable power close to the throne. Five such prominent groups served the emperor: the Nakatomi and the Imbe in religious capacities, and in military matters the Otomo (hereditary bodyguards of the emperor), Kumebe (Corporation of Soldiers), and Mononobe (Corporation of Armorers). Another reference to the five families as continuing the five-clan organization of the horse-riding people is the story of the five wondrous princes who were born of Amaterasu's jewels, which Susano-o chewed and spat out as a magical mist.

Summary At any rate, the divine origin of Shinto and of the Japanese nation was established through the bringing down to earth of the Celestial Matsuri, deeply rooted in phallicism and shamanism, complete with high priests, a phased ritual, sacred symbols, prayers, and formulas, and with a central deity—the sun goddess, Amaterasu.

But, in addition to all this, there was Uzume the female shaman, the deity of sexual attraction, who, at the Eight Crossroads of Heaven, eased a problem that nearly prevented the celestial heritage from taking its intended course.

THE CELESTIAL HERITAGE

The myth of Prince Ninigi's descent from heaven to earth is the account of the creation of the people of Japan in the image of their celestial deities, complete with a religious system and a heavenly prince, an ancestor of emperors. A subplot to this drama is the account of the meeting of two phallic deities, Ame-no-Uzume-no-Mikoto and Saruta-hiko-no-Mikoto, who by order of Prince Ninigi are given to each other as man and wife. Thereby, these powers too are established as being divine, full members of the Shinto pantheon, even though they began their careers at a much lower social level.

In the *Kojiki,* the myths about Ninigi are separated chronologically from the account of the Celestial Matsuri by a series that describes the consolidation of the land by earthly kami and the pacification of the land by heavenly kami. These myths presumably account for the invasion, settling, conquest, and development of the country. When all that had been accomplished, the earth was made ready to receive its divine prince. The following version of this advent is based on both the *Kojiki* and the *Nihongi.*

Prince Ninigi's Escort   When the sun goddess was assured that the land had been subdued and that the forces of Izumo would cooperate in receiving her representative, Amaterasu selected Prince Ninigi as her envoy to rule over the land. Preparing Ninigi for his journey, Amaterasu and Taka-mi-musubi, the High Integrating Deity, gave him a number of instructions. They also selected an escort to assist him in fulfilling his responsibilities. Then Amaterasu entrusted Ninigi with the sacred symbols of office: the divine Eight-hand Mirror, Yata-no-Kagami; the Fire-quelling Sword (or Grass-cutting Sword, according to some), Kusanagi-no-Tsurugi; the sacred jewels; and the sacred spear. As she gave him these treasures, Amaterasu said: "My child, when thou lookest upon this mirror, let it be as if thou wert looking at me. Let it be with thee on thy couch and in thy hall, and let it be with thee a holy mirror. . . ."[1]

She also instructed the deity Omoi-kane (Thought-includer) to take in hand her affairs and carry on the government below.[2] And Amaterasu gave to Ninigi some rice ears from the sacred garden, to be planted on earth. The *Kojiki* mentions one further gift, the Ten Treasures, which have been discussed in relation to Uzume's chanting of the magic numbers.

The Imperial Edict While all the deities who had been selected to go with Prince Ninigi waited, Amaterasu issued an imperial edict: "The Heavenly Ancestors (i.e., Amaterasu-o-mi-kami and Takami-Musubi) caused Ame-no-koyane, Futo-tama and Ame-no-uzume to descend from Heaven, in attendance upon the Heavenly Grandson, and then issued the following Imperial Edict: 'We, on our own part, shall worship in the Sacred Precincts of Divine Fences and Heavenly Rock Boundaries on behalf of the Heavenly Grandson, and ye, Ame-no-koyane and Futo-tama, shall go down to the Central Land of Reed-plains with the Divine *himorogi* and reverently pray to the Kami for the welfare of the Heavenly Grandson, guarding him in your attendance under the same roof against all emergencies, and serving him with the rice of the consecrated paddy-fields of which we partook in Heaven above—the original rice-seeds brought thence here below—and Futo-tama shall perform his duties on the Earth with the Kami belonging to different hereditary corporations just as they were wont to do in Heaven.' Thus those Kami were transferred from Heaven to the suite of the Heavenly Grandson when he descended to this Earth."[3]

The entourage of attendants assembled to escort Ninigi to earth included, in addition to the five ritualists already mentioned (who had also participated in the Celestial Matsuri), Toyo-uke-hime-no-Kami (Deity of Luxuriant Food), Ame-no-Tajikara-o-no-Kami (Hand-strength Male Deity), Omoi-kane-no-Kami (Deity Thought-includer), Ame-no-Oshi-no-Mikoto (Heavenly Great Wondrous Deity), Ama-tsu-Kuma-no-Mikoto (His Augustness Heaven's Round Eyes), Ame-no-Iwato-wake-no-Kami (Deity Rock Door-opener of Eternal Night), Toyo-Iwamado-no-Kami (Luxuriant

Rock True Gate Deity), Saruta-hiko (Monkey Rice Field Prince), and several others.

Among all those gods, Saruta-hiko was an earth deity, and he did not take part in the ceremony held in front of Amaterasu's cave dwelling. Neither did the food deity Ugadama-no-Mikoto.

The Phallic Deities of the Eight Crossroads Before Prince Ninigi descended to earth, he sent scouts to find out the condition of the land. They came back and reported: "In Ame-no-yachimata [Eight Crossroads of Heaven] we met a deity seven fathoms tall, the length of whose nose is seven hands. A brilliance shines from his mouth and from his posteriors, which lights up the heaven and the earth; his eyes are like eight-hand mirrors."[4]

Ninigi instructed his scouts to learn who this awesome deity was. Upon returning, they reported that they were unable to face him because his brilliance made them dizzy. Then Ninigi commanded Ame-no-Uzume-no-Mikoto, saying: "Thou art superior to others in the power of thy looks. Thou hadst better go and question him."[5]

So Uzume went, and when she approached the deity she bared her breasts, pushing down the band of her garment below her navel, and with a mocking laugh asked him his name and why he was blocking the road. He identified himself as the earth deity Saruta-hiko, and said that he was merely waiting to escort Prince Ninigi's party downward to the Central Land of Reed Plains.

Uzume returned to heaven and reported to Ninigi in detail. Then Ninigi was safely escorted by means of the Floating Bridge of Heaven to the peak of Kushifuru, in Hyuga Province in Kyushu. After looking about, and finding himself satisfied, he built a palace and dwelt there. He then ordered Uzume to become the bride of Saruta-hiko, and she acquired the title Duchess of Saru, or Sarume-kimi, Monkey Female Duchess.

Not long after that, Saruta-hiko went out fishing, his hand was caught by a giant shellfish, and he drowned. As his body sank to the bottom of the sea, he was given the name Bottom-touching August Spirit. Now Uzume called all the fishes of the sea together, and they pledged to serve Prince Ninigi, all except for the *bêche-de-mer*, which refused to open its mouth. For this reason Uzume slit open its mouth with her dagger. Thus, when the first fruits were offered to the emperor each year, in the province of Shima (present-day Mie Prefecture) some were always offered to Ame-no-Uzume as well.

The Meaning of the Myth In the two myths in which Uzume appears, she is revealed as a female shaman, a dancing miko, a deity of sexual attraction, and a wise woman, superior because of her beauty. She plays her role as the charming, irresistible female with flair and effectiveness—and confidence.

Saruta-hiko, as he is first encountered at the Eight Crossroads of Heaven, is described as a giant with blazing eyes and dazzling light emanating from his mouth and buttocks. He identifies himself as an earth god. The "saru" of his name means monkey or ape, and these creatures serve as messengers to Yama-no-Kami, the mountain deity. Stone carvings of monkeys are often found along the road-sides of agricultural villages. Colonies of monkeys still roam through some forests in Japan.[6] The monkey's sexual activity distinguishes him, along with the horse, as a most exemplary phallic symbol. Saruta-hiko, as a symbol of sexual robustness standing at the Eight Crossroads of Heaven and giving forth a blinding radiance, could well be cast in the image of a monkeylike creature, such as the hamadryad baboon, which has bright scarlet buttocks and flashing red eyes. At least this is one reasonable explanation for Saruta-hiko's physical characteristics as they are described in the myth, even though the baboon was not present in Japan.

The story of Saruta-hiko's death by drowning seems to be a curious turn of events, upon first reflection. However, when we note that three deities were born from his drowning, we recognize that his death was an act of self-sacrifice similar to that of Ugadama, the food deity. Her death assured the productivity of the land; his assured the productivity of the sea. Thus, in fishing villages at the time of the Dosojin festival, the ritual of purification is performed by taking mikoshi out to sea to meet the spirit of the kami, who ensures a good harvest. The shintai, or manifestation of the god, placed within the mikoshi is usually a phallus-shaped stone. Saruta-hiko's relationship with field and mountain deities of fertility is extended to the domain of the sea.

The creation myths, the Celestial Matsuri, and the celestial heritage disclose the interest and concern of the recorders of those stories in the affairs of their country on several different but interrelated levels. The myths reveal ancient religious practices that were intended to effect agricultural fertility through rituals based on magic, the sacrifice of animal and human life, and the worship of the sun goddess and of a host of other deities. The course of events in the development of early Japanese culture followed the pattern normal to human societies, going from conflict through compromise to synthesis. Nevertheless, it is apparent that at any stage in Japan's early history there were many overlapping and conflicting beliefs dating from prehistoric times, and that these included animism, phallicism, hero and ancestor worship, and more than one form of shamanism. These pre-Shinto concepts do not have neat or exact lines of demarcation; and while they seem to be religious in character, in that they pay respect to the great forces of nature, like all creeds of uneasy men they are also influenced by the deeper motives of fear and yearning.

Inasmuch as many modern scholars of Shrine Shinto assiduously avoid any reference to folk cult beliefs based upon phallicism, it is especially interesting to observe that Saruta-hiko and Uzume, the two most popular and useful deities of folk religion or of cult Shinto, were recognized as being very important religious entities and were included in the Shinto pantheon by the authority of those who compiled the official records of ancient times.

There should be no surprise, then, in the fact that the phallic gods should have become the most popular deities in all of Shinto. This was possible precisely because they were created at the folk level and continue to be worshiped by the masses. While there are thousands of deities, or kami, most of these are of local character, relating to specific villages, sites, or shrines. Notwithstanding the cults of some powerful kami—such as Hachiman, god of war and guardian of the nation, whose shrines are scattered throughout Japan—the influence of these kami is limited, while the power of the phallic deities is universal. At the level of folk worship, people generally revere Saruta-hiko and Uzume above Amaterasu, the symbolic ancestor of the nation, since this man-wife deity, as Dosojin, is at the very root of the two most important human concerns—the reproduction of their own kind and the getting of food. The joining of the goddess of cereals, Ugadama, with the phallic deities Saruta-hiko and Uzume, to form a triad is both logical and efficient, since thereby one deity is made to serve both needs. The gods in this triad, together with several other deities, are installed at Fushimi-Inari Shrine near Kyoto, and all of them together are called Inari-sama, or simply Inari. Inari's messenger is the white fox, and commonly the fox is mistaken for the deity—which is natural enough, since once upon a time the fox was regarded as the kami of rice.

RICE AND CEREMONY

The beauty of the Japanese landscape owes a great deal to the cultivation of rice. In the lowland areas, fields bright green with rice shoots extend as far as the eye can see. Occasional farmhouses, all but concealed by closely spaced tall trees that provide the farm compound with shelter from wind and sun, float in a sea of bluish green as the watered paddies reflect the azure sky. In some places almost every usable plot of land has been reserved for the growing of rice. The great masses of people who have migrated to the cities live there in crowded contrast to those who dwell in the idyllic spaciousness of the countryside. The crowding of human beings in the islands of Japan is apparent only in the cities. The countryside is still the Central Reed Plain of mythology. Parts of the mountain country, too, have been disciplined by rice paddies, contained by terraces built up with stone walls, rising above one another, often to the brow of a high hill. The earth to fill those terraces was carried on weary backs from nearby forests hundreds of years ago. The water irrigating those fields flows by gravity from the highest terrace to the next below it, until the lowest level has been reached. In the latter part of summer, when irrigation is stopped, the fully grown rice covers the fields like a sea of undulating green moss. When one stands at the edge of such a sea in a remote mountain valley overhung by an early morning mist, the beauty and the power of nature are felt with a sense of mystery and wonder.

Rice Planting and Harvest   The planting of rice begins with preparations in February, when the emperor prays for divine assistance for the people who work in the fields. Ceremonies are held at the Grand Shrines at Ise, asking the gods to bless the rice seeds. A little later, priests in a number of shrines hold ceremonies where rice in the form of mochi is offered the resident deities, thereby renewing favorable relations with them for the coming year.

During the cool first days in May, farmers sow the rice seed in order to obtain the seedlings. These will be transplanted to the paddies in June, and there will grow until they mature sometime in September or October. By the end of May, the actual transplanting is started. It continues, field by field, through the month of June and into July. The emperor himself participates ceremonially in the labor of planting rice, just as it is done throughout all Japan, by personally setting out rice shoots in the fields of the Shugaku-in Palace gardens, north of Kyoto.

Each year fields all over the country are planted according to neighborhood schedules so that periodically each farmer in an area can be assured an early harvest. The transplanting is done cooperatively, and often large fields are finished in a day. This backbreaking work is performed mostly by women, who stand shin deep in the flooded fields, rooting seedling after seedling in the soft mud an arm's length below. The work never stops, in rain or sunshine, in heat or in cold, as long as there is light to work by. It is an extraordinarily beautiful sight to watch a lake of muddy water turning green as the thousands of fragile spiky shoots are set out in advancing rows during the course of only a few hours.

The rice-transplanting festival, the Ta-ue Matsuri, which is observed throughout the country, is said to have been originated in the third century A.D. by Empress Jingu. Upon returning from her expedition to Korea, she introduced many new ideas and techniques, including the systematic cultivation of rice. The empress chose a plot of ground at Sumiyoshi Shrine near Naniwa (present-day Osaka) for the first planting of rice, and this was done with appropriate religious safeguards. In places like Sumiyoshi Shrine the rice-planting ceremony is still very elaborate and formal. It includes ceremonial dances, purification rituals, and the planting of seedlings by elected women, and all these rites are watched by a large number of people. In other places the ceremony may be performed by a Shinto priest dressed in a special costume and wearing a white mask. Here the ritual may be mainly a dance of wild gyrating movements, performed not in a shrine but out-of-doors on the floor of a small pavilion. In a ceremony held recently at a Shinto shrine in the Five Lakes district of Mount Fuji, musicians who sat on the floor in one corner of the pavilion included a farmer, a municipal clerk, a small-businessman, a young priest, and a schoolteacher. The little wooden pavilion stood under towering cryptomeria trees, part of a mountain forest. The eerie dance drama had no spectator other than those of us who had stumbled upon it, drawn from afar by the music like his followers to the sounds of the Pied Piper.

In such rituals, the prayers for a good harvest invoke the deities to control the elements of nature in its many moods so that the growing season goes well—that the rains will come on time and in proper amounts; that typhoons do not flatten the rice when it is half grown, thus burying the green heads to rot in mud; and that flocks of birds do not rob the ripening heads of their seeds. The most disastrous of all the calamities that can affect the rice crop is drought. Although Japan appears to be a lush, verdant garden, perpetually green, the months of summer often bring severe dry spells. At such times, the god of rain is enjoined, through a variety of schemes, enchantments, threats, bribes, and prayers, to abate his wrath and to send down the rain upon the thirsting land.

Farmers in the Kyoto district climb to the top of Mount Atago, where they bind a statue of Jizo with ropes of rice straw, promising to release him as soon as he intervenes with the gods to make rain.[1] Here Jizo performs the same service as Dosojin.

The farmers of the Ninabe district in Aomori Prefecture gather at Gongen Shrine on Mount Orizume. They offer sakè to the shrine's god, and require the chief priest to drink with them. When the opportune moment arrives, they throw the priest into the pond, and back in again as he tries to come out. This is repeated time and again, until the priest is subdued and quietly remains immersed in the pond. The reason for this ritual lies in the belief that the shrine's deity, being fond of the priest, will bring rain to save his faithful servant from the cruel treatment of the farmers.[2]

Methods vary with place and people. Thus, "the farmers of the lake district around Mount Fuji consider the five Fuji lakes as sacred and protect them against defilement, but when they desire rain in a season of drought, they purposely throw dried cattle bones into the lake in the belief that this pollution will raise the ire of the *kami* of the lakes so that they will make it rain as punishment."[3]

The customs for bringing rain seem to be based upon two principles: that of appeasement and that of irritation. Almost all mountains, streams, and rivers have kami, or tutelary deities. In order to obtain rain in times of drought, farmers follow local practices of making offerings of food, sakè, prayers, and dances to those deities in the belief that they have been offended and therefore are withholding the rain. Or, acting on the other principle, some farmers will commit an act of despoliation in order to irritate the deities so that in retaliation they will "punish" the people by causing bad weather and rain. These customs show a great variety and originality in method, and most of them have been employed since ancient times.

Festivals of the Year   The festivals held throughout the year in Japan are almost without number. There are thousands of shrines and temples, and each has its tutelary kami, who is honored at least once annually. Ceremonies to respect the rice deity, Inari, are performed throughout the country, and each village holds a festival of its own.

The most important festivals nationally are those recognized by Shrine Shinto and the Imperial Household. The most important festival of all is the Daijo-sai, which occurs soon after a new emperor is enthroned. This ceremony is based upon the annual Autumn Festival of New Rice Crops, the Niiname-sai, and is preceded by the Pacification Ceremony, the Chinkon-sai, and also by elaborate year-long preliminaries involved in growing and harvesting the sacred rice which is to be used on that occasion.

The following partial list of festivals connected with the growing and harvesting of rice is drawn from Kato's *Study of Shinto*:

I. The Great Festival: Daijo-sai, or Great Harvest Festival; performed at the ceremony of the investiture of the emperor.
II. The Middle Festivals
    1. The Toshigoi or Kinen-sai, Festival for Praying for a Rich Harvest; held on the fourth day of the second month.
    2. The Tsukinami Matsuri, or Monthly Festivals; held on the eleventh day of the sixth and twelfth months.
    3. The Kanname-sai, or Autumn Festival of Thanksgiving, at the Ise Grand Shrines, on which occasion new rice of the year is presented to the ancestral sun goddess; held on the eleventh day of the ninth month.
    4. The Niiname-sai (Shinjo-sai), or autumn Festival of New Rice Crops; performed regularly in the years between the rare occurrences of the Daijo-sai.
    5. Kamo-no-Matsuri, Festival of the Kamo Shrines, the guardian shrines of the old capital, Kyoto; held during the fourth month.
III. The Lesser Festivals
    Under this category are listed thirteen festivals dedicated to the deities of various well-known shrines and to the deity of wind and the deity of fire, and to appeasing the evil deities of epidemic pestilences.

The festivals dedicated to the deities of rice, besides those listed in Kato's second category, include those held in thousands of villages and local shrines. Examples of these are the Hatsu-uma-sai, Festival of the First Day of the Horse, performed especially at Fushimi-Inari Shrine but also in many other places; the Ta-ue Matsuri, Rice-transplanting Festival, of which a spectacular version is performed at Sumiyoshi Shrine near Osaka; the Kanname-sai, Autumn Festival of Thanksgiving, performed at Ise on behalf of the emperor's ancestors; and all of those festivals dedicated to deities like Dosojin, Yama-no-Kami, Ta-no-Kami, Otoshi-no-Kami, and others connected with rice fields and rice growing.

These annual rice ceremonies, and the careful preparations for them, indicate how completely and intimately the religious ideas of the people were associated with rice. Rice was life itself, and its supply depended upon the efficacy of the rituals that solicited the cooperation of the kami of nature. At the folk level, Inari-sama responded to the farmers' needs. At the state level, in response to the imperial edict issued by the sun goddess, the emperor must achieve a spiritual reunion with his heavenly ancestor by performing the Great Harvest Festival, the Daijo-sai. The mythological Celestial Matsuri performed by Uzume and the Great Harvest Festival performed by the emperor, because of certain shamanistic elements shared in common, establish the fact that both have their roots in very ancient beliefs and practices.

Floyd H. Ross, in *Shinto: The Way of Japan,* has given a detailed account of the Daijo-sai as it is performed today. The brief description of the dual ceremony that follows indicates certain ritual phrases and shamanistic symbols that appear in the Celestial Matsuri. Thus, the similarity in form and the elements shared in common by the Celestial Matsuri, the imperial Daijo-sai, and the commoners' Dosojin festival are established.

Daijo-sai: The Great Harvest Festival The exact date for the Daijo-sai is decided by court officials a year in advance and is announced to the people. Later, two rice fields near Kyoto, one to the east and one to the west, are selected by tortoise-shell divination for growing the rice to be used in the great ceremony. The fields are fenced and purified, according to ancient ritual. A small shrine is built nearby, dedicated to the eight kami of agriculture. Two of these are already familiar to us: Ugadama-no-Mikoto (also known as Miketsu-no-Kami), deity of food, and Ame-no-Uzume-no-Mikoto (or Omiya-no-Me-no-Kami, Great Palace Female Deity). The first four sheaves of rice to be gathered at harvest time are offered to the eight deities at the little shrine, and then these same sheaves are reserved for use by the new emperor in the Daijo-sai ceremony. For one month before that important occasion, he practices abstinence and limits his daily routines and duties.[4]

A few days before the ceremony, two small identical pavilions are built within the palace grounds at Kyoto. These pavilions are called the Yuki-den and Suki-den, and they accommodate the deities of heaven and the deities of earth, respectively.[5] The interior of each pavilion is bare of furnishings except for two food mats placed side by side, one for the kami and one for the emperor.

To the west of the food mat of the kami is the kami seat, a dais built of eight layers of tatami, covered with a length of white raw silk. A triangular pillow, known as the *saka makura,* "hill pillow," is laid at the head of this dais. Upon this couch are placed a simple folded garment made of white silk, a fan, a comb, and a pair of slippers.[6] This altar-seat is the symbol of the couch upon which Prince Ninigi kept the Three Sacred Treasures that Amaterasu gave him before he came down to earth: the divine mirror, the sacred sword, and the hallowed jewels.[7]

The mirror is identified as the shintai of the sun goddess, and apparently the articles of apparel placed upon the couch are for her use. The triangular pillow is reminiscent of the hiichi, the black cloth pillow that is hung in the ceremonial tree at the Dosojin festival.

Chinkon-sai: The Great Pacification Ceremony: The Chinkon-sai is held on the eve of the Daijo-sai and is a preparation for it, in that it is intended to pacify the fourfold mitama of the new emperor and to integrate body and spirit into a harmonious whole, thus ensuring his well-being and usefulness to the nation.

The ceremony consists of four parts: abstinence, purification, exorcism, and spirit pacification. The emperor enters his personal meditation shrine, the *shinden,* and sits before the altar. The shrine is dedicated to the eight musubi, the initial creator deities, who were born of themselves in the Plain of High Heaven. The tatami of the shinden are so arranged as to provide nine squares, upon which these eight deities are accommodated according to rank. The ninth place in the center of the room is occupied symbolically by the group as a whole. The emperor makes the nine round out to ten, the perfect or magical number: the tenth level of existence connotes spiritual perfection, the state of being a kami.

With a prayer, the chief priest exhorts the eight kami to descend to their places by way of the himorogi placed upon the altar. Next, the Ten Sacred Treasures that Prince Ninigi brought with him in his descent from heaven are placed before the kami. These are of four kinds: mirrors, swords, jewels, and scarves. Then, while a virgin priestess, a miko, just outside the sacred room but in view of the emperor, begins to dance upon an upturned tub, with a spear in one hand and jingling bells in the other, the chief priest takes a silk cord from a box and holds it before him. The dancer strikes the tub with the shaft of the spear, and at each blow the priest ties a knot in the cord until he has made ten. Then the chief priest takes the emperor's sacred robes from another box and shakes them out ten times. The tying of the ten knots and the shaking of the robes ten times have their precedent in Uzume's chanting of the magic numbers one to ten, and in the ten sacred treasures. In this instance, their ritual use helps the emperor to reach the spiritual level of a kami.

The Chinkon-sai closes as the silk cord, the ceremonial garb, and the treasures are put away. The emperor prepares for the Great Harvest Festival, the Daijo-sai, which begins forthwith.[8]

The Ritual of the Daijo-sai   In the evening, after the conclusion of the Chinkon-sai, the emperor, clad in white robes made of raw silk, proceeds from his personal meditation shrine to the first of the two pavilions. The court musicians set the rhythms for the "Song of Pounding Rice." Outside, young dancing girls mime the motions of pounding rice in the old way, with mortar and pestle. A high priest waits for the emperor in the outer room of the Yuki-den as he recites prayers. The procession that escorts the emperor includes a colorful assembly of priests and female attendants who carry the utensils and items needed for the sacred food offering. Entering the Yuki-den first, two female attendants conduct the emperor into the inner chamber. He takes his seat upon a hard mat. The priest reads sacred prayers addressed to the kami of heaven and to the sun goddess. Offerings of steamed rice, millet, and white and black sakè are made to the kami. The emperor partakes of the same foods. Following a brief rite of purification, the emperor withdraws and is escorted to the Suki-den, where the ceremony is repeated, this time addressed to the earth deities who are enshrined at Ise, especially to Toyo-uke-hime-no-Kami, goddess of cereals. Fully twenty-four hours are consumed in the double ceremony of the Chinkon-sai and the Daijo-sai, in which both the sun goddess, Amaterasu, and the food goddess, Toyo-uke (or Ugadama), the two principal kami at the Inner and Outer shrines of Ise, respectively, are venerated.[9]

The Emperor as Kami   By means of the Chinkon-sai, the emperor pacifies and purifies his spirit; and in the Daijo-sai he expresses his gratitude to the great deities of heaven and earth, most especially to Amaterasu and to Toyo-uke. Toward the end of the Daijo-sai, once in each pavilion, the emperor offers rice to these deities and eats some of it himself, thereby acknowledging Amaterasu's gift of the first rice seeds, which Prince Ninigi brought down from heaven, and Toyo-uke's continuing beneficence in producing plentiful crops.

Early agricultural people were reluctant to taste the yearly first fruits of any crop until some pious ceremony had been performed that made it safe for them to do so. The reason for this reluctance appears to lie in the feeling that the first fruits either are the property of a deity or actually contain a divinity. In Japan, the first deity of rice, Inari, was believed to be the spirit of the growing rice plant, which dwelt within it, and the harvested grain was thought to be divine. Ross has pointed out the significance of sharing food, as symbolized in the ritual of the Daijo-sai: "In Oriental society generally, to eat together meant to become a member of that group, an intimate member. By eating the same food with *kami*, whether the main *kami* in the ceremony was a goddess of food or Amaterasu (the Sun-Goddess), the emperor belonged to the class of *kami*: he was accepted as having the same qualities as the *kami*."[10]

Ross's conclusion was that the emperor is a "living *kami*" or a kami incarnate. The emperor's mind-heart, his *kokoro*, is the mind-heart of a kami.[11] The direct participation of the emperor on behalf of the welfare of the nation, to ensure its food supply, illustrates the attitude of Japanese toward nature. It stands in marked contrast to that of people in Western or Christian nations, who seem to regard nature as a resource to be conquered and exploited for man's aggrandizement. The Japanese have never regarded nature as unfriendly or hostile, or as a warehouse to be looted—at least until recently.

The manner in which such fundamental attitudes toward nature and life, forming slowly at the folk level, developed in Japan into national acceptance is reflected in the rise to prominence of Inari, the primeval spirit of rice.

THE DEITIES OF RICE AND SEX

The great era of building Shinto shrines covered a period of about five hundred years, from the founding of the Naiku, or Inner Shrine, at Ise in 4 B.C.,* to the construction of the Geku, the Outer Shrine, of Ise in A.D. 478.[1] This proliferation showed how completely the mythological deities had been accepted into the system of Shinto. With the introduction of Buddhism in Japan, about A.D. 552, native religious ideas were faced with great competition. Magnificent Buddhist temples and monasteries appeared, on mountaintops and in cities as well, to lure converts to a new faith. Buddhism gave great impetus to Chinese learning and culture, and tried to monopolize religious thought by its efforts to absorb indigenous Japanese traditions, including the deities that had risen out of nature worship and spiritism. In spite of Buddhist influence upon the nobility and imperial family at the court, however, the great mass of the people throughout the rest of the country were very slow to give up the familiar deities that they had inherited from their forefathers.

At the beginning of the Nara period (646–794), these beliefs in nature deities were recognized officially when arrangements were made in 711 to allow the worship of the deity of rice at Fushimi on Mount Inari.[2] The origin, development, and rise to ascendancy of Fushimi-Inari Shrine illustrate the manner in which people gradually change their ideas about their gods. At Fushimi-Inari, as elsewhere, the first deities to be enshrined were real objects or animal spirits.

*The corrected date appears to be the twenty-sixth year of the reign of Emperor Suinin, or A.D. 275.

But in the course of only a few centuries these gradually acquired human form.

Fushimi-Inari Shrine The first large structure at this site was built in A.D. 832. After that, its appeal as a place of worship was indicated by the addition of other deities, and by the favors bestowed upon them and upon the shrine by the imperial court. As time went on, imperial patronage elevated the stature of this shrine and extended the popularity of worship to a very broad base, which eventually became also a very powerful one.[3] "During the Heian period (794–1185) the many historical references to the Inari Shrine at Fushimi, and Inari worship show its development from a farmers' fertility cult to a nationwide worship."[4] Those historical references indicate three trends: (a) the effort of Shinto to regain its hold upon the ruling classes as the official religion; (b) the recognition by the rulers of the strength of nature worship and their effort through it to gain favor with the people; and (c) the struggle between Buddhism and Shinto, and, eventually, the adaptability of the Buddhist hierarchy. When Buddhism failed to eradicate folk-cult beliefs and their deities, it moved to absorb them, although it placed native deities in a position subordinate to its own. The amalgamation of Buddhist and Shinto deities, as they appear in sculptured form, is visual evidence of the compromises effected between the two religions.

While the imperial court supported Buddhism, it was put under pressure to support the Shinto heritage. For example, the court extended its recognition to Inari worship by raising the rank of the shrine at Fushimi. However, Buddhism also moved to benefit from the persisting popularity of nature worship by building Buddhist temples on the grounds of the shrine at Fushimi (as well as at many other places), and by participating in official Shinto ceremonies. In that way, the Buddhist effort was successful in making Shinto gods appear to be manifestations of buddhas and of many different bodhisattvas.

Rise to Prominence of Fushimi-Inari Shrine At any rate, the rise to prominence of Fushimi-Inari Shrine moved another step forward when, in 908, the minister Fujiwara Tokihira constructed three buildings there. In 942, Emperor Suzaku raised Fushimi-Inari Shrine to the rank of Sho-ichi, or Higher First Class. Sometime after 1072, Fushimi-Inari Shrine as a whole became one of the twenty-two most important shrines in the nation. By 1178 it ranked sixth among the seven most important. During the Kamakura period (1185–1336), Buddhism reached the peak of its influence, while Shintoism in general waned, as did Fushimi-Inari Shrine with it.

Even so, in 1239 the shrine moved into third place among the nation's five most important Shinto shrines. The strength and constancy of Inari worship persisted for the next six hundred years, and in 1871 Inari was raised to the rank of Kampei Taisha, Grand National Shrine, the highest possible designation.[5] Thus, Fushimi-Inari became a place for "national worship and this meant that all matters relating to the country at large as well as matters of international relations were reported to the deities enshrined there."[6] The cult of Inari passed through many vicissitudes in the course of its history without losing its hold upon the people, eventually becoming a national cult having a close relationship with the imperial family.

The purpose of tracing the origin and development of Fushimi-Inari Shrine is to focus, finally, on the nature of the deities to whom this place is dedicated. Who are these deities? And why are they worshiped there, in one of the three most important shrines in Japan?

The cult of Inari started with farmers in their reverence for the spirit of rice, and in the course of time it became popular with merchants, artisans, government officials, and a branch of the imperial family. Nine major deities are honored at Fushimi-Inari, and many lesser ones whose shrines are scattered on the mountainside. Today, the average worshiper makes no effort to distinguish among the varied deities of the Inari pantheon but addresses himself to Inari-sama, an inclusive name that gathers all the several spirits into one.

The Major Deities of Fushimi-Inari Shrine   D. C. Buchanan, who lived next to Fushimi-Inari Shrine near Kyoto for a year, and spent about ten years in making a thorough study of the Inari cult throughout Japan, identified its deities, according to rank, as follows:

"First is Uga-no-mitama-no-kami, Food August Spirit Deity; the second is Saruta-hiko-no-Mikoto, Monkey Rice-field Prince; the third is O-ichi-hime, Great First Princess, who also is recognized as being the deity of sex attraction, Ame-no-Uzume-no-Mikoto, Heaven-alarming Female Augustness. These three function as a triad, and their messenger is the fox. The fourth and fifth deities are Onamochi and O-toshi-no-kami. The former is a son of Susano-o and is known under many names, including Okuni-nushi and Daikoku, one of the Seven Gods of Luck."[7]

Another source[8] identifies the five most important deities of Fushimi-Inari Shrine as being Ame-no-Minaka-nushi, Taka-mi-musubi, Kami-musubi, Saruta-hiko, and Uga-no-Mitama. The first three are creator-deities who preceded Izanagi and Izanami in the mythic hierarchy.

Still another source states that these deities are Ame-no-Minaka-nushi, Izanagi, Izanami, Ho-musubi, and Uga-no-Mitama. (But in 1973 one of the priests at Fushimi-Inari Shrine told this writer that Izanagi and Izanami had never been included among its pantheon.)

The deity who appears in all three reports is Uga-no-Mitama, while Saruta-hiko appears in two. But no one questions the fact that the shrine is dedicated to the deity of rice. Six additional deities connected with the growing of rice are included in the top ranks of the Inari pantheon, as well as seven minor deities of good luck, who have risen to recognition because of their popularity among all segments of the Japanese people.

Origins of the Rice Deity The religious customs and practices of the people of the prehistoric period apparently were based upon elements of phallic worship, sun worship, burial cults, and indigenous as well as imported shamanism, all designed to deal with the unpredictable behavior of nature and the spirit world. The belief in the magic power by which the rice plant grew from a single tiny seed to reproduce a thousandfold was reinforced by worshiping the rice plant as being divine. Later, the plant was considered to be the dwelling place of the spirit that had the power to make it grow. In time, this deity of the rice plant was known as Inari. Hirata Atsutane in 1811 derived the meaning of Inari in this way: *ine* means "rice plant" and *nari* is "flowering" or "fertile." Thus Inari is the deity of the flowering or fertile rice plant. A second derivation and a simpler one is based on *ine,* rice plant, and *naru,* to grow: the growing rice plant is the symbol of the deity[10]

Thus, Inari—the deity of the growing rice plant—became the first deity of food long before the Japanese began to put their mythology into writing. The personification of Inari followed much later, as did the extension of calendrical practices and sun worship to the creation of the sun goddess, Amaterasu. The deity of food, Inari, conceived in prehistoric times as the spirit of rice, sometimes also appeared in the form of a fox, inasmuch as foxes often were seen frolicking or running through rice fields. The fox was believed to be another embodiment of the spirit in the rice plant. When foxes were observed coupling in a rice field, peasants reasoned that the animals were fertilizing the rice plants. The prime belief of phallic cults held that, by performing the sexual act at the times of seed sowing and of harvest, human beings could magically influence the growth and development of rice plants. This was an extension of their own procreative powers. In this respect, divine foxes were regarded as being omnipotent.[11]

The first manifestation of the deity Inari is told in two separate

THE MYTHIC ROOTS

accounts, one Shinto and the other Buddhist in origin. The Shinto version stated that it occurred in the reign of Empress Gemmei, on the first day of the horse—that is, on February 11—in A.D. 711. That is regarded as the official date of the founding of Inari Shrine at Fushimi.[12]

Shinto Version of Inari One day a rich man, a descendant of a teacher from China, amused himself by shooting arrows at a target of mochi cakes. The spirit of the rice deity, which lives in all forms of rice, of course, was deeply offended by such inconsiderate and abusive treatment, and in the form of a white bird flew away to a mountain perch in a tall cryptomeria tree. The frightened man realized the sinfulness of his act in so misusing the food, a divine gift. To make amends, he built a shrine to the deity of rice upon the very spot where the bird had rested, and he was not punished.[13]

The Shinto account of the origin of Inari reflects a tie with China, where the worship of grain deities began in very ancient times. The earliest inhabitants of Japan undoubtedly worshiped food deities before rice was introduced into the country. The very date on which Inari appeared confirms this: "The first day of the Horse of the second month, according to the old lunar calendar, is the first day of spring and therefore the time to begin seed planting. Hence it is most fitting that the spirit of rice should appear at that time."[14]

Buddhist Version of Inari One day Kobo Daishi (or Kukai; 774–835), the great Buddhist teacher, met an old man carrying sheaves of rice. The old man said to him, "I am called Shiba Mori Choja Inari-tomi [Rice-wealth] and I live in Naikai-bo Temple at Hachijo [in Kyoto]. If you dedicate a shrine to me I will always assist you in propagating your teachings." Because he recognized the old man as the deity of rice, Kobo Daishi built a shrine at Mount Inari. Later, this little shrine was removed and taken to Naikai-bo Temple, where it became a shelter for mikoshi.[15]

Original Inari Shrines No trace remains of the original shrines mentioned in either of these legends, but in 923 the first of the permanent buildings of Fushimi-Inari Shrine was erected on what is believed to be the same spot. At any rate, by 927 three shrines are mentioned in Book Nine of the *Engishiki* as existing on Mount Inari. The divinity of the main shrine was Uga-no-Mitama-no-Kami (also known as Ugadama), the spirit of rice in the storehouse. The second shrine was dedicated to Susano-o, the rainstorm deity, Uga-no-Mitama's father; and the third one to Kamu-Oichi-hime, Divine Great Majesty Princess, her mother.[16]

The Evolution of Inari   As is the custom in Japan, these three shrines were called the shrines of Mount Inari, after the place rather than the deities. The region around this mountain, including its foothills, was developed with extraordinarily rich rice fields, so that, appropriately, the spirit of rice was worshiped here. But before these three shrines were built, a single shrine already existed on Mount Inari. It was dedicated to the Three Foxes, regarded as the deities of growing rice. Although the earliest shrine of the Three Foxes was different from that of the rice spirit, Ugadama, after many years passed no distinction between them was made, and gradually the records referred to "the shrine of Inari" as if it were one shrine dedicated to one divinity.

The shrine of Inari gained national recognition in this way: "In 827, the Emperor Junna's illness was explained by diviners as being a curse due to the felling of the trees at the 'Shrine of Inari,' whereupon the Emperor bestowed the lowest degree of the fifth rank upon the deity of that shrine in order to have the curse taken away. And in 843, the Emperor Nimmyo raised the same deity to the highest degree of the fifth rank."[17]

Later emperors bestowed still higher rank upon the three shrines, but always as upon a single deity. And for this reason, M. W. de Visser concluded: "I see in the fox shrine called Myobu-sha, or Tome-sha (Fox Temple), the root source of the whole Inari cult. As stated above, the Court Ladies, Myobu, all belonged to the fifth rank, and it is quite probable that the original name Tome-sha, or Fox Shrine, was changed to Myobu-sha after the three female fox-divinities worshipped there had obtained that rank in 827. For they were considered as one and the same with the Spirit of the Rice, and accordingly, the rank was bestowed alike upon the whole of the complexion."[18]

The appearance of the rice spirit in the shape of a fox in Japanese folk worship is consistent with similar manifestations of the spirit of corn in Europe, Egypt, and China, where it appeared as gander, goat, hare, cat, fox, wolf, dog, cock, goose, cow, pig, horse, and many other creatures. The foxes of Mount Inari were worshiped as deities of rice until the anthropomorphic concept of the female spirit of rice prevailed, thereby demoting the foxes to the role of messengers. De Visser was "convinced that not the messenger-foxes became Inari herself but that the fox-goddesses of Mt. Inari had to give way to a human divinity of the same nature, and were degraded to the rank of messengers."[19]

The stag of Kasuga, the dove of Hachiman, the crow of Kumano, the snowy heron of Kebi, the snake of Suwa, the tortoise of Matsuo, all were considered messengers of deities in Japan's olden times.

These were evidences of survivals of older cults in which the animals themselves had been deities.

The Pantheon at Fushimi-Inari Shrine A large number of divinities are enshrined in various temples and sites on Mount Inari, but the main ones worshiped there are phallic deities of agricultural fertility. Two of these are also deities of procreation. In addition to the five earlier named—Ugadama-no-Mikoto, Oda-no-Mikoto, Oichi-Hime, Onamochi, and Otoshi-no-Kami (these last two together were also called Tanaka-Okuni)—these four are installed there: Waka-toshi-no-Kami (Young Harvest Deity), Natsu-taka-no-Kami (Summer High Sun Deity), Aki-hime-no-Kami (Autumn Princess Deity), and Kuku-toshi-no-Kami (Stern Harvest Deity). These four together are known as Shi Daijin, the Four Great Deities.[20]

Also, ten subsidiary deities are worshiped at different shrines on the slopes of Mount Inari. Several are leading figures in old legends, while others are obscure. Some of the more important shrines are Byakko-sha, the White Fox Shrine, honoring the marvelous magical powers of the white fox, who can grant wealth, health, and success if properly approached; Choja-no-Yashiro, the Wealthy Man Shrine, which preserves the Shinto legend of the mochi-cake target and the first worshiping of Inari as the spirit of food; a shrine for five deities, who include the spirit of Hiruko, the "leech-child" sun god who was set adrift by Izanagi and Izanami (Hiruko is also identified with Ebisu, one of the Seven Gods of Luck); and another shrine for five other deities, the most important of whom is Hachiman, the god of war. One of the most significant of all the Mount Inari establishments is the Ise-no-Ryogu-sha, which represents the spirits of the two main shrines of Ise, combining worship of the sun goddess, Amaterasu, with that of the food goddess, Uke-mochi-no-Kami or Toyo-uke-no-Kami.[21]

Ugadama: The Food Spirit The first and central deity of the Inari pantheon, Uga-no-Mitama-no-Kami, is worshiped on the third peak of Mount Inari, at Mannaka-Shimo-no-Yashiro, the Central Lower Shrine. Actually, two deities are combined at this shrine to make Ugadama: they are Kuku-no-Kami (Stern Elder Deity), who is the deity of trees, and Kaya-no-Hime-no-Kami, who is the goddess of grasses and weeds. These two presences show that the primary spirits of the Inari pantheon include both the deity of food and the watchful guardian of the home. Inasmuch as Japanese houses use timbers for structural frames, grasses for tatami mats, and rushes for thatching, it is not to be wondered at that carpenters and contractors are among the most ardent worshipers at Fushimi-Inari Shrine.[22]

Uga-no-Mitama is known under many names, nearly all of which are based upon sounds meaning "food" or "meal": *ke, ka, ge,* and *ga.* The honorific "u" (or "o") added to these gives *uke, uka, uge, oge,* and *uga,* which are incorporated in the four names most commonly used to identify the food goddess: Uga-no-Mitama-no-Kami (Food August Spirit Deity), Toyo-uke-hime-no-Kami (Luxuriant Food Princess Deity), Uke-mochi-no-Kami (Food-possessing Deity), and Ogetsu-hime-no-Kami (Great Food Princess Deity).[23]

In the *Kojiki,* Uga-no-Mitama-no-Kami is the daughter of Susano-o, the rainstorm god, and of Kamu-Oichi-hime (Divine Great Majesty Princess), herself the daughter of Oyama-tsumi-no-Kami (Great Mountain-possessor August Deity). It is most fitting that the goddess of food, the spirit of rice, should come from the union of the rainstorm god with the daughter of the great mountain deity.[24] Concerning this genealogy, we find the following: "But Susano-o himself also married another wife, Kamu-O-ichi-hime, a daughter of O-yama-tsu-mi-nu-kami (Great Mountain Kami). . . . She gave him two sons . . . and Uga-no-mitama (August Spirit of Food), who later became the main kami worshipped under the name of Inari."[25]

The *Nihongi,* however, states that Izanagi and Izanami created Uga-no-Mitama-no-Mikoto when they were hungry. Izanagi and Izanami have been identified as the deities of the sky and the earth, respectively.[26] Recognition of the fact that the union of the Sky Father and the Earth Mother should produce food shows that the makers of Japanese myths in prehistoric times had logical and discerning minds.[27]

The *Kojiki* tells about another of their descendants, Toyo-uke-hime-no-Kami (Luxuriant Food Princess Deity), who, as the daughter of Waka-musubi-no-Kami (Young Wondrous Producing Deity), was the grandchild of Izanami.[28] The spirit of this goddess is said to dwell in the Outer Shrine at Ise. The Inner Shrine at Ise, as we have seen, is dedicated to Amaterasu.

The Second Major Deity: The Earth Spirit   The second main deity of Fushimi-Inari Shrine is worshiped on the second peak of the mountain. He is Oda-no-Mikoto (Great Rice Field Augustness). He is also known under the names Otsuchi-no-Mi-oya-no-Kami (Great Earth August Ancestor Deity), Saruta-hiko (Monkey Rice Field Prince), Yachimata-no-Kami (Eight Crossroads Deity), Sae-no-Kami (Preventive Deity), and Dosojin (Earth Ancestor Deity).

The same Chinese ideographs can be read either as Tsuchi-no-Kami or as Dosojin, and both are translated as Earth Ancestor Deity. These names epitomize the whole mystery that led to the deification of the earth and of the rice field. The soil is held to be the origin of life, its ancestor, and therefore divine. Man's most valued food for sustaining life, rice, is obtained from the soil of a field. Thus, in awe and in gratitude, both the earth and the field are deified.[29]

Saruta-hiko is a phallic deity, and the importance of the role he played in fertility rites is shown by the fact that he is included in two very interesting and important myths. He is the child of Otoshi-no-Kami (Great Harvest Deity) and Ame-shiru-Karu-mizu-hime (Heaven-governing Fresh Princess of Karu). The third deity of the Inari pantheon is Uzume, the wife of Saruta-hiko, and she appears in the same myths.

The Third Major Deity: The Goddess of Sexual Attraction As Buchanan has noted: "The third deity of the original Inari trinity is, like the first, a goddess, and is worshipped on the first peak of the mountain at a place called Minami-no-za-kami-yashiro (Southern-seat-upper-shrine)."[30]

Here she is known as Oichi-hime (Great First Princess). She is popularly called Uzume (Dread Female), a name which is derived from Ame-no-Uzume-no-Mikoto. She is also known as Omiya-hime (Great Palace Princess), Miyabi-no-Kami (Graceful Deity), Sarume-kami (Monkey Duchess, or Duchess of Saru), Oyama-hime (Great Mountain Princess),[31] and Omiya-no-Me (Great Palace Female).[32]

These varied names identify this goddess as the phallic counterpart of Saruta-hiko: she is a deity both of human fecundity and of agricultural fertility. As Ame-no-Uzume-no-Mikoto and Miyabi-no-Kami, she is the goddess of sexual attraction and "is the patron deity of all professional singers, dancers, musicians, and actors. Geisha and professional prostitutes, who seek to allure men by means of physical attractions, flock to her shrine."[33]

The genealogy of Ame-no-Uzume is not mentioned specifically in either the *Kojiki* or the *Nihongi*. She does appear very prominently, however, in spectacular and eventful myths which identify her as a phallic deity or a deity of sexual attraction. She is much more than just a sensational character, as we have seen in the study of the ritual dance she performed before the Cave of Heaven. Although Ugadama alone is the central deity of agriculture, the goddess of food representing the fertility of the earth, Saruta-hiko and Uzume together, as man and wife, symbolize the universal principle of sex, of life replenishing itself. This principle is expressed through the sexuality suggested by similar male and female figures in corn-, rice-, and wheat-growing cultures throughout the world. Thus: "In the islands of Bali and Lombok, when the time of harvest has come, the owner of the field himself makes a beginning by cutting 'the principal rice' and binding it into two sheaves, called 'husband and wife.' Hence, when people of Bali bring the two sheaves, the husband and wife, into the barn, they say, 'Increase ye and multiply without ceasing.' . . . The pinch of hunger sometimes drives individuals to eat up the rice of these two sheaves, but the wretches who do so are viewed with disgust by their fellows and branded as pigs and dogs. Nobody would ever sell these holy sheaves with the rest of their profane brethren."[34]

Another illustration, this one from Java, resembles an ancient practice of Europeans respecting their corn spirit: "Before the reapers begin to cut the rice, the priest or sorcerer picks out a number of ears of rice, which are tied together, smeared with ointment, and adorned with flowers. Thus decked out, the ears are called the padi-penganten, that is, the Rice-bride and groom; their wedding feast is celebrated, and the cutting of the rice begins immediately afterwards."[35]

In Japan, Dosojin sculptures depicting man-and-wife deities frequently are found at the edges of rice paddies, and at harvest time two small sheaves of rice are placed as offerings against the sides of such images. Thus, Saruta-hiko, Uzume, and Ugadama are connected with the spirit of rice. These three divinities in human form seem to have succeeded to the role originally held by the three foxes of Mount Inari, the first three deities relating to the spirit of rice to be worshiped in that place. Further evidence of Saruta-hiko's and Uzume's connection with Inari is observed in the shrines dedicated to Dosojin, which frequently are painted red (as are Inari shrines) and where the symbols of the white fox and the phallus are found.

Oyama-hime and Oichi-hime   The two names Oichi-hime (Great First Princess) and Oyama-hime (Great Mountain Princess) refer to the primary deity of Mount Inari. She resides upon the first, or southern, peak of the mountain, from which she overlooks and protects the rice fields upon the slopes and plains below.[36]

In Japan, there are two types of mountain kami, those that govern the peaks, ridges, valleys, and slopes of the mountains as such, and those that are spirits of agriculture. The first type is worshiped by woodcutters and charcoal-makers, while the second is worshiped by farmers. The two types are not necessarily mutually exclusive. The highest-ranking mountain kami, as we have seen, is Oyama-tsumi-no-Kami, the father of Kamu-Oichi-hime (whose shortened epithet, Oichi-hime, is one of the names given to the deity of sex, Ame-no-Uzume-no-Mikoto). In the *Kojiki,* Kamu-Oichi-hime and Susano-o produced Uga-no-Mitama-no-Mikoto. Thus, by deduction, the deity of sex, Uzume, would appear to be the mother of the deity of food. This apparent blood relationship reaffirms the connection between human sexuality and agricultural fertility. At any rate, a large number of mountain deities are descended from one related to Oyama-tsumi. Herbert has listed ten in the "governing" category and five in the "agricultural" category.[37] In addition, many special or local mountain kami are known throughout Japan.

Agricultural kami of mountain regions descend to the fields as snakes, in accordance with the ancient and general belief that the supernatural spirit of the earth takes the form of a snake. A snake, therefore, is thought to be the manifestation of a yama-no-kami. The creative force of the earth that is stored in the mountain must find its way into the fields in order to make plants grow. This spirit, or mitama, "is considered to be identical with Chibo-shin (Mother-Earth) who keeps revived constantly as snakes, coming out of the mountains into the fields in spring to become the god of the fields (Ta-no-kami), and returning to the mountains in the fall to become the god of the mountains (Yama-no-kami). Thus Ta-no-kami and Yama-no-kami are identified with the Snake God."[38]

Sarume-kimi and Omiya-hime Aston made two references to the "dread female," Uzume. One related to the name of Saru-no-Kami, and the other to her role as the Great Palace Female: "She was the ancestress of the Sarume, or 'monkey female,' who performed religious dances (kagura) at Court and delivered inspired utterances. Hirata identifies this deity with 'O-miya-hime (Great-palace-female),' worshipped as one of the eight gods of the Jingi-kwan, or Department of Religion. She represents the chief lady officials of the palace as a class . . . from another point of view she is a type of the wise woman, sorceress, or prophetess. She was prayed to for long life, for protection from evil by night and by day, for honours and for posterity."[39]

The name Sarume-kimi (Monkey Female Duchess) was given to Uzume as a reward or an honorary title for services rendered to Prince Ninigi upon his descent to earth. The *Kojiki* stated that females alone held this title and that the *sarume* were women who performed *saru-mai,* or comic monkey dances, in honor of the gods. The sarume also were regarded as mediums, and in later times were called miko. Moreover, as is well known, the monkey is regarded as the messenger of mountain kami. Different kinds of animals carved in stone, and known as *o-tsukai,* messengers or guardians, are nearly always found at entrances to shrines and temples, especially in country places. Among these images, those of monkeys are encountered frequently.

Oyama-kui (Great Mountain Integrator) is one of those deities whose o-tsukai is a monkey "because his original temple, the Hie-taisha, is situated in wooded hills (Hiei-san) where many specimens can be seen. More often than not, a statue of a monkey, sometimes dressed in human clothes, is found near branch shrines, as in the case of the Tokyo Hie-jinja."[40]

If the pattern of the succession of deities is followed—as we have seen is the case at Fushimi-Inari, where the three foxes, the original deities of rice, were succeeded by three anthropomorphic deities—then we can conclude that monkey deities were succeeded by deities in human form, namely, Saruta-hiko, Monkey Rice Field Prince, and Sarume-kimi, Monkey Female Duchess.

Of further interest is the fact that Oyama-kui, popularly known as Sanno (which is probably a Buddhist appellation), is worshiped in the form of stone monuments, upon which are carved figures of monkey. Sanno is a very unusual deity, being both male and female at the same time. In the Sanno Festival of Mount Hiei near Kyoto, held April 12–14, this dual deity is married in a ceremony on one evening and bears children on the next, and these children are worshiped in the temple throughout the following year. Thus, Oyama-kui, or Sanno, is connected with human fertility rituals as well as with agricultural fertility. In this respect, Sanno is very similar to Dosojin shown as a couple, and this explains why in some places the Dosojin festival is called the Sanno festival.[41]

Summary   Three of the deities whom we first met in mythological accounts have been identified as being the three main deities at Fushimi-Inari Shrine, one of the most important centers of official Shinto. These three deities are Ugadama, Saruta-hiko, and Uzume. As phallic gods of food production, they are associated with rice, rice fields, and mountain watersheds. In addition, Saruta-hiko and Uzume are recognized also as being the couple-deity in roadside sculptures called Dosojin, or Earth Ancestor Deity. In this form, they are the spirit of sexual attraction and human increase.

The utilization of the power of human sexual activity for the purpose of effecting a greater yield of crops logically leads to concentrating the attributes of all related deities in one divine being. In Japan, this composite divinity—the triad Saruta-hiko, Uzume, and Ugadama—is known as Inari-sama, or simply as Inari. It represents the religious expression of the integration of sex and food, the most vital forces in nature, in the daily lives of the Japanese people.

At present, of course, the daily needs of the people are vastly more complicated than they were in prehistoric times, and so the Japanese have systematically expanded the attributes of Inari-sama. In doing so, they have given this deity the power to grant them all kinds of boons unknown to their ancestors: success in business, passing examinations, winning lawsuits, safety on the highways, amassing wealth—good fortune in all its modern contexts and connotations. The mountainside behind the main shrines at Fushimi-Inari is dotted with thousands of small shrines, consisting of stone altars flanked and backed by stone monuments dedicated to Inari. These little shrines, like the largest ones, are guarded by images of foxes, ranging in size from tiny to big, in number from two to six and sometimes even more. Small porcelain foxes and miniature torii in wood have been offered at these altars by the millions. Every day, but especially on a Sunday (which is the holiday from work for most Japanese), Fushimi-Inari's countless shrines are visited by thousands upon thousands of people: adults of all ages, babies, toddlers, teen-agers, the aged, the rich, the poor, the believers and the seekers.

The style of worship established in earlier times is very much alive today, although its purposes may have been changed and enlarged. The numbers of petitioners who come to Fushimi-Inari show that many members of the present industrial society of Japan seem to have retained the ability to live in an "integrated" or "organic" way.

This ability is a characteristic found in early cultures but is not easily achieved by modern ones: "Indeed, one of the major differences separating the people of the early cultures from the people of today is precisely the utter incapacity of the latter to live their organic life (particularly as regards sex and nutrition) as a sacrament. . . . For the modern they are simply physiological acts, whereas for primitive man they were sacraments, ceremonies by means of which he communicated with the *force* which stood for life itself."[42]

An example of this idea comes from ancient Rome. There, in the temple of the goddess Vesta, a god identified as Priapus was represented by a phallic image. But the two deities together formed a single one known as Pabulum, or Food.[43]

For the common people of Japan, in rural communities especially, the deity of food and sex is expressed simply in the form of Dosojin. It does not matter now whether this man-wife deity is thought of as consisting of Saruta-hiko and Uzume, or of Izanagi and Izanami, or of some other combination of male and female forces. For the official expressions of Shrine Shinto, the deity of food and sex is Inari. And the fact that Inari encompasses a great number of deities only emphasizes the processes of syncretization that have occurred since man (and his gods) were created.

DEITIES OF RICE AND SEX

263

The innate capacity of the early Japanese to pattern their organic life in harmony with nature, maintained through the centuries, has molded Japanese character and given artistic expression to their daily activities. The pre-Shinto heaven was here on earth, and life was a love of working within nature. The love of creating, in whatever form, was a sacred, magical act to be enjoyed here and now, not in some far-off Promised Land.

While it is true that life in Japan is no longer as simple as once it was for most people, it is still governed by these uncomplicated basic attitudes. The outward manifestations may be modified in response to changing political, social, and economic pressures, but the creative life force still persists within. As they have demonstrated several times before in their history, the people of Japan are showing once again that they are capable of absorbing and adapting the influences of other cultures without sacrificing the values that are fundamental to Japanese character and life.

APPENDIX:
GLOSSARY OF ROADSIDE DEITIES

THE LATE KAMAKURA PERIOD (1185–1336) seems to have been the time when stone roadside deities first appeared and spread throughout the Japanese countryside. Following that initial acceptance, the greatest popularity of these images was reached during the Muromachi period (1336–1568) and then again in the Edo period (1603–1868).[1] This expression of creative folk art was both abundant and ecumenical: while it began by portraying animistic phallic emblems and deities, it soon invited Buddhist divinities to take their place among the native originals. While the couple Dosojin was the predominant figure in the earliest days, eventually other deities of Buddhist origin, such as Jizo, became equally popular. Because of this commingling, and as a matter of convenience to the people, similar powers were ascribed to most of these roadside deities without regard for their provenance.

The widespread interchange of attributes among these many folk deities makes it difficult sometimes to distinguish between those of indigenous Shinto origin and those influenced by Buddhist ideas imported from China and India. Nowadays, the Buddhist deities appear to be more numerous among the stone images found along Japan's roads.

These divinities usually are considered to be native to Japan: Dosojin, Sae-no-Kami, Saruta-hiko, Sanno, Konsei-sama, Tajikara-o-no-Mikoto, Kojin, Fujin, Raishin, and Suijin. The remainder are Buddhist: the Buddha himself; several of the bodhisattvas, including Kannon, Jizo, and Miroku Bosatsu; Koshin; Mari-shiten; Emma-o; and an assortment of *tengu*, goblinlike creatures.

The Seven Gods of Luck, amalgamations of Shinto and Buddhist deities, as well as a few lesser creatures of the religious imagination, also appear. Descriptions of these, too, are included in this glossary.

Bato Kanzeon. Guardian deity of horses. Buddhist. Usually this deity, whose name literally means "Horse-headed Kanzeon," is represented as a human figure wearing a crown or hat on which a horse's head (*bato*) is carved. Sometimes he is shown with three faces, each having three eyes, and with a single body having four pairs of arms, each hand holding a different Buddhist symbol. Some of these images are seated, and a rare few are on horseback. Bato Kanzeon can be represented also in the form of an upright shaft of stone, six feet or more in height, on which his name is carved. He is considered to be in charge of the salvation of those who have fallen into the realm of animals, Chikusho-do,[2] and is regarded as the guardian deity of horses, farm animals, and human travelers. His image is placed beside roads and near mountain passes. Drivers of automobiles should also worship Bato Kanzeon. *See also* Kannon, Kanzeon.

Dosojin. Earth Ancestor Deity or Road Ancestor Deity. Shinto. Dosojin is the Japanese phallic deity supreme, helping to ensure abundance in agriculture and human fecundity, protecting against sickness and evil spirits, and serving as a guardian spirit of roads and of travelers upon them. Dosojin is unique, being represented in sculptured form as a male-and-female, husband-and-wife pair, symbolizing the phallo-ktenic principles of procreation and prevention—the safeguarding against death through sexual activity.

Emma-o. Buddhist. The king and judge of the dead to Buddhists, Emma-o presides over a tribunal consisting of ten judges or kings, their clerks, scribes, and witnesses. Ju-o-kyo, the faith of the Ten Kings (*Ju-o*), is a popular belief derived from a combination of Buddhism and Taoism in China. Often the Ten Kings, in sculptured form, were made small enough to be portable. They were placed on altars for use in rituals and then put away again for safekeeping. They were borrowed and loaned back and forth among small rural shrines and temples.

Eventually Emma-o was separated from the tribunal, to be depicted thereafter as a single figure. Usually he is shown with a red face and a fierce expression, a flowing beard, and long canine teeth protruding over his lips. His headdress is a crown bearing on it the ideogram meaning "king" (*o*).

Five Elements. Taoist/Buddhist. An unusual image is that of the five elements, whose symbols are carved on a "rock tower" or on an upright natural stone. The elements are earth, water, fire, air (or wind), and ether (or spirit), or, on occasion, metal, symbolized by the square, circle, triangle, inverted semicircle, and tama, or jewel. These five elements are related to the five precepts of the Buddha: not to kill living things, not to commit adultery, not to tell lies, not to steal, and not to drink intoxicating beverages.

Fudo Myo-o. Buddhist. Fudo is one of the five terrible manifestations of the Buddha, which are the counterparts of the Buddha's five benevolent manifestations. Fudo is called "The Overcomer" and "The Immovable" (*fudo*), and he is always depicted with a fierce expression.[3] Sometimes he is shown seated on the brink of a precipice, sometimes standing on a rock surrounded by flames. He holds a sword and a rope, and a flamelike halo frames his head. He is regarded as a deity of fire, but actually the flames symbolize the power of the intellect or the attainment of buddhahood. With his sword he combats the three poisons of greed, anger, and delusion; with his rope he binds those who oppose the Buddha's teachings.[4]

Fujin and Raishin. The wind deity and the thunder deity. Shinto. These two gods are associated with agriculture. They originate in mythology as Shinatobe-no-Mikoto and Kura-Okami, respectively, children of the fire deity, Kagutsuchi. Often they are represented in stone as roadside gods, or their images are placed where the ravages of wind and thunder are likely to be severe.

Fujin, the wind deity, is shown carrying a bag full of wind over his shoulders, his hair windblown. At the beginning of the typhoon season farmers place paper strips in the fields, dedicating them to Fujin.

Raishin, the thunder deity, is shown wearing a necklace of drums. He is associated with Susano-o, the rainstorm deity, because thunder often accompanies rain. Because the darting tongue of a snake recalls the flash of lightning, sometimes Raishin is represented in the form of a snake.[5]

Jizo. Sanskrit: Kshitigarbha. Buddhist. Jizo, originally a bodhisattva, a being destined for buddhahood who devotes himself to helping all beings attain enlightenment before entering nirvana himself, is popularly regarded as a protector of children, guarding them from epidemic diseases and other maladies. He is represented as a Buddhist priest, in simple long robes, carrying a staff in one hand and a tama in the other, waiting at the gate of the underworld, where Buddhist spirits must confront the tribunal headed by Emma-o, who passes judgment on them. Jizo is also involved in cases of spirit possession in which children serve as mediums.

Kaiko-dama Dai-Myojin. The silkworm-cocoon deity. Shinto. This is the guardian of silk production, usually represented in the form of a man whose face resembles a cocoon, and who wears a headdress shaped like a house roof crowned with a tama. In some cases he is represented by a large cocoon on which his name is written.

Kannon, Kanzeon. Sanskrit: Avalokiteshvara. Buddhist. The representation of this deity is both ancient and widespread, having been found in Arabia, Sri Lanka, India, China, Tibet, and Korea, as well as Japan. It has been revered both as a male and as a female divinity, although in China and Japan it usually is female. Originally Kannon, or more properly Kanzeon, is a bodhisattva, whose name means "Regarder of the Cries of the World" and who personifies compassion.

The deified Kannon of folk religion, popularly known in English as the "goddess of mercy," is depicted in many ways and has many titles but always is a deity of infinite compassion. Her most notable form is as Senju Kannon, or Kannon of the Thousand Hands, which by their very number exemplify her versatility and compassion. She carries such Buddhist emblems as the wheel, rosary, lotus flower, incense burner, fan, bow and arrow, goad or spear, rope, ax, fly whisk, scroll, begging bowl, hare, moon, cock, sun, medicine flask, vase, various musical instruments, willow branch, crystal ball, sacred fungus, and a small image of the Buddha or of Kannon herself.[6]

Besides Bato Kanzeon, who is one aspect of Kannon, there are many other Kannon of varied attributes, such as Gyoran Kannon, represented with a carp; Anoku Kannon, seated on a rock near a waterfall; Nyoirin Kannon, the omnipotent, a seated figure with one knee raised and the right cheek resting on the right hand: Ryugu Kannon, seated on a dragon; Junimen Kannon, with eleven small heads atop and around the larger main head; Sho Kanzeon, her right hand lifted in blessing, her left hand holding a lotus blossom; Juntei Kannon, with nine arms; Fuken Kannon, with eight arms; and many others.[7]

Kojin. Shinto. Kojin is the god of the hearth, and usually his shrine is placed near the fireplace or stove in the kitchen. When he is enshrined in the garden, he is known as Ji-Kojin, Ground Kojin. Occasionally Kojin is represented in the form of thin plates of stone inscribed with characters reading "Sampo Kojin" (Three Treasures Kojin), "Kojin-o" (King Kojin), and other epithets.

Kojin is seen also as an image with three faces and six arms, carrying a bow, arrows, sword, lance, saw, and bell. It is similar to the image of Bato Kanzeon, but instead of wearing a crown with the image of a horse on it, Kojin has flamelike hair. Some sculptures are inscribed with the characters reading "Wago-no-Kami" (God of Harmonious Existence), "Hi-no-Yojin" (Guard Against Fire), or "Kaho-Jinka-no-Sampo" (Three Treasures of the House of the Lucky).[8]

Konsei Dai-Myojin. Root of Life Great Shining Deity. Shinto. Popularly called Konsei-sama, this name is given to natural stones that have phallic shapes, stones carved in the form of a phallus and a kteis, stones carved in the image of Sanno (a female monkey with genital organs exposed), or stone carvings of men and women in sexual postures. Konsei-sama may be regarded as being the same as Sae-no-Kami and Dosojin.

Koshin. The deity of roads. Buddhist. Koshin goes by several names, such as

Shomen Kongo and Koshin Shomen. He can be traced to an aboriginal deity of India known as Blue-faced Kongo (Aomen Kongo, in Japanese). According to the teachings of Taoism, on the night of the Day of Koshin, when all is quiet, a worm known as Sanshi, who lives in a person's body, leaves that body and flies up to the god of heaven to tell of the evil deeds performed by the person in whom it dwells. In order to prevent this from happening while they slept, people used to sit up all night at that critical time.[9]

The Koshin image shows a fiercely scowling, rugged male with two, four, six, or eight arms, holding a bow, arrow, rope, club, sword, and a miniature image of a partially naked woman. Two hands are folded in prayer. He has a third eye placed vertically in the middle of his forehead. The emblems of the sun and the moon, often shown riding on clouds, are depicted in the upper corners of the composition. Three monkeys, a cock and a hen, *oni* (ogres), and an *amanojaku* often are included, dramatizing the design. (An amanojaku is a demon in stunted human form, usually shown beneath the feet of Koshin. Such a demon represents the baser aspects of man, such as envy, greed, and pride, which must be subdued in striving toward self-realization, the attainment of buddhahood.)

Koshin is associated with Sanno, too, and in such cases is represented by the same kind of image of a female monkey as is Sanno. Saruta-hiko is linked with Sanno and Koshin, and he is honored on the Day of the Monkey, along with Koshin.[10]

Kuyo-to. Prayer tower. Buddhist. These so-called towers usually are not more than six to eight feet high and are dedicated to the memory of the dead. As a group, they are called *tsukimachi kuyo-to,* "moon-awaiting prayer towers." These towers, made of stone, represent Nyoirin Kannon as the principal deity but are found also as representations of Koshin-kuyo (Koshin prayers), Koshin-to (Koshin towers), Niju-san-ya-kuyo (Twenty-third-night prayers), and so on. There are also prayer towers with such phrases as *Namu Amida Butsu,* "Homage to Amida Buddha," written on them.

The old custom called for men and women to gather on designated days to eat, drink, talk, or recite Buddhist sutras while waiting for the moon to rise. Their talk often turned to sex and to childbirth, and to prayers for safe delivery. In some regions, these meetings were held for unmarried women only, in others for married women, or for old women or old men only.

Marishiten. Goddess of light. Buddhist. This deity has a martial aspect. Usually she is represented as mounted on a boar, but sometimes she rides an elephant, tiger, dragon, or snake. She has three faces, the middle and right ones being of gentle expression, the left one fierce and menacing. Marishiten is in the center, Bishamon-ten on the left, and Daikoku on the right. She is depicted with eight arms, carrying the sun, the moon, a spear, a bow and arrow, a sword, and a war fan. She has the mysterious power to make herself invisible, so that neither sun nor moon can see her and neither fire nor water can destroy her. This is an important power in battle, and therefore she is worshiped by warriors.[11] She is of Hindu origin, being a transformation of Marichi Deva, who is the offspring of Brahma and is the goddess of light. Marishiten is also called "Queen of Heaven." The dragon is one of her symbols.

Miroku Bosatsu. Sanskrit: Maitreya Bodhisattva. Buddhist. This deity is some-times referred to as the "Buddhist Messiah," who will come to earth five thousand years after Sakyamuni Buddha's entry into Nirvana. His present dwelling is the Tushita Heaven, the Heaven of the Contented Ones, a sacred region (like the

Christian Paradise) which is the home of the bodhisattvas, those beings who are destined to become buddhas. Sakyamuni Buddha once dwelt there, and Miroku now presides over it. He watches over devout members of the Buddhist faith, and he prays eternally for the happiness of humankind.[12]

In Japan, Miroku sculptured in the round is represented in a seated position, with his left foot on the ground, his right foot on his left knee, right elbow on right knee, and left hand on right ankle. His head is slightly bent, his right hand supports his chin or cheek, and there is a little stupa (a phallic emblem) on his crown. Because of his posture, many untutored people think of him as the "god of toothache."

Oni. Ogres. These are mischievous little demons, equipped with claws, sharp teeth, malignant eyes, and square heads with two small horns. Sometimes they swarm in bands of hundreds. Occasionally, one may be converted to Buddhism, in which event his horns are sawed off by priests and he goes on his way carrying the bell and umbrella of a monk.[13]

On February 3, when the ceremony of exorcism called Oni-yarai is held, dried beans are thrown about the house to aid in casting out such devils.

Roku Jizo. The Six Jizo. Buddhist. The single Jizo developed into the form known as Roku Jizo through the six incarnations Jizo experiences as he reveals himself in the six lower realms of the ten realms of existence (hell, the animal world, the world of hungry ghosts, the world of warlike demons, the human world, and the heavenly realm) during the time between the Buddha's death and the emergence of Miroku Bosatsu to save the world. In Japan, Roku Jizo appears as a group of six almost identical figures, either as statues or as figures engraved on a stone slab. Each figure differs from the others only slightly, either in posture or in the emblem held in the hand.

According to Lafcadio Hearn, "Jizo was a woman 10,000 *ko* [*kalpas*] before this era and became filled with desire to convert all livings things of the Six Worlds and Four Births. By virtue of the Supernatural Powers, she multiplied herself and simultaneously appeared in all the Six States of Sentient Existence at once, and converted the dwellers thereof."[14]

Sambiki Saru. The Three Monkeys. Buddhist/Shinto. Mizaru, with hands over his eyes, sees no evil; Kikazaru, covering his ears, hears no evil; and Iwazaru, with hands over mouth, speaks no evil. The monkey is the messenger of Yama-no-Kami (deity of the mountains). The worship of Sanno originated in that offered to Yama-no-Kami, and the emblem of Sanno is a female monkey. Buddhist images in the form of Koshin, expressing the principle of human fecundity, became amalgamated with images of Sanno as a monkey. Monkeys appear in a great variety of forms on many Buddhist roadside sculptures, but almost never on sculptures of Dosojin. This seems odd, inasmuch as Saruta-hiko (Monkey Rice Field Prince) is linked with Dosojin. The Three Monkeys have become very popular, and appear in the form of toys and decorations that have no connection with their religious significance.[15]

Sanno. Mountain King. Shinto. Sanno is represented by a female monkey with genital organs painted red, or by carvings of one, two, three, or as many as twenty-four monkeys on a stone slab. The sex of the monkeys in such a group varies, being male, female, or neuter. However, where there is only one monkey, usually it is female.

Saruta-hiko. Monkey Rice Field Prince. Shinto. Saruta-hiko is represented by a phallic stone, which often is enshrined in the same place that is dedicated to the rice deity, Inari, whose symbol is the fox. Saruta-hiko is the male partner in couple Dosojin sculptures. In origin he is connected with Ta-no-Kami (deity of the rice fields) and with Sanno.

Seven Gods of Luck. Buddhist/Shinto. These seven personages are among the most popular of folk sculptures in Japan, since they relate to the physical and material well-being of all people. In the course of time they have been included in the Shinto pantheon, and are honored as a group in one of the lesser shrines at Fushimi-Inari Shrine near Kyoto. The seven gods are Ebisu, Daikoku, Bishamonten, Benzaiten (or Benten), Hotei, Jurojin, and Fukurokuju.[16] This is the order in which they are usually depicted and in which they will be discussed below.

1. Ebisu, the god of daily food. Ebisu, or Hiruko, was a child of Izanagi and Izanami, the creator-deities of Japanese mythology. Because Hiruko was deformed, being legless, his parents felt that they could not accept him as their own and set him adrift in a camphorwood boat. Hiruko is thought to have represented the sun for a cult of sun worshipers in times preceding the domination of Amaterasu as sun goddess.

Besides being legless, Ebisu is deaf and cannot hear the summons which calls all the other deities to Izumo in October for their annual convention. He stays behind and participates in the Ebisu-ko, a festival held in his honor on October 20.

Ebisu is a deity of honest dealing, and is shown with a beard, laughing, holding a fishing pole or a *tai* (sea bream). He wears a two-pointed hat. He hates chickens, having been deceived by them at one time. Occasionally he is shown with Daikoku, and then male characteristics are given to Daikoku and female attributes to Ebisu, the pair being depicted as man and wife.

2. Daikoku, the god of wealth. The popular version of this deity shows a short, stout, jolly man standing or sitting on two bales of rice, carrying a large wooden mallet in his right hand and a bag slung over his left shoulder or on his back. Sometimes he stands with Ebisu, who assists him with the heavy bag of treasure. Daikoku's "lucky mallet" has the power to confer wealth with one stroke.

This deity has a counterpart in both Shinto and Buddhism. His Shinto parallel is Okuni-nushi, also known as Onamochi. The Buddhist god Mahakara, the deity of procreation, who embodies the yin and the yang, or the female and male principles, also resembles Daikoku. The male and female principles are shown symbolically on Daikoku's mallet, which bears the design of a pear-shaped tama with three rings.

Moreover, Daikoku is found as a member of several triads of deities, one being that of Marishiten, Bishamonten, and Daikoku. Here he is depicted as a three-headed man, standing on two bales of rice or on a running boar. The central figure is Marishiten, with Daikoku and Bishamonten standing at either side.

3. Bishamonten, the god of war. Also known as Tamonten, this deity, a god of war to the Japanese, is identified with the Hindu divinity Vaisravana, guardian king of the north. He is also identified with the Hindu god of riches, Jambhala,[17] and the Chinese god of wealth, Ts'ai-shen[18] or Ta-wan.[19] According to myth, Bishamonten appeared in a vision as a venerable old man and thereby saved the life of Prince Shotoku (574–622) of Japan during his war in defense of Buddhism. Because of this association, Bishamonten is shown in full armor. He has a fierce expression and carries a small pagoda in his right hand, a three-pronged spear in his left.

Although he is one of the Seven Gods of Luck, Bishamonten is seldom invoked at the home altar. While not strictly a god of war, he is associated with military power and glory and is one of the guardians of heaven. According to Hindu mythology, Mount Meru (or Sumeru), where the thirty-three Deva Kings dwell, is paved on its four sides with gold, silver, lapis-lazuli, and crystal. Bishamonten is believed to live near this mountain and to guard it well. People think that "to those that pray to him, he can grant good fortune more swiftly than the flight of an arrow from the bow."[20]

4. Benzaiten, the goddess of love, beauty, and music. Also known as Benten, this deity is of Hindu origin, deriving from Sarasvati (or Lakshmi), who is the daughter of Sagara, the Hindu dragon king, and is herself the goddess of streams and seas. Benten is said to have come to Japan in a boat with six male companions: Hotei, Jurojin, Daikoku, Ebisu, Fukurokuju, and Bishamonten (later her husband).

In Japan, Benten is worshiped at her shrine on the island of Enoshima, near Kamakura, and elsewhere, but her main shrine, Itsukushima, is on the island of Miyajima, near Hiroshima. Often she is represented with a serpent or a dragon coiled around the rock upon which she sits. And she is variously depicted with four or eight hands, each holding a different Buddhist symbol: a sword, wheel, ax, rope, bow and arrow, tama, and key. Her crown takes various forms, sometimes being surmounted by a phoenix, sometimes by three flaming jewels, sometimes by a Shinto torii beneath which is coiled a white snake having the face of an old man with bushy white eyebrows. Often she is depicted riding a dragon and playing a *biwa*, a Japanese instrument somewhat resembling a lute.

Benten is also known as the White Snake Lady. The snake, besides being a symbol of fertility and sexuality, is associated with rivers, seas, and water generally, and therefore Benten is regarded as an agricultural deity who assures the fertility of rice fields, which require flooding in the early stages of rice growing. Thus, she is associated with Ugadama, the goddess of grain.

Benten's promiscuity has provoked countless tales. She has had an enormous number of lovers among both demigods and humans. At Seimei-ji temple in Toyokawa, Aichi Prefecture, for example, "there is a Benten festival that celebrates her predilection for handsome horse drivers. She took one away with her and that was the last that was heard of him—hence this festival that features charms in the shape of well-endowed horses."[21]

5. Hotei, the god of happiness. Hotei is the most popular of the Seven Gods of Luck. He is very short and very fat, with a bulging stomach, and is laughing joyously as he carries on his back a linen bag (*hotei*) in which are stowed many precious things. Hotei is regarded as a Buddhist monk, and is thought to have been a Chinese Taoist priest in the tenth century. He is often shown carrying a rosary and a clam shell, such as itinerant priests used for a begging bowl. He puts his sack to many uses: sometimes he sleeps in it, sometimes carries a couple of children in it. Many folk carvings in wood show Hotei with a phallic head and rounded, folded arms covered by voluminous sleeves, the whole sculpture representing the male genital organs.

6. Jurojin, the god of longevity and wisdom. He is depicted as a tall, solemn old man with a white beard, dressed as a scholar, and accompanied by a deer or a crane. He carries a scroll in one hand and a staff in the other. He is grave, serious, yet kind. It is thought that Jurojin is but a variant of Fukurokuju. Jurojin often wears a mitered hat on which is drawn the disk of the sun. Designs employing the bamboo, plum, and pine, the last an emblem of longevity, as are the crane and the deer, are shown about his person.

7. Fukurokuju, the god of good fortune and longevity. This deity is portrayed as an old bearded dwarf with a very elongated head, who is dancing and singing. His name means "fortune, prosperity, and longevity," and he carries a bamboo-leaf fan or a sacred tama, or is in the company of a crane, tortoise, or stag, all three of which are symbols of long life. Fukurokuju is fun-loving and boisterous by nature. He is regarded as a scholar, but unquestionably he is also a phallic deity offering promise of long life. Fukurokuju, Jurojin, and Hotei are represented with elongated phallic heads so proportioned that their meaning is very clear. Jurojin and Fukurokuju almost certainly were the same deity at one time.

Shogun Jizo. Shinto. Jizo became amalgamated with the guardian deity of Kyoto, the premodern capital of Japan, who was represented by a warrior on horseback. These equestrian figures were erected at the borders of the capital and beside burial mounds as protective blocking deities. Jizo riding a horse is called Shogun Jizo, or Jizo of Victorious Armies (*shogun*).[22]

Suijin. The god of water. Shinto. Suijin is worshiped as the source of freshwater supplies, such as springs, wells, ponds, lakes, irrigation ditches, and rivers. Images of Suijin are made of stone and represent a coiled snake with its large sleepy head resting upon the topmost coil, or a snake with the head of an old man, or a beautiful woman crowned with a torii, a coiled snake, or both.

Suijin is an amalgamation of the deity Ugadama, goddess of cereals, and the deity Benten, goddess of love, beauty, music, learning, and eloquence, as well as the sea. The cultivation of rice and other crops is inseparably connected with water, and the people believed that the sacred replenishing water came from within the earth as well as from beyond the sea where the deities lived.[23]

Tajikara-o-no-Mikoto. Hand Strength Male Deity. Shinto. This is the male deity who, in the myth that tells of the retreat of the sun goddess, grasped her by the arm and drew her from the cave in which she had hidden herself. Tajikara is greatly honored for this deed, but he is little regarded in folk worship and sculptures of him are rare.

Tengu. Taoist/Buddhist. Goblins or spirits. Tengu are mythical creatures, like the unicorn, phoenix, and dragon. They appear in sculptured form as half-man, half-bird, with wings and claws, and sometimes a large beak or an elongated nose, because of which they are associated with Saruta-hiko. Tengu move through the air with great ease. They live in the mountains in the topmost branches of trees. They are considered to be lesser divinities, messengers of the deities of mountains. Tengu are associated with the male and female principles. They are supposed to be born from eggs, and in carvings are often shown emerging from eggshells or rolling eggs before them. Along with the fox and the badger, tengu seem to have evolved from Chinese ideas of magic, sorcery, and witchcraft.[24]

REFERENCE NOTES

AUTHOR'S PREFACE

1. Ichiro Hori, *Folk Religion in Japan,* pp. 18–19.
2. Carl Gustav Jung, "A Psychological Commentary," in W. Y. Evans-Wentz, *The Tibetan Book of the Dead,* p. xliv.

CHAPTER I

1. D. C. Buchanan, "Inari: Its Origin, Development and Nature," p. 24.
2. Genchi Kato, *A Study of Shinto: The Religion of the Japanese Nation,* p. 15.
3. Erich Neumann, *The Origins and History of Consciousness,* vol. 1, p. xxii, fn. 7.
4. Ibid., p. 19.
5. Kenkichi Ito, *Sei no Shakujin* (Stone Gods of Sex), pp. 62–70.
6. Ibid.
7. Ibid., pp. 94–102.
8. Eiichi Ashida, *Doso no Kamigami* (Gods of Doso), p. 6.

CHAPTER II

1. Quoted in Eiichi Ashida, *Doso no Kamigami* (Gods of Doso), p. 11.
2. Ibid.
3. Ibid.
4. Hachiro Daigo, *Dosojin—Robo no Sekibutsu* (Dosojin: The Roadside Stone Buddhas), vol. 2, p. 23.
5. Hachiro Daigo, *Robo no Sekibutsu* (The Roadside Stone Buddhas), vol. 1, p. 128.
6. Ashida, *Doso no Kamigami,* p. 31.
7. Ibid., p. 5.
8. Kenkichi Ito, *Sei no Shakujin* (Stone Gods of Sex), p. 25.
9. Ibid., p. 32.

10. Ibid., pp. 50–51.
11. Ashida, *Doso no Kamigami,* p. 26.
12. Ito, *Sei no Shakujin,* pp. 179–81.
13. Ibid.
14. Ashida, *Doso no Kamigami,* p. 29.
15. Daigo, *Dosojin—Robo no Sekibutsu,* vol. 2, p. 144.
16. Ibid.
17. Ito, *Sei no Shakujin,* pp. 176–79.
18. Daigo, *Dosojin—Robo no Sekibutsu,* vol. 2, pp. 35–36.
19. Ashida, *Doso no Kamigami,* p. 29.

CHAPTER III

1. Kenkichi Ito, *Sei no Shakujin* (Stone Gods of Sex), p. 200.
2. Kanagawa-ken Kyoiku Iinkai (Kanagawa Prefecture Board of Education), "Oiso no Dosojin Matsuri" (The Dosojin Festival of Oiso), pp. 1–60.
3. Eiichi Ashida, *Doso no Kamigami* (Gods of Doso), p. 27.
4. Ito, *Sei no Shakujin,* p. 72.
5. Kanagawa-ken, "Oiso no Dosojin Matsuri," pp. 2–4.
6. Ibid., pp. 16–17.
7. Ito, *Sei no Shakujin,* pp. 200–201.
8. Kofu Daini Kotogakko Shakai Kenkyu-bu (Kofu Second High School Social Studies Club), *Zusetsu Kai no Dosojin* (An Illustrated Account of Dosojin in Kai Province), p. 61.
9. Ibid.
10. Ibid., pp. 61–63.
11. Erich Neumann, *The Origins and History of Consciousness,* vol. 1, p. 239, fn. 51.
12. Frederick Starr, "Ema," pp. 1–12.
13. Ito, *Sei no Shakujin,* pp. 201–14.
14. Ibid.
15. Kofu Daini Kotogakko, *Kai no Dosojin,* p. 59.

16. Kanagawa-ken, *Oiso no Dosojin Matsuri,* pp. 5–12.
17. Tamotsu Yato, *Naked Festival.*
18. Ibid., p. 159.
19. Ibid., p. 166.
20. Genchi Kato, "The Naoe Matsuri," pp. 113–16.
21. Kanagawa-ken, *Oiso no Dosojin Matsuri,* pp. 1–66.
22. Yato, *Naked Festival,* p. 159.
23. Hideo Nishioka, *Nihon Seishin-shi* (The History of Japanese Phallicism), p. 286.
24. Yato, *Naked Festival,* p. 156.
25. Ito, *Sei no Shakujin,* p. 210.
26. Ibid.
27. Ibid.
28. Hachiro Daigo, *Dosojin—Robo no Sekibutsu* (Dosojin: The Roadside Stone Buddhas), vol. 2, pp. 100–101.
29. Ibid., p. 101.
30. Kofu Daini Kotogakko, *Kai no Dosojin,* p. 60.
31. Ashida, *Doso no Kamigami,* p. 19. Jiro and Taro are the names of a couple Dosojin sculpture in the locality.

CHAPTER IV

1. J. Edward Kidder, *Japan Before Buddhism,* pp. 81–84.
2. Genchi Kato, *A Study of Shinto: The Religion of the Japanese Nation,* p. 19, quoting the *Kojiki.*
3. Ibid., p. 11, quoting the *Man'yoshu,* vol. 3.
4. Ibid., p. 9.
5. William George Aston, *Shinto: The Way of the Gods,* p. 27.
6. Ibid., p. 9.
7. Kato, *A Study of Shinto,* p. 31.
8. Aston, *Shinto: The Way of the Gods,* pp. 27–30, quoting the *Kojiki.*
9. Kato, *A Study of Shinto,* p. 37.
10. Ibid., p. 39.
11. Ibid., p. 28.
12. Aston, *Shinto: The Way of the Gods,* p. 26.
13. Karl Florenz, "Ancient Japanese Rituals," p. 3.
14. J. Edward Kidder, *The Birth of Japanese Art,* p. 78.

15. W. L. Schwartz, "The Great Shrine of Idzumo," pp. 640–42.
16. Ibid., pp. 657–58.
17. Ichiro Hori, *Folk Religion in Japan,* pp. 74–80.
18. Ibid., pp. 111–19.
19. Ibid., p. 143.
20. Carmen Blacker, "Ten Worlds of the Mountain Sleeper," p. 123.
21. Hori, *Folk Religion in Japan,* p. 79.

CHAPTER V

1. Genchi Kato, *A Study in the Development of Religious Ideas Among the Japanese People as Illustrated by Japanese Phallicism,* p. 5.
2. Ibid., pp. 8–9.
3. *Larousse Encyclopedia of Mythology,* p. 133.
4. Edmund Buckley, *Phallicism in Japan,* p. 27.
5. Heinrich Zimmer, *Myths and Symbols in Indian Art and Civilization,* p. 140.
6. Buckley, *Phallicism in Japan,* p. 27.
7. J. Edward Kidder, *The Birth of Japanese Art,* p. 7.
8. Ibid., p. 24.
9. Ibid., p. 7.
10. Ibid., p. 70.
11. J. Edward Kidder, *Early Japanese Art,* p. 17.
12. Mircea Eliade, *Patterns in Comparative Religion,* p. 333.
13. Ibid., p. 334.
14. Ibid., p. 357.
15. William George Aston, *Shinto: The Way of the Gods,* p. 196.
16. George De Vos and Hiroshi Wagatsuma, *Japan's Invisible Race,* p. 18.
17. Kato, "Development of Religious Ideas," p. 20.
18. Donald Richie and Kenkichi Ito, *The Erotic Gods,* p. 15.
19. Ibid., p. 104.
20. Kato, "Development of Religious Ideas," p. 10.
21. Richie and Ito, *The Erotic Gods,* p. 20.
22. Kato, "Development of Religious Ideas," p. 19.
23. Buckley, *Phallicism in Japan,* p. 12.

24. Daniel C. Holtom, "The Political Philosophy of Modern Shinto," p. 178.

25. Buckley, *Phallicism in Japan,* p. 12.

26. Jean Herbert, *Shinto: The Fountainhead of Japan,* pp. 357–58.

27. Aston, *Shinto: The Way of the Gods,* p. 306.

28. Ibid., p. 188.

29. Ibid., p. 216.

30. Kunio Yanagita, *Shakujin Mondo* (Questions and Answers About Stone Gods), p. 75.

31. Ibid., p. 74.

32. Herbert, *Shinto: The Fountainhead of Japan,* p. 209.

33. Ichiro Hori, *Folk Religion in Japan,* p. 112.

34. Ibid., p. 117.

35. Aston, *Shinto: The Way of the Gods,* p. 307.

36. Yanagita, *Shakujin Mondo,* p. 109.

37. Richie and Ito, *The Erotic Gods,* p. 137.

38. Carmen Blacker, "Ten Worlds of the Mountain Sleeper, "p. 125.

39. Richie and Ito, *The Erotic Gods,* p. 137.

40. Ibid, pp. 136, 137.

41. Kenji Kawaguchi, *Dosojin no Furusato o Tazunete* (Visiting the Home of Dosojin), p. 194.

Chapter VI

1. Mircea Eliade, *Shamanism,* p. 259.

2. Ibid., pp. 270–71.

3. D. C. Buchanan, "Inari: Its Origin, Development and Nature," p. 24.

4. Daniel C. Holtom, "Some Notes on Japanese Tree Worship," p. 11.

5. Eliade, *Shamanism,* pp. 17–23.

6. William George Aston, *Nihongi,* vol. 1, pp. 178–81.

7. Felicia Bock, translation of chapter 30 of the *Wei Chih* in the *San Juo Chih* (unpublished manuscript), pp. 19–22.

8. J. Edward Kidder, *Japan Before Buddhism,* pp. 160–200.

9. J. Edward Kidder, *Early Japanese Art,* pp. 98–105.

10. Ibid., p. 108.

11. Ibid., p. 109.

12. Eliade, *Shamanism,* p. 462.

13. Ibid., p. 464, quoting M. Eder.

14. Ibid., p. 465.

15. Jeremiah Curtin, *A Journey into Southern Siberia,* p. 46.

16. Eliade, *Shamanism,* p. 192.

17. Buchanan, "Inari," p. 97.

18. Ichijo Kaneyoshi, *Kuji Kongen Shinsaku* (New Thoughts on Court Rites and Court Ceremonies), vol. 1, pp. 43–46.

19. W. E. Castle, "The ABC of Color Inheritance in Horses."

20. J. Edward Kidder, *The Birth of Japanese Art,* p. 143.

21. Ichiro Hori, *Folk Religion in Japan,* pp. 182–83.

22. Ibid., p. 206.

23. Ibid., pp. 207–8.

24. Kidder, *Early Japanese Art,* p. 133.

25. Ibid., p. 100.

26. Eliade, *Shamanism,* pp. 169–75.

27. Percival Lowell, "Esoteric Shinto," pp. 112–15.

28. R. J. Kirby, "Doing Nothing and Divination," pp. 195–213.

29. William George Aston, *Shinto: The Way of the Gods,* pp. 340–41.

30. Ibid., p. 341.

31. Ibid.

32. Ibid., p. 344.

Chapter VII

1. Basil Hall Chamberlain, *Kojiki,* p. i.

2. Ibid., p. xcvii.

3. Ibid., p. xxvii.

4. Ibid., p. 44.

5. Ibid., p. 46.

Chapter VIII

1. Erich Neumann, *The Origins and History of Consciousness,* vol. 1, p. 103.

2. Basil Hall Chamberlain, *Kojiki,* p. 19.

3. Jean Herbert, *Shinto: The Fountainhead of Japan,* p. 254.

4. J. Edward Kidder, *Japan Before Buddhism,* p. 116.

5. William George Aston, *Shinto:*

The Way of the Gods, pp. 89–90, quoting Chamberlain, *Kojiki*, pp. 20–21.

6. Chamberlain, *Kojiki*, p. 22.

7. Ibid.

8. Eliade, *Shamanism*, p. 271.

9. Aston, *Shinto: The Way of the Gods*, p. 113.

10. Chamberlain, *Kojiki*, pp. 32–36.

11. Ibid., pp. 38–39.

12. Ibid., pp. 39–40.

13. Aston, *Shinto: The Way of the Gods*, p. 94.

14. Chamberlain, *Kojiki*, pp. 40–41.

15. Ibid., p. 44.

16. Hachiro Daigo, *Dosojin—Robo no Sekibutsu* (Dosojin: The Roadside Stone Buddhas), vol. 2, p. 19.

17. Chamberlain, *Kojiki*, pp. 44–46.

18. Ibid., p. 51.

19. Kidder, *Japan Before Buddhism*, p. 116.

20. J. Edward Kidder, *Early Japanese Art*, p. 10.

21. Aston, *Shinto: The Way of the Gods*, p. 188.

22. Neumann, *Origins and History of Consciousness*, vol. 1, p. xvi.

23. Mircea Eliade, *Myths, Dreams, and Mysteries*, p. 182.

24. Neumann, *Origins and History of Consciousness*, vol. 1, p. 39.

25. Ibid., pp. 120–21.

26. Chamberlain, *Kojiki*, p. 70.

27. Ernest M. Satow, "The Shinto Temples of Ise," pp. 125–26.

28. Neumann, *Origins and History of Consciousness*, vol. 1, p. 54.

29. James G. Frazer, *The Golden Bough*, p. 431.

30. Eliade, *Myths, Dreams, and Mysteries*, p. 184.

31. Ibid., p. 188.

32. Neumann, *Origins and History of Consciousness*, vol. 1, p. 106.

CHAPTER IX

1. Basil Hall Chamberlain, *Kojiki*, pp. 61–62.

2. William George Aston, *Shinto: The Way of the Gods*, pp. 297–300.

3. Mircea Eliade, *Shamanism*, pp. 111–12.

4. Ibid., pp. 237–38.

5. Japanese National Commission for UNESCO, *Japan: Its Land, People and Culture*, pp. 83–84.

6. Ibid., p. 85.

7. Ibid.

8. Namio Egami, *The Formation of the People and the Origin of the State in Japan*, p. 49.

9. W. L. Schwartz, "The Great Shrine of Idzumo," p. 502.

10. Ibid., p. 534.

11. Ibid.

12. Ibid., pp. 537–38.

13. Ibid., p. 538.

14. Karl Florenz, "Ancient Japanese Rituals," p. 83.

15. Egami, *Formation of the People*, p. 85.

CHAPTER X

1. Ernest M. Satow, "The Shinto Temples of Ise," p. 129.

2. Ibid., p. 130.

3. Ibid., pp. 130–31.

4. Basil Hall Chamberlain, *Kojiki*, p. 65.

5. Jean Herbert, *Shinto: The Fountainhead of Japan*, p. 169.

6. Chamberlain, *Kojiki*, pp. 64–65.

7. John F. Embree, *Suye Mura: A Japanese Village*, p. 99.

8. Ibid., p. 102.

9. Mircea Eliade, *Shamanism*, p. 154.

10. Satow, "The Shinto Temples of Ise," p. 131.

11. Eliade, *Shamanism*, p. 168.

12. Ibid., pp. 168–75.

13. Ibid., p. 171.

14. Ibid., pp. 168–75.

15. Ibid., p. 173, fn. 131.

16. Aston, *Shinto: The Way of the Gods*, p. 89.

17. Satow, "The Shinto Temples of Ise," pp. 131–32.

18. Aston, *Shinto: The Way of the Gods*, p. 293.

19. Chamberlain, *Kojiki*, p. 86.

20. Herbert, *Shinto: The Fountainhead of Japan*, p. 334.

CHAPTER XI

1. William George Aston, *Nihongi,* vol. 1, p. 83.
2. Basil Hall Chamberlain, *Kojiki,* p. 130.
3. Jean Herbert, *Shinto: The Fountainhead of Japan,* pp. 359–60, quoting the *Kogoshui.*
4. Aston, *Nihongi,* vol. 1, p. 77.
5. Herbert, *Shinto: The Fountainhead of Japan,* p. 356.
6. Michael Conners, "The End of the Land," p. 159.

CHAPTER XII

1. James A. Rabitt, "The Sacredness of Rice," p. 216.
2. Ibid., pp. 216–17.
3. Ibid.
4. William George Aston, *Shinto: The Way of the Gods,* pp. 269–82.
5. Ibid., p. 169.
6. Floyd H. Ross, *Shinto: The Way of Japan,* pp. 88–91.
7. This reconstruction is based on information obtained from Satow, Ross, and Herbert.
8. This reconstruction is based on information obtained from Satow, Ross, and Herbert.
9. Ross, *Shinto: The Way of Japan,* p. 93.
10. Ibid., p. 94.

CHAPTER XIII

1. Ernest M. Satow, "The Shinto Temples of Ise," p. 126.
2. D. C. Buchanan, "Inari: Its Origin, Development and Nature," p. 59.
3. Ibid., pp. 78–84.
4. Ibid., p. 79.
5. Ibid., pp. 59–77.
6. Ibid., p. 84.
7. Ibid., pp. 86–102.
8. Jean Herbert, *Shinto: The Fountainhead of Japan,* p. 508.
9. Ibid.
10. Buchanan, "Inari," pp. 6–7.
11. Ibid., p. 20.
12. Ibid., p. 15.
13. Ibid., pp. 15–17.
14. Ibid., p. 16.
15. Ibid.
16. M. W. de Visser, "The Fox and the Badger in Japanese Folklore," p. 134.
17. Ibid., p. 141.
18. Ibid., p. 142.
19. Ibid., p. 143.
20. Buchanan, "Inari," pp. 86–98.
21. Ibid., pp. 99–100.
22. Ibid., pp. 86–90.
23. Ibid., pp. 87–88.
24. Ibid., p. 87.
25. Herbert, *Shinto: The Fountainhead of Japan,* p. 318.
26. Daniel C. Holtom, *Modern Japan and Shinto Nationalism,* pp. 43–47.
27. Buchanan, "Inari," p. 88.
28. Ibid., p. 91.
29. Ibid.
30. Ibid., p. 93.
31. Herbert, *Shinto: The Fountainhead of Japan,* p. 358.
32. William George Aston, *Shinto: The Way of the Gods,* p. 184.
33. Buchanan, "Inari," p. 93.
34. James G. Frazer, *The Golden Bough,* p. 418.
35. Ibid.
36. Buchanan, "Inari," p. 93.
37. Herbert, *Shinto: The Fountainhead of Japan,* p. 469.
38. Hachiro Daigo, *Robo no Sekibutsu* (The Roadside Stone Buddhas), vol. 1, p. 7.
39. Aston, *Shinto: The Way of the Gods,* p. 184.
40. Herbert, *Shinto: The Fountainhead of Japan,* p. 103.
41. Ibid., p. 199.
42. Mircea Eliade, *Patterns in Comparative Religion,* p. 31.
43. Robert Briffault, *The Mothers,* vol. 3, p. 18.

APPENDIX

1. Kenkichi Ito, *Sexual Stone Gods* (privately printed, 1965), pp. 57–61.
2. Hachiro Daigo, *Robo no Sekibutsu* (The Roadside Stone Buddhas), vol. 1, p. 117.
3. Maude Rex Allen, *Japanese Art Motives,* p. 110.

4. Henri L. Joly, *Legend in Japanese Art,* p. 75.

5. Daigo, *Robo no Sekibutsu,* vol. 1, p. 110.

6. Allen, *Japanese Art Motives,* pp. 98–102.

7. Joly, *Legend in Japanese Art,* pp. 204–6.

8. Daigo, *Robo no Sekibutsu,* vol. 1, p. 96.

9. Ibid., p. 125.

10. Ibid.

11. Allen, *Japanese Art Motives,* p. 102.

12. Ibid.

13. Joly, *Legend in Japanese Art,* pp. 126–27.

14. Lafcadio Hearn, *Glimpses of Unfamiliar Japan,* vol. 1, p. 128.

15. Allen, *Japanese Art Motives,* pp. 60–61.

16. Ibid., pp. 115–30.

17. *Larousse Encyclopedia of Mythology,* p. 777.

18. Ibid., p. 403.

19. Allen, *Japanese Art Motives,* p. 127.

20. Ibid.

21. Donald Richie and Kenkichi Ito, *The Erotic Gods,* p. 165.

22. Daigo, *Robo no Sekibutsu,* vol. 1, p. 72.

23. Ibid., p. 110.

24. Allen, *Japanese Art Motives,* p. 49.

BIBLIOGRAPHY

LIST OF ABBREVIATIONS

MNM = Monumenta Nipponica Monograph
TASJ = *Transactions of the Asiatic Society of Japan*
TYKS = *Teihon Yanagita Kunio Shu* (Collected Works of Kunio Yanagita)

SOURCES IN ENGLISH

BOOKS

Allen, Maude Rex. *Japanese Art Motives.* Chicago: A. D. McClurg & Co., 1917.

Anesaki, Masaharu. *Art, Life and Nature in Japan.* Boston: Marshall Jones Co., 1933.

————. *History of Japanese Religion.* London: Routledge & Kegan Paul, 1938.

————. *Japanese Mythology.* The Mythology of All Races, vol. 8. Edited by C. J. A. MacCulloch. Boston: Marshall Jones Co., 1928.

————. *Religious Life of the Japanese People.* Tokyo: Kokusai Bunka Shinkokai, 1961.

Aoki, Michiko Yamaguchi, trans. *Izumo Fudoki.* MNM. Tokyo: Sophia University, 1971.

Aston, William George, trans. *Nihongi: Chronicles of Japan.* London: Kegan Paul, Trench, Trubner & Co., 1896.

————. *Shinto: The Ancient Religion of Japan.* London: Constable, 1910.

————. *Shinto: The Way of the Gods.* London: Longmans, Green & Co., 1905.

Bauer, Helen and Carlquist. *Japanese Festivals.* New York: Doubleday, 1965.

Beardsley, Richard K.; Hall, John W.; and Ward, Robert E. *Village Japan.* Chicago: University of Chicago Press, 1959.

Bock, Felicia, trans. *Engi-Shiki: Procedures of the Engi Era.* 2 vols. MNM. Tokyo: Sophia University, vol. 1, 1970; vol. 2, 1972.

Bownas, Geoffrey. *Japanese Rainmaking and Other Folk Practices.* London: Allen and Unwin, 1963.

Briffault, Robert. *The Mothers.* 3 vols. New York: The Macmillan Co., 1927.

Brown, Sanger, II. *The Sex Worship and Symbolism of Primitive Races.* Boston: R. G. Badger, 1916.

Buckley, Edmund. *Phallicism in Japan.* Chicago: University of Chicago Press, 1895.

Campbell, Joseph. *The Hero with a Thousand Faces.* New York: Pantheon Books, 1961.

Casal, U. A. *Five Sacred Festivals of Ancient Japan.* MNM. Tokyo: Sophia University, 1967.

Chamberlain, Basil Hall, trans. *Kojiki, or Records of Ancient Matters.* Supplement to *TASJ* vol. 10, 1882; reprinted Tokyo: Asiatic Society of Japan, 1906.

Clark, Grahame. *World Prehistory: A New Outline.* London: Cambridge University Press, 1969.

Cles-Reden, Sibylle von. *The Realm of the Great Goddess*. London: Thames & Hudson, 1961.

Curtin, Jeremiah. *A Journey into Southern Siberia*. Boston: Little, Brown and Co., 1909.

Czaplicka, M. A. *Aboriginal Siberia*. Oxford: Clarendon Press, 1914.

———. *My Siberian Year*. London: Mills and Brown, 1916.

De Vos, George, and Wagatsuma, Hiroshi. *Japan's Invisible Race: Caste in Culture and Personality*. Berkeley and Los Angeles: University of California Press, 1967.

Earhart, H. Byron. *A Religious Study of the Mount Haguro Sect of Shugendo: An Example of Japanese Mountain Religion*. MNM. Tokyo: Sophia University, 1970.

Egami, Namio. *The Beginnings of Japanese Art*. Translated by John Bester. New York and Tokyo: Weatherhill/Heibonsha, 1973.

———. *The Formation of the People and the Origin of the State in Japan*. Tokyo: Toyo Bunko, 1964.

Eliade, Mircea. *Myths, Dreams, and Mysteries*. New York and Evanston, Ill.: Harper & Row, 1960.

———. *Patterns in Comparative Religion*. Translated by Rosemary Sheed. London and New York: World, 1958.

———. *Shamanism: Archaic Techniques of Ecstasy*. New York: Pantheon Books, 1964.

Embree, John F. *Suye Mura: A Japanese Village*. Chicago: University of Chicago Press, 1931.

Etter, Carl. *Ainu Folklore*. Chicago, New York, and Toronto: Wilcox & Follett Co., 1949.

Evans-Wentz, W. Y. *The Tibetan Book of the Dead*. New York: Galaxy Books, Oxford University Press, 1960.

Frazer, James G. *The Golden Bough*. New York: The Macmillan Co., 1927.

Getty, Alice. *The Gods of Northern Buddhism*. Oxford: Clarendon Press, 1914.

Gordon, Antoinette. *The Iconography of Tibetan Lamaism*. Rutland, Vt., and Tokyo: Charles E. Tuttle Co., 1959.

Griffis, William Elliot. *The Mikado's Empire: History of Japan from 660 B.C. to 1872 A.D.* New York: Harper and Bros., 1876.

———. *The Religions of Japan*. New York: Charles Scribner's Sons, 1912.

Groot, Gerard. *The Prehistory of Japan*. New York: Columbia University Press, 1951.

Gunsaulus, Helen C. *The Japanese New Year's Festival, Games and Pastimes*. Chicago: Field Museum of Natural History, 1923.

Harada, Jiro. *Japanese Gardens*. Boston: C. T. Branford, 1956.

Hearn, Lafcadio. *Exotics and Retrospectives*. Boston: Little, Brown and Co., 1905.

———. *Glimpses of Unfamiliar Japan*. Vol. 1. New York: Houghton, Mifflin and Co., 1894.

———. *In Ghostly Japan*. Boston: Little, Brown and Co., 1894.

———. *Japan: An Attempt at Interpretation*. Rutland, Vt., and Tokyo: Charles E. Tuttle Co., 1955 (reprint).

———. *Kokoro: Hints and Echoes of Japanese Inner Life*. New York: Houghton, Mifflin and Co., 1896.

———. *Kotto: Being Japanese Curios, with Sundry Cobwebs*. London: The Macmillan Co., 1910.

Herbert, Jean. *Shinto: The Fountainhead of Japan*. New York: Stein and Day, 1967.

Holtom, Daniel C. *Modern Japan and Shinto Nationalism: A Study of Present-day Trends in Japanese Religions*. Rev. ed. Chicago: University of Chicago Press, 1947; reprinted New York: Paragon Reprint Corp., 1963.

Hori, Ichiro. *Folk Religion in Japan*. Chicago and London: University of Chicago Press, 1968.

Ienaga, Saburo. *History of Japan*. Tokyo: Japan Travel Bureau, 1953.

Japanese National Commission for UNESCO. *Japan: Its Land, People and Culture*. Tokyo: Printing Bureau, Ministry of Finance and Ministry of Education, 1964.

Joly, Henri L. *Legend in Japanese Art*. New York and London: John Lane Co., 1908.

Kasai, Shigeo. *Hachijo: Isle of Exile*. New York and Tokyo: Weatherhill, 1973.

Kato, Genchi. *Gleanings from Ancient Stories*. Tokyo: Meiji Japan Society, 1925.

————. *A Study in the Development of Religious Ideas Among the Japanese People as Illustrated by Japanese Phallicism*. Supplement to *TASJ* (series 2) vol. 1, 1924.

————. *A Study of Shinto: The Religion of the Japanese Nation*. Tokyo: Meiji Japan Society, 1926.

Kenrick, Vivienne. *Horses in Japan: Customs, Legends, History and Mythology*. Tokyo: Hokuseido Press, 1964.

Kidder, J. Edward. *Ancient Japan*. New York: John Day Co., 1965.

————. *The Birth of Japanese Art*. New York and Washington, D.C.: Frederick A. Praeger, 1965.

————. *Early Japanese Art: The Great Tombs and Treasures*. London: Thames & Hudson, 1964.

————. *Japan Before Buddhism*. London: Thames & Hudson, 1959.

————. *The Jomon Pottery of Japan*. Ascona, Switzerland: Artibus Asiae, 1957.

Kitagawa, Joseph M. *Religion in Japanese History*. New York and London: Columbia University Press, 1966.

Komatsu, Isao. *The Japanese People: Origins of the People and the Language*. Japanese Life and Culture, vol. 1. Tokyo: Kokusai Bunka Shinkokai, 1962.

Larousse Encyclopedia of Mythology. New York: Prometheus Press, 1960.

Lebra, William P. *Okinawan Religion: Belief, Ritual and Social Structure*. Honolulu: University of Hawaii Press, 1966.

Leonard, Jonathan Norton, and the editors of Time/Life Books. *Early Japan*. Great Ages of Man: A History of the World's Cultures. New York: Time/Life Books, 1968.

Lowell, Percival. *Occult Japan*. Boston: Houghton, Mifflin and Co., 1895.

Maraini, Fosco. *Meeting with Japan*. New York: Viking Press, 1960.

Monro, Neil G. *Prehistoric Japan*. Yokohama: privately printed, 1911.

Mukerjee, Radhakamal. *The Flowering of Indian Art*. New York: Asia Publishing House, 1964.

Munsterberg, Hugo. *The Folk Arts of Japan*. Rutland, Vt., and Tokyo: Charles E. Tuttle Co., 1961.

Neumann, Erich. *The Great Mother*. New York: Pantheon Books, 1963.

————. *The Origins and History of Consciousness*. 2 vols. Translated by R. F. C. Hull. New York: Harper Torchbooks/The Bollingen Library, Harper and Brothers, 1962.

Norbeck, Edward. *Takashima: A Japanese Fishing Community*. Salt Lake City, Utah: University of Utah Press, 1954.

Nozaki, Kiyoshi. *Kitsune: Japan's Fox of Mystery, Romance and Humour*. Tokyo: Hokuseido Press, 1961.

Ono, Sokyo. *Shinto: The Kami Way*. Rutland, Vt., and Tokyo: Charles E. Tuttle Co., 1962.

Otto, Alexander, and Holbrook, Theodore S. *Mythological Japan, or The Symbolism of Mythology to Japanese Art*. Philadelphia: Drexel Biddle, 1902.

Philippi, Donald L., trans. *Kojiki*. Tokyo: Princeton University Press and University of Tokyo Press, 1968.

———. *Norito: A New Translation of the Ancient Japanese Prayers.* Tokyo: Institute for Japanese Culture and Classics, Kokugakuin University, 1959.

Ponsonby-Fane, R. *Divine Spirits of Shinto and Hirota Jinja.* Kyoto: Kamikomo, 1934.

Richie, Donald, and Ito, Kenkichi. *The Erotic Gods: Phallicism in Japan.* Tokyo: Zufushinsha, 1967.

Ross, Floyd H. *Shinto: The Way of Japan.* Boston: Beacon Press, 1965.

Sakurai, Tokutaro. *Japanese Festivals: Annual Rites and Observances.* Tokyo: International Society for Educational Information Press, 1970.

Sansom, George B. *Japan: A Short Cultural History.* New York: Appleton-Century-Crofts, 1962.

Skeat, Walter W. *Malay Magic.* New York: Dover Publications, 1967.

Swann, Peter C. *Art of the World.* New York: Crown, 1966.

Tsunoda, Ryusaku; De Bary, William T.; and Keene, Donald. *Sources of Japanese Tradition.* New York: Columbia University Press, 1958.

Westrop, H. M. *Primitive Symbolism in Phallic Worship.* London: G. Redway, 1884.

Yanagita, Kunio. *Our Ancestors: The Japanese Family System.* Translated by Fanny Hagin Mayer and Yasuyo Ishiwara. Tokyo: Japan Society for the Promotion of Science, 1970.

Yato, Tamotsu. *Naked Festival.* New York and Tokyo: Walker/Weatherhill, 1968.

Zimmer, Heinrich. *The Art of Indian Asia.* Completed and edited by Joseph Campbell. 2 vols. Bollingen Series 39. New York: Pantheon Books, 1955.

———. *Myths and Symbols in Indian Art and Civilization.* Edited by Joseph Campbell. Bollingen Series 6. New York: Pantheon Books, 1946.

PERIODICALS

Aoyagi, Mizuho. "Stones from the Past." *This Is Japan* 9 (1962): 114–15.

Blacker, Carmen. "Ten Worlds of the Mountain Sleeper." *This Is Japan* 16 (1969): 122–29.

Buchanan, D. C. "Inari: Its Origin, Development and Nature." *TASJ* (series 2) 12 (1935): 1–191.

Carnes, Pack. "Kyushu: The Land of Amaterasu." *This Is Japan* 16 (1969): 118–21.

Castle, W. E. "The ABC of Color Inheritance in Horses." *The Cattleman*, September, 1948, pp. 122–28.

Conners, Michael. "The End of the Land." *This Is Japan* 17 (1970): 152–59.

Coville, Cabot. "Shinto, Engine of Government." *TASJ* (series 3) 1 (1948): 1–23.

Dickins, F. V. "The Seven Gods of Happiness." *TASJ* 8 (1880): 427–61.

Dietz, Robert S., and Holden, John C. "The Breakup of Pangea." *Scientific American* 223 (1970) no. 4: 30–41.

Eastlake, F. Warrington. "Equine Deities." *TASJ* 11 (1883): 260–85.

———. "The Kirin." *TASJ* 13 (1885): 211–23.

Fairchild, William P. "Shamanism in Japan." *Folklore Studies* 21 (1962): 1–122.

Florenz, Karl. "Ancient Japanese Rituals." *TASJ* 27 (1900): 1–112.

Groot, Gerard. "An Essay on Early Japanese History." *TASJ* (series 3) 1 (1948): 24–46.

Gubbins, J. H. "The Feudal System in Japan Under the Tokugawa Shoguns." *TASJ* 15 (1887) part 2: 3–142.

Holtom, Daniel C. "The Meaning of Kami." *Monumenta Nipponica* 3 (1940) part 1: 1–27; 3 (1940) part 2: 32–53; 4 (1941) part 2: 25–68.

————. "The Political Philosophy of Modern Shinto: A Study of the State Religion of Japan." *TASJ* 49 (1922): 1–325.

————. "Some Notes on Japanese Tree Worship." *TASJ* (series 2) 8 (1931): 1–19.

Hori, Ichiro. "Japanese Folk Beliefs." *American Anthropologist* 61 (1959): 405–24.

Ikeda, Sanshiro. "Worship by the Wayside." *This Is Japan* 9 (1962): 110–13.

Kato, Genchi. "The Naoe Matsuri." Translated by Daniel C. Holtom. *TASJ* (series 2) 8 (1931): 11–136.

Kellogg, E. R. "Spring and Autumn Fires in Japan." *TASJ* 46 (1918): 1–48.

Kidder, J. Edward. "Haniwa: The Origin and Meaning of the Tomb Sculptures." *TASJ* (series 3) 9 (1966): 51–68.

Kirby, R. J. "Ancestral Worship in Japan." *TASJ* 38 (1911): 233–67.

————. "Doing Nothing and Divination." *TASJ* 41 (1913): 195–213.

————. "Ukemochi-no-Kami: The Shinto Goddess of Food." *TASJ* 38 (1910): 39–56.

Kitagawa, Momo-o. "Ancient Buddhas in Granite and Rock." *This Is Japan* 9 (1962): 96–105.

Lay, Arthur Hyde. "Japanese Funeral Rites." *TASJ* 19 (1891): 507–44.

Lowell, Percival. "Esoteric Shinto." *TASJ* 21 (1893) part 1: 106–35; 21 (1893) part 2: 152–97; 21 (1893) part 3: 241–70; 22 (1894) part 4: 1–26.

Maraini, Fosco. "The Enchanted Castle of 'Safe' Myths." *This Is Japan* 16 (1969): 112–17.

Monro, Neil G. "Primitive Culture in Japan." *TASJ* 34 (1906): 1–212.

Ninomiya, Shigeaki. "An Inquiry Concerning the Origin, Development, and Present Situation of Eta in Relation to the History of Social Classes in Japan." *TASJ* (series 2) 10 (1933): 49–111.

Norbeck, Edward. "Pollution and Taboo in Contemporary Japan." *Southwestern Journal of Anthropology* 8 (1952): 269–85.

————. "Yakudoshi: A Japanese Complex of Supernatural Beliefs." *Southwestern Journal of Anthropology* 11 (1955): 105–20.

Rabitt, James A. "Rice in the Cultural Life of the Japanese People." *TASJ* (series 2) 19 (1940): 187–258.

Satow, Ernest M. "Ancient Japanese Rituals." *TASJ* 7 (1879): 95–126, 409–55; 9 (1881): 183–211.

————. "Notes on Loochoo." *TASJ* 1 (1874): 1–8.

————. "The Revival of Pure Shinto." *TASJ* 3 (1875): 1–87.

————. "The Shinto Temples of Ise." *TASJ* 2 (1874): 113–39.

Schwartz, W. L. "The Great Shrine of Idzumo." *TASJ* 41 (1913): 495–555.

Smith, Robert J. "Ihai: Mortuary Tablets, the Household and Kin in Japanese Ancestor Worship." *TASJ* (series 3) 9 (1966): 83–102.

Snellen, J. R., trans. "Shoku Nihongi: Chronicles of Japan, Continued from 697–791 AD." *TASJ* (series 2) 11 (1934): 151–239; 14 (1937): 209–78.

Spencer, Robert Steward. "The Noro, or Priestesses of Loo Choo." *TASJ* (series 2) 8 (1931): 94–112.

Starr, Frederick. "Ema." *TASJ* 48 (1920): 1–22.

Visser, M. W. de. "Fire and Ignes Fatui in China and Japan." *Mitteilungen des Seminars für Orientalische Sprachen* 17 (1914): 97–193.

————. "The Fox and the Badger in Japanese Folklore." *TASJ* 36 (1908) part 3: 1–159.

————. "The Snake in Japanese Superstition." *Mitteilungen des Seminars für Orientalische Sprachen* 14 (1911): 267–321.

————. "The Tengu." *TASJ* 36 (1908) part 2: 25–99.

Whymant, A. Neville. "The Oceanic Theory of the Origin of the Japanese Language and People." *TASJ* (series 2) 3 (1926): 15–81.

Abe, Michiyoshi. *Kyushu Sei Suhai Shiryo* (Data on the Worship of Sex in Kyushu). Oita: Hareruya Shoten, 1963.

Arai, Tsuneyasu. *Nihon no Matsuri to Geino* (Festivals and Entertainments of Japan). Tokyo: Yoshikawa Kobunkan, 1956.

Araki, Sueo, ed. *Himerareta Chokoku-shu* (A Collection of Hidden Sculptures). Tokyo: Asoka Shobo, 1951.

Ariga, Kizaemon. *Sonraku Seikatsu: Mura no Seikatsu Soshiki* (Village Life: The Organization of Life in Villages). Tokyo: Kokuritsu Shoin, 1958.

Ashida, Eiichi. *Shashin-shu: Doso no Kamigami* (Photographic Collection: Gods of Doso). Fujisawa: Ikeda Shoten, 1963.

Chunichi Eigasha, ed. *Matsuri no Nihon* (The Japan of Festivals). Nagoya: Chunichi Eigasha, 1964.

Daigo, Hachiro. *Robo no Sekibutsu* (The Roadside Stone Buddhas). Vol. 1 of 2 vols. Tokyo: Shinju Shoin, 1965.

———. *Dosojin—Robo no Sekibutsu* (Dosojin: The Roadside Stone Buddhas). Vol. 2 of 2 vols. Tokyo: Shinju Shoin, 1966.

Fujibayashi, Sadao. *Sei Fudoki* (Sexual Customs). Minzoku Mingei Sosho (Folklore and Folk Art Series). Tokyo: Iwasaki Shoten, 1958.

Fujisawa, Eigen, ed. *Nihon Sei Fuzoku-shi* (History of Japanese Manners and Customs Concerning Sex). Tokyo: Yuzankaku Shuppansha, 1963.

Furuno, Kiyoto. *Genshi Shukyo* (Primitive Religion). Tokyo: Kadokawa Shoten, 1964.

Hagiwara, Tatsuo. *Chusei Saishi Soshiki no Kenkyu* (A Study of the Organization of Festivals and Rites in the Middle Ages). Tokyo: Yoshikawa Kobunkan, 1962.

———. *Matsuri Fudoki* (An Encyclopedia of Festivals). 2 vols. Tokyo: Shakai Shisosha, 1965.

Higo, Kazuo. *Kodai Densho Kenkyu* (A Study of Ancient Traditions). Tokyo: Kawade Shobo, 1938.

———. *Nihon ni okeru Genshi Shukyo no Kenkyu* (A Study of Primitive Religion in Japan). Tokyo: Tokai Shobo, 1950.

———. *Nihon Shinwa Kenkyu* (Studies in Japanese Mythology). Tokyo: Kawade Shobo, 1938.

Hisaki, Yukio. *Nihon no Shukyo: Minshu no Shukyo-shi* (Japanese Religions: A History of Folk Religion). Tokyo: Kobundo, 1965.

Hori, Ichiro. *Minkan Shinko* (Folk Beliefs). Tokyo: Iwanami Shoten, 1951.

———. *Waga Kuni Minkan Shinko-shi no Kenkyu* (A Study of the History of the Folk Beliefs of Our Nation). Osaka: Sogensha, 1953.

Horiguchi, Sozan. *Jizo Bosatsu Ritsuzo* (Standing Statues of the Bodhisattva Jizo). Tokyo: Geien Junreisha, 1955.

Ichijo Kaneyoshi. *Kuji Kongen Shinsaku* (New Thoughts on Court Rites and Court Ceremonies). Edited by Nasanao Sekine. 2 vols. Tokyo: Rikugokan, 1909.

Ikeda, Sanshiro. *Shinshu no Sekibutsu* (Stone Buddhas of Shinshu). Tokyo: Toho Shobo, 1966.

Ikeda, Yasaburo. *Otoko to Onna no Minzoku-shi* (A Folk History of Man and Woman). Tokyo: Kodansha, 1965.

Ishigami, Ken. *Ishi no Densetsu* (Legends of Stone). Tokyo: Sekaisha, 1963.

Ishikawa, Sanshiro. *Kojiki Shinwa no Shin Kenkyu* (A New Study of the Myths in the Kojiki), Tokyo: Jiipusha, 1950.

Ito, Kenkichi. *Ishigami no Setto* (Stone Gods). Fuji City: Fuji Museum, 1963.

————. *Robo no Seizo: Sekushii Dosojin Junrei* (Roadside Sex Images: Pilgrimage to Sexy Dosojin). Tokyo: Zufushinsha, 1965.

————. *Sei no Mihotoke* (Buddhas of Sex). Tokyo: Zufushinsha, 1965.

————. *Sei no Shakujin: Sotai Dosojin Ko* (Stone Gods of Sex: On the Couple Dosojin). Tokyo: Yamato Keikokusha, 1965.

————, and Endo, Hideo. *Dosojin no Furusato: Sei no Ishigami* (The Homeland of Dosojin: Stone Gods of Sex). Tokyo: Yamato Shobo, 1972.

Kawaguchi, Kenji. *Dosojin no Furusato o Tazunete* (Visiting the Homeland of Dosojin). Tokyo: Tokyo Bijutsu Kabushiki Kaisha, 1968.

————. *Wasurerareta Kami to Hotoke* (Forgotten Gods and Buddhas). Tokyo: Kinseisha, 1965.

Kita, Sadakichi. *Fukujin Kenkyu* (A Study of the Gods of Luck). Tokyo: Nihon Gakujutsu Fukyukai, 1941.

Kofu Daini Kotogakko Shakai Kenkyu-bu (Kofu Second High School Social Studies Club). *Zusetsu Kai no Dosojin* (An Illustrated Account of the Dosojin of Kai). Kofu: Chiho Shoin, 1959.

Kondo, Kihaku. *Kodai Shinko Kenkyu: Inari Shinko Ron* (A Study of Ancient Religion: On the Worship of Inari). Tokyo: Kadokawa Shoten, 1963.

Krauss, Friedrich S. *Nihon no Sei to Shuzoku: Minzokugaku-jo no Kosatsu* (The Sex and Customs of the Japanese: An Ethnological Study). Trans. by Ichiro Yasuda. Tokyo: Togensha, 1965.

Kubo, Tokutada. *Koshin Shinko no Kenkyu: Nempu-hen* (A Study of the Worship of Koshin: A Chronological Record). Tokyo: Teikoku Shoin, 1963.

Maeda, Taku. *Sosen Suhai no Kenkyu* (A Study of Ancestor Worship). Tokyo: Aoyama Shoin, 1965.

Manabe, Kozei. *Jizoson no Sekai* (The World of Jizo). Tokyo: Aoyama Shoin, 1959.

Matsumoto, Nobuhiro. *Nihon no Shinwa* (The Myths of Japan). Tokyo: Shibundo, 1956.

————. *Nihon Shinwa no Kenkyu* (Studies in Japanese Mythology). Tokyo: Dobunkan, 1931.

Matsuoka, Shizuo. *Kiki Ronkyu* (A Study of the *Kojiki* and *Nihon Shoki*). 20 vols. Tokyo: Dobunkan, 1931–34.

————. *Nihon Koyu Minzoku Shinko* (Indigenous Japanese Folk Beliefs). Tokyo: Toko Shoin, 1941.

Matsuyama, Yoshio. *Yamaguni no Kami to Hito* (Deities and People of the Mountain Provinces). Tokyo: Miraisha, 1961.

Meishida, Daijo. *Shakujin Sekibutsu Shinko no Kenkyu* (A Study of the Worship of Stone Gods and Buddhas). Tokyo: Yamaoka Shoten, 1962.

Meishin Chosa Kyogikai (Committee on the Investigation of Superstitions, Ministry of Education). *Nihon no Zokushin* (Popular Beliefs in Japan). Tokyo: Hihodo, 1949.

Mitsuishi, Mukusaburo. *Seishin to Sekibutsu* (Sex Gods and Stone Buddhas). Ueda, Nagano Prefecture: Ueda Ogata Shiryo Kanko-kai, 1966.

Miyamoto, Tsuneichi, ed. *Nihon Sairei Fudoki* (An Encyclopedia of Japanese Festivals). Tokyo: Keiyusha, 1963.

Murakami, Shigeyoshi. *Kindai Minshu Shukyo-shi no Kenkyu* (A Study of the History of Recent Popular Religions). Kyoto: Hozokan, 1963.

Murayama, Setsu. *Kojiki Kaidoku: Kami to Sei to Ango* (Deciphering the *Kojiki*: Gods, Sex, and Symbols). Tokyo: Hobunsha, 1956.

Nishioka, Hideo. *Nihon Seishin-shi* (The History of Japanese Phallicism). Tokyo: Takahashi Shoten, 1961; 2nd ed. 1967.

Nishiyama, Isao. *Jinja to Saishi: Jodai Shinto-shi no Kenkyu* (Shrines and Rites: A Study of the History of Ancient Shinto). Tokyo: Shibundo, 1964.

Obayashi, Futoyoshi. *Nihon Shinwa no Kigen* (The Origin of Japanese Myths). Tokyo: Kadokawa Shoten, 1965.

Oka, Masao, ed. *Nihon Minzoku no Kigen* (The Origin of the Japanese People). Tokyo: Heibonsha, 1958.

Osaka Yomiuri Shimbunsha, ed. *No no Hotoke: Furuki Shomin no Kokoro* (Buddhas of the Fields: The Minds of the Common People of the Past). Osaka: Naniwasha, 1965.

Ota, Koboku. *Bi no Sekibutsu* (Stone Buddhas of Beauty). Tokyo: Shigi Shoin, 1962.

Ota, Saburo. *Sei Suhai* (Sex Worship). Nagoya: Reimei Shoten, 1956.

Sakai, Usaku. *Ine no Matsuri* (Rice Festivals). Tokyo: Iwasaki Shoten, 1958.

Sasaki, Takami. *Tokai no Butsuzo* (Buddhist Statues of Tokai). Nagoya: Nagoya Tetsudo, 1961.

Sasaya, Ryozo. *Kodai Nihon no Minzoku to Seikatsu* (The Customs and Daily Life of Ancient Japan). Tokyo: Azuma Shuppansha, 1962.

Sawa, Ryuken. *Nihon no Butsuzo* (Buddhist Statues of Japan). Tokyo: Shibundo, 1963.

Shibusawa, Keizo, ed. *Emakimono ni yoru Nihon Jomin Seikatsu Ebiki* (The Life of Japanese Commoners Depicted in Picture Scrolls). 2 vols. Tokyo: Kadokawa Shoten, 1965–68.

Shimizu, Chomei. *Sagami Michi no Kami Zu-shi* (An Illustrated Account of the Deities of the Roads in Sagami). Tokyo: Hatano Shoten, 1965.

Taeda, Mikihiro, and Noguchi, Yoshimaro. *Nihon no Dogu* (Clay Figurines of Japan). Tokyo: Kinokuniya Shoten, 1959.

Takabatake Kotogakko Shakai-han (Takabatake High School Social Studies Club). *Takabatake no Sekihi Sekibutsu* (Stone Monuments and Buddhas of Takabatake). Takabatake, Yamagata Prefecture: Takabatake no Sekihi Sekibutsu Kanko-kai (Society for the Publication of Stone Monuments and Stone Buddhas of Takabatake), 1958.

Takagi, Susumu. *Seishin Fudoki* (An Encyclopedia of Deities of Sex). Tokyo: Shinchosha, 1961.

Takeda, Hisayoshi. *Dosojin*. Tokyo: Arusu, 1941.

———. *Noson no Nenju Gyoji* (Annual Events of Farming Villages). Tokyo: Ryuseikaku, 1943.

———. *Robo no Sekibutsu* (Roadside Stone Buddhas). Tokyo: Daiichi Hoki Shuppan Kabushiki Kaisha, 1971.

Takemura, Fumio. *Sei, Kami, Ningen, Sekkusu* (Sexuality, Gods, Man, and Sex). Tokyo: Toto Shobo, 1965.

Takeno, Choji. *Kojiki no Minzokugaku-teki Kosatsu* (An Ethnological Study of the *Kojiki*). Tokyo: Waseda University Press, 1950.

Taniguchi, Tetsuo, and Katayama, Setsuzo. *Nihon no Sekibutsu* (Stone Buddhas of Japan). Tokyo: Asahi Shimbunsha, 1958.

Tozuka, Takaichiro. *Noyama no Hotoke* (Buddhas of the Fields and Mountains). Tokyo: Kongosha, 1963.

Tsukushi, Shinshin. *Amaterasu no Tanjo* (The Birth of Amaterasu). Tokyo: Kadokawa Shoten, 1962.

Wakasugi, Kei. *Hojo Sekibutsu* (Stone Buddhas of Hojo). Tokyo: Chikuma Shobo, 1963.

———. *No no Hotoke* (Buddhas of the Fields). Tokyo: Sogen Shinsha, 1963.

———. *Sekibutsu Junrei* (A Pilgrimage to Stone Buddhas). Tokyo: Sogen Shinsha, 1960.

Wayama, Tetsuko. *Inshi to Jashin* (Obscene Shrines and Evil Gods). Tokyo: Hakubunkan, 1918.

Yanagita, Kunio. *Densetsu* (Legends). Tokyo: Iwanami Shoten, 1940.

———. *Fuko-naru Geijutsu* (Unfortunate Art). Tokyo: Chikuma Shobo, 1953.

———. "Imo no Chikara" (The Power of Women). *TYKS*, vol. 9, pp. 1–219. Tokyo: Chikuma Shobo, 1962.

———. "Josei to Minkan Densho" (Women and Popular Legends). *TYKS*, vol. 8, pp. 315–447. Tokyo: Chikuma Shobo, 1962.

———. "Miko Ko" (On the Miko). *TYKS*, vol. 9, pp. 221–301. Tokyo: Chikuma Shobo, 1962.

———. "Misaki-gami Ko" (On the God of the Promontory). *TYKS*, vol. 30, pp. 158–68. Tokyo: Chikuma Shobo, 1964.

———. *Nihon no Matsuri* (Festivals of Japan). Tokyo: Kadokawa Shoten, 1956.

———. "Sai no Kawara no Hanashi" (The Tale of Sai no Kawara). *TYKS*, vol. 27, pp. 277–81. Tokyo: Chikuma Shobo, 1964.

———. *Shakujin Mondo* (Questions and Answers About Stone Gods). Tokyo: Shogensha, 1942.

———. *Shinju-hen hoka Go-hen* (A Chapter on Divine Trees and Five Other Chapters). *TYKS*, vol. 11. Tokyo: Chikuma Shobo, 1963.

———. *Shinto to Minzokugaku* (Shinto and Folklore). Tokyo: Meiseido Shoten, 1943.

———. *Sogo Nihon Minzoku Goi* (Comprehensive Glossary of Japanese Folklore). 4 vols. Tokyo: Heibonsha, 1955–56.

———. "Sosen-gami" (Ancestral Deities). *TYKS*, vol. 27, pp. 326–35. Tokyo: Chikuma Shobo, 1964.

———, and Hori, Ichiro. *Jusan-zuka Ko* (On the Thirteen Tumuli). Tokyo: Sanseido, 1948.

Yoshiga, Hideo. *Ta no Kami: Nihon no Inasaku Girei* (The Deity of Rice Fields: Festivals and Rituals of Rice Cultivation in Japan). Tokyo: Heibonsha, 1959.

Yuzankaku, ed. "Sei-teki Sairei ni Tsuite" (On Sexual Festivals and Rites). *Sei Fuzoku* (Sexual Customs), vol. 3. Tokyo: Yuzankaku, 1959.

PERIODICALS

Ashida, Eiichi. "Michi no Kami" (The Roadside Gods). *Nihon Bijutsu Kogei* (Japanese Arts and Crafts), no. 321 (June, 1965), pp. 22–29.

———. "Koshiji no Dosojin" (The Dosojin of Koshiji). *Mingei Techo* (Folk Art Notebook), no. 164 (January, 1972), pp. 8–15; no. 165 (February, 1972), pp. 24–30; no. 166 (March, 1972), pp. 24–27.

Gotemba-shi Bunkazai Chosa Iinkai (Committee for the Investigation of the Cultural Properties of Gotemba City). "Gotemba no Dosojin" (Dosojin of Gotemba). *Bunkazai no Shiori Dainishu* (Cultural Properties Guide No. 2; 1960), pp. 1–46.

Harada, Toshiaki. "Buraku Saishi ni okeru Shamanizumu no Keiko" (Shamanistic Tendencies in Village Rites). *Minzokugaku Kenkyu* (Ethnological Studies) 14 (1949), no. 1: 7–13.

Ikeda, Sanshiro. "Shinshu no Dosojin Kenkyu" (A Study of the Dosojin of Shinshu). *The Mingei*, no. 42 (November, 1961), pp. 6–21.

———. "Shinshu no Sekibutsu" (Stone Buddhas of Shinshu). Catalogue of the Exhibition of Stone Buddhas of Shinshu, Fifth Festival of Art and Culture, Matsumoto City Museum, October, 1964, pp. 18–24.

Kanagawa-ken Kyoiku Iinkai (Kanagawa Prefecture Board of Education). "Oiso no Dosojin Matsuri" (The Dosojin Festival of Oiso). *Kanagawa-ken Minzoku Shirizu 2* (Kanagawa Prefecture Ethnology Series 2; 1962), pp. 1–76.

INDEX

211, 231; phallic symbols of, 212; *mitama* of, 213; *see also* Izanagi and Izanami

Izanagi and Izanami: identified with Dosojin, 31; and Ame-no-Nuboko, 162; creation of islands and deities by, 167, 201–2, 205–7, 215; and the Heavenly Pillar, 182; courtship of, 207–9; as sky and earth deities, 258

Izanami, death of, 209–10, 216, 217; *see also* Izanagi and Izanami

Izu Dosojin, 51

Izumo Fudoki (Chronicles of the Izumo Area), 225

Izumo, Great Shrine of, 157, 223, 233

jewels, 38–39, 228; *see also* Ten Sacred Treasures

Jimmu, emperor, 154, 204, 234

Jingu, empress, 151, 155, 163, 165, 167, 207, 244

Jizo, 169, 178, 266–67; festival of, 189; as rainmaker, 245; six incarnations of, 269; as horse-riding statue, 272

Joya-sai, 53

Junna, emperor, 256

jussha, 188–89

Kagutsuchi, 148, 167, 209, 214

Kaiko-dama Dai-Myojin, 267

kami, 149, 154, 248; emperor as, 249–50; see also *mitama*

kami-age, 61, 230

Kami-musubi, 253

kami-oroshi, 57, 230

Kamo-no-Matsuri, 246

Kamu-Oichi-hime, 253, 255, 258, 259, 260–61

Kangiten, *see* Shoten

kannagi, 188; see also *miko*

Kanname-sai, 246, 247

Kanna-zuki, 49

Kannon, 265, 267

Kanzeon, *see* Kannon

Kato, Genchi, 148, 151, 246; quoted, 162

Kaya-no-Hime-no-Kami, 257

kegare, 153, 208

kezurikake, 60

Kibi-hime-no-Mikoto, 45

Kinen-sai, 175, 246

Kirby, R. J., 192

Kishin, 45

Kobo Daishi, 255

Kogoshui (Gleanings from Ancient Stories), 200

Kojiki (Record of Ancient Matters), 44, 165, 199–200; phallicism in, 167–68

Kojin, 267

Konjaku Monogatari, 169

Konsei Dai-Myojin, 46, 170, 267

Koshin, 28, 178, 267–68

ko system, 157–58

kuchiyose, 188, 189

Kuji Kongen, 187

Kuku-no-Kami, 257

Kuku-toshi-no-Kami, 257

kunado, 211

Kunado-no-Kami, 35, 45, 171, 173, 176; identified with Dosojin, 31; and divination, 194, 195; birth of, 210

Kuyo-to, 268

leech-child, *see* Hiruko

longevity symbols, 60

lustration, 191

magatama, see jewels

mani, see jewels

Marishiten, 268

masks, 190

Mata-no-Kami, 45, 170

matchmaking deities, 45; offerings to, 48

Michiae-no-Matsuri, 169, 171–72, 173, 174

Michi-no-Kami, 31

Miketsu-no-Kami, *see* Ugadama

miko, 186, 188, 195, 248, 261

mikoshi, 64, 65, 240

Miroku Bosatsu, 268–69

mirrors, 228, 229, 238, 248; *see also* Ten Sacred Treasures

mitama, 153, 182–83; concept of, 149–52; of Izanagi, 213; of the emperor, 248; see also *kami*

Mitama Furishiki, 234

Mitoshi-no-Kami, 166–67, 187

Miyabi-no-Kami, 259

monkeys, 46, 240, 262, 269

Mononobe hereditary corporation, 235

mountain beliefs, *see* Shugendo sect

Mount Fuji, 148, 170

musubi, 181, 248

Musubi-no-Kami, 51

Nakatomi hereditary corporation, 192, 235

naked festivals, 63, 64, 166

Natsu-taka-no-Kami, 257

nembashira, 56

Nembutsu sect, 158

Neumann, Erich, 30

New Year: decorations of, 53, 57; ceremonies of, 54

night festivals, 168, 175

Nihongi (Chronicles of Japan), 44, 199, 200

Nihon Montoku Tenno Jitsuroku (The Authentic Japanese History of the Reign of the Emperor Montoku), 168
Niiname-sai (Shinjo-sai), 246
Ninigi-no-Mikoto, 67, 154–55, 204, 234, 235, 248; descent from heaven of, 237–38, 239
Nintoku, emperor, 184
norito, 68, 171–72, 220, 224, 230
numbers, magic of, 193, 233, 235, 249

o-bashira, 194, 212
ochoya, 62
Oda-no-Mikoto, 258
offerings, 230, 239; to Dosojin, 49, 59–61; to ancestral spirits, 156; for rain, 245; at Daijo-sai, 249
Ogetsu-hime-no-Kami, 258
o-hagi, 48
Oharai Kotoba, 152, 153
Oichi-hime, *see* Kamu-Oichi-hime
Oide, 194
Okame, 58, 59
okamori, 62
Okuni-nushi-no-Mikoto, 45, 150, 157, 207, 223, 233, 234, 253
Omiya-hime, 259, 261
Omiya-no-Me-no-Kami, *see* Uzume
Ommyodo sect, 158, 160
Omoi-kane-no-Kami, 228, 238
Onamochi, *see* Okuni-nushi-no-Mikoto
oni, 269
Oni-e, 50
Onogoro, 206, 207
o-shimboku, 56
Otoshi-no-Kami, 247, 253, 259
Otsuchi-no-Mi-oya-no-Kami, *see* Oda-no-Mikoto
o-tsukai, 261–62
outdoor shrines, 152
Oyama-hime, 259, 260
Oyama-kui, 262
Oyama-tsumi-no-Kami, 170, 258, 260

pacification ceremony, *see* Chinkon-sai
pagodas, 28, 38, 39
phallicism: deities in, 43, 44; placing of objects, 161; myths of, 161–62; symbols in, 162, 164–65, 176–78, 205, 206, 212–13; connection with stones, 162–63; dualism in, 163; procreative aspect of, 163; preventive aspect of, 163–64; in prehistory, 164–65; in agriculture, 165–67; reforms against, 168; shrines connected with, 169–71; festivals connected with, 174–75
pollution, 152–53
pond festivals, 64–65

purification, 63–65, 152–54; ritual of, 211; of sites, 230

Raishin, 266
rape, symbolic, 224
religious societies, see *ko* system
rice cultivation, 221–22, 243; rituals connected with, 244–46; festivals connected with, 246–50
rice deity, *see* Inari
roadside sculptures, *see* Dosojin
Ross, Floyd H., 247, 250
Ryobu Shinto, 192

sacrifice: of humans, 185, 216; of horses, 186, 187, 224
Sae-no-Kami, 31, 45–46, 214; worship of, 169; festivals for, 171–72, 207; and divination, 194, 195; at Fushimi-Inari Shrine, 258
Sagami, 31
Sagicho Matsuri, 54, 173–74
Sai-no-Kami, 31, 46, 48–49
sakaki, 152, 183, 190, 228
salt, 153
Sambiki Saru, 269
Sankuro festival, 50, 54; hut for, 62; *see also* Dosojin festival
Sanno, 46, 262, 269
saru-ishi, 45
saru-mai, 261
Sarume-kimi, 239, 261–62
Saruta-hiko-no-Mikoto, 270; identified with Dosojin, 29, 30, 31, 48; identified with Hyottoko, 57; as tree-fork deity, 60; as phallic deity, 169, 239–41, 259; and Uzume, 204, 237, 239; death of, 239, 240; at Fushimi-Inari Shrine, 253, 254, 258
Sato Shinen, 162
Satow, Ernest, 227, 232, 233
Saya-no-Kami, 50
scapegoats, 63–64
scarves, *see* Ten Sacred Treasures
Seiwa, emperor, 172, 173
Seven Gods of Luck, 57–59, 270–72
shamanism, 151; women in, 30, 155, 165, 186, 188, 189; in Japan, 186–87, 240; crowns used in, 186, 189, 190, 232; horses in, 187; cults in, 188–89; symbols in, 189–90; use of drugs in, 190–91; and divination, 192; drums used in, 232–33; *see also* shamans
shamans, 231–32; and ecstasy, 182, 190–91; role of, 183–84, 221; training of, 184, 189; *see also* shamanism
Shi Daijin, 257
shimboku, see *o-shimboku*

The "weathermark" identifies this book as a publication of John Weatherhill, Inc., publishers of fine books on Asia and the Pacific. Editor in charge, Suzanne Trumbull. Book design, typography, and layout of illustrations, Dana Levy. Production supervision, Mitsuo Okado. Composition, Kwangmyong Printing Co., Seoul. Letterpress printing, Kenkyusha Printing Co., Tokyo. Gravure platemaking and printing, Nissha Printing Co., Kyoto. Binding, Makoto Binderies, Tokyo. The text is set in 12-point Monotype Bembo with hand-set Bulmer and Caslon Open Face for display.